AF621890

बेगूसराय
का
इतिहास एवं पुरातत्व

(आलेख-संग्रह)

History & Archaeology
of
Begusarai

बेगूसराय
का
इतिहास एवं पुरातत्व

(आलेख-संग्रह)

History & Archaeology
of
Begusarai

संपादक

डॉ. शैलेश कुमार सिन्हा

उप संपादक

डॉ. अमिय कृष्ण

लक्की इन्टरनेशनल

नई दिल्ली (इंडिया)- 110080

संस्करण 2026
आई. एस. बी. एन. 978–93–83514–51–9

© संपादक

सर्वाधिकार सुरक्षित।

इस पुस्तक का कोई भी अंश संपादक की लिखित पूर्व आज्ञा के बिना पूर्णतः या अंशतः इस रूप में न तो प्रकाशित किया जाए और न ही किसी भी तरह की फोटो कॉपी, यांत्रिक या कहीं और संगृहीत की जाए।

लेजर तथा पुस्तक सज्जा
नई दिल्ली

कवर फोटो
सूर्य, संग्रहालय जी. डी. कॉलेज, बेगूसराय

सम्पर्क : शैलेश कुमार सिन्हा, पावर हाउस रोड, राजेन्द्र नगर,
बेगूसराय, (बिहार) 851101
मो. 9939803797

प्रकाशक

लक्की इन्टरनेशनल
एच–16/1922, संगम विहार,
नई दिल्ली (इंडिया)- 80
e-mail: luckybk05@yahoo.co.in,
Phone: 07838260289, 9871911248

भूमिका

क्षेत्रीय इतिहास एवं पुरातत्व विषयक लेखन एक चुनौतीपूर्ण कार्य है। इस विषय पर शोध आलेख का लेखन बाह्य स्त्रोतों एवं पथ प्रदर्शक पूर्व कार्यों के अभाव में कभी –कभी दुष्कर हो जाता है।

बेगूसराय जनपद इतिहास एवं पुरातत्व की दृष्टि से अत्यंत समृद्ध है। इतिहास की पुनर्रचना हेतु अनेकानेक साधन यहाँ यत्र–तत्र बिखरे पड़े हैं। ये समस्त साधन क्षेत्रीय इतिहास को मुखरित करने हेतु आतुर प्रतीत होते हैं। यह अत्यंत आश्चर्य का विषय है कि इस समृद्धि के बावजूद मुख्य धारा के इतिहास में बेगूसराय एवं इसके समान कई अन्य क्षेत्रों का उल्लेख नहीं हुआ है। मुख्य धारा का इतिहास केन्द्र के परितः सीमित हो गया प्रतीत होता है। इतिहास की दृष्टि क्षेत्र (परिधि) से केन्द्र की ओर अधिक प्रासंगिक होता है न कि केन्द्र से क्षेत्र (परिधि) की ओर।

बेगूसराय जनपद इतिहास ही नही, इतिहास–लेखन की दृष्टि से भी उर्वर है। इतिहास – लेखन की स्थानीय समृद्ध परम्परा देश के स्वतंत्रता–काल से ही राष्ट्रीय फलक पर अपनी छाप छोड़ती रही है। अनवरत शोध लेखन एवं इतिहास संबंधी गोष्ठियों ने इस क्षेत्र में इतिहास से संबंधित चेतना विकसित की है। वर्तमान में भी इस विषय का आकर्षण बना हुआ है एवं लेखन कार्य शोध आदि की प्रवृति बनी हुई है।

किसी भी विषय में शोध हेतु पूर्व–कार्य महत्वपूर्ण भूमिका का निर्वहन करते हैं। पुरातत्व के क्षेत्र में एवं विशेषकर क्षेत्रीय पुरातत्व के क्षेत्र में तो पूर्व के शोध कार्य एकमात्र पथ–प्रदर्शक हैं। इसके बल पर नये तथ्य स्थापित हो सकते हैं अथवा पूर्व –उद्घाटित तथ्यों को नयी दिशा मिल सकती है। इस दृष्टि से हमने पूर्व कार्यों को संकलित कर पुस्तकाकार एक स्थल पर उपलब्ध कराने का एक प्रयास किया है जिससे नयी पीढी के शोधार्थियों को एक दिशा मिल सके एवं साथ ही साथ जागरूक सुधी जन लाभान्वित हो सकें। शोध आलेखों में व्यक्त धारणाओं की संपुष्टि करने वाले चित्रों को भी इस संकलन में स्थान प्रदान किया जा रहा है।

संकलित शोध – आलेखों में से कुछ अब सामान्यजनों एवं एक हद तक युवा शोधार्थियों को उपलब्ध नहीं रहे। इन्हें उपलब्ध कराना भी हमारा उद्देश्य रहा है। कतिपय कारणों से बेगूसराय के इतिहास व पुरातत्व विषयक कुछ शोध आलेख प्रस्तुत संकलन में समाहित नहीं हो सके हैं। आलेखों की अनुपलब्धता सर्वाधिक महत्वपूर्ण कारण हैं। भविष्य में हम उन शोध – आलेखों को अपने संकलन में समाहित करने हेतु आशान्वित हैं।

प्रस्तुत संकलन में जिन लेखकों के शोध आलेख सम्मिलित किए गये हैं, हम उनके प्रति अपना आभार व्यक्त करते हैं। इन आलेखों को प्रकाशित करने वाली पत्र पत्रिकाओं एवं प्रकाशन संस्थान के प्रति भी हम आभारी हैं। उचित समय पर उनके सकारात्मक एवं सजग कदम के बल पर ही हम आज इन शोध आलेखों को आपके सम्मुख प्रस्तुत कर पा रहे हैं।

संकलन में सम्मिलित शोध आलेखों को उनके प्रकाशन वर्ष के आधार पर क्रमबद्ध प्रस्तुत किया गया है जिससे विषयवस्तु के उद्घाटित होने का भी सही–सही आकलन किया जा सके।

आपके बहुमूल्य सुझावों एवं विचारों हेतु प्रतीक्षारत् ।

संपादक

List of Contributors

Prof. Radhakrishna Choudhary
Dr. Akhileshwar Kumar
Dr. R. C. Prasad
Dr. Arun Kumar Sinha
Dr. Thakur Harendra Dayal
Dr. Avinash Chandra Verma
Dr. Jagdeshwar Pandey
Prof. Phuleshwar Singh
Dr. Piyush Gupta
Dr. Umesh Chandra Dwivedi
Dr. Ram Shekhar Singh
Mr. Umesh Kumar Singh
Dr. Shailesh Kumar Sinha
Dr. Surendra Kumar
Dr. Prabal Gupta
Mr. Jitendra Karzi
Mr. Ram Chandra Paswan

Dr. Jaideva Mishra

Dr. Mukesh Kumar

Dr. Permanand Singh

Dr. Radhaswami

Miss Kiran Bala Sinha

Dr. Amiya Krishna

Mr. Manas Ranjan Manvansh

Dr. Sushant Kumar

Dr. Anil Kumar

Dr. Yashvir Kumar Singh

Dr. Kundan Kumar

Dr. Km. Ranjana

अनुक्रम

हिन्दी आलेख

Appendix

Description of The Plates.

(Bulletin Series No. 1* G.D. College Begusarai)

Naulagarh Image Inscription.

1. The Image[1] :-

The present image is probably that of Vishnu.

2. The Inscription, on the pedestal of the image reads :-

Line 1 :- **Om Sri Vigrahpaldeva rajye samvat 24 krimitiya sau -**

Line 2 :- **ndika ? Mahamati duhitra Dhammajiyapatnya Asokaya ka..**

Note :- The last two words are not distinct.

Importance of the word "Krimi"

While preparing the manuscript for the Press, the article[2] of Dr. Dinesh Chandra Sarkar came out discussing about the ancient city of Krmila. According to the learned scholar there were two Bhuktis, viz, Srinagarbhukti (also identified with Pataliputra) and Tribhukti. On the basis of recent discoveries, Dr. Sarkar has found out a Krmila Visaya (district) forming the part of Srinagarbhukti and while discussing its exact location he observes, "nothing can be said definitely until further evidence is forthcoming."

The mention of the word "**Krimi**" in our inscription may also throw some light on the contemporary history. The only Visaya (district) forming part of Tirabhukti division is Kaksa-Visaya (district), though its exact situation has not yet been satisfactorily located. It may be consectured that this area, where our inscription has been found, also formed a Visaya (district) of Tirabhukti with Naulagarh as its headquarters.

The Inscription :- Line I **Om Sri Vigrahapaladeva rajya samvat 24 Krimitiya San ....**

Line II **ndika ? Mahamati duhitra Dhammajiyapatiya Asokaya ka ....**

The Naulagarh Stone Image Inscription is a brilliant discovery and adds a new list to the already existing Pala records spread over different parts of our country. The discovery is unique in the sense that it throws a flood of light on the Pala History in North Bihar. The inscription refers to king Vigrahpaldeva but it does not say as to which of the three Vigrahpaldevas can this be attributed. This is a common phenomenon of all such Pala records wherever there have been two or three kings of the same name and instances to this effect are not lacking. Hence we will have to judge this inscripiton from various standpoints and fix the name of actual king. On the grounds, given below, this inscription may be attributed to king Vigrahapal III.

a) The existing political condition of Pala kingdom during the regin of king Vigrahpaldeva III.

b) The uncertainty about the chronology of Vigrahpala III.

c) To what extent does the present image come under mediaeval school of eastern art in the 11th &12th centuries?

d) The Script of the Inscription.

Before dwelling at length upon the points raised above, it is better to give below the findspots of three Vigrahpalas in Bihar and also the known length of their successive reigns.

a) Find spots :-

1) Vigrahpala I- year 3- Two identical Bihar Buddha image Inscriptions.
2) Vigrahpala II[3] or III year 3 (2?) - Kurkihar Image Inscription.
Vigrahpala II[3] or III year 19 - Kurkihar Image Inscription.
Vigrahpala II[3] or III year 19 - Kurkihar Image Inscription.
3) Vigrahpala III .... year 5[4] - Gaya Akshayvat Temple Inscription.
Vigrahpala III --- year 13[5]- Bihar Budha Image Inscription.

b) Known lengths & approximate dates :-

1) Vigrahpala I or Surpala - 3 years- 850 A.D. (850-854)
2) Vigrahpala II 26 years (?) - 960 A.D. (960-988)
3) Mahipala I (988-1035)
4) Nayapala 1035 A.D.
5) Vigrahpala III 1054 A.D. ....
Mahipala II ...... 1070[6]

Let us now take up the points one by one. The Pala power had begun to crack up by the time of Vigrahapala I. He did not take much interest in the political activities and was a man of pacific and religious dispostion. By the time of Vigrahpala II three well - defined kingdoms had come to stay.

a) Chandra Kingdom comprising east and south Bengal.

b) Kamboja and Pala Kingdom proper comprising Anga and Magadh

c) Gopala II and Vigrahpala II had the curious misfortune of losing the paternal territory of the dynasty, though ruling over other parts of the kingdom.

The disintegration had set in. The Palas were losing their political hold not only in Bengal but also in Bihar. The findspots of Mahipal I's inscription show that he was in possession of South and North Bihar. No other Pala records were upto this period were found and people believed that Pala rule was limited to South Bihar. Jayswal was of opinion that the Palas ruled over undivided Bengal and Bihar excluding Mithila.[7] Another authority stated, "it is not exactly known what influence the Palas exercised over Tirhut in the IInd century A.D."[8] It is not certain whether Mahipala inherited or conquered North Bihar, but the fact remains that North Bihar was included in his dominions. That he ruled over Tirhut is now proved by the Imadpur Image Inscription. Mahipal had attempted to retrieve the lost position of Palas and it is quite likely that he might have conquered North Bihar. Mahipala's success could not be manintained for long by his successors. The Pala Kings came into conflict with the Kalachuris and Karna advanced upto the borders of West Bengal. According to Ramcharita[9] Vigrahpaladeva III defeated Karna and married his daughter Yannvansri. Both Nayapal and Vigrahpala III lost hold over West Bengal[10]. While the political power of the Palas was on the wane, Chalukya invasion under Vikaramaditya took palce on the regin of Vigrahpaldeva III. The Somavamsi ruler, Mahasiva Gupta Yayati, of Orissa also invaded Bengal in the middle of the 11th century A.D. Thus Palas were reduced to non-entity and the Pala power in Magadha was simply a shadow. An inscription from Gaya of 5th regnal year of king Vigrahpaladeva III says about the use of a new dynasty in Gaya, handed by Sudraka, Thus it is evident that Pala sovereignty was crumbling and their suzerainty over Magadha was reduced to a mere name.

From what we have seen above, it is evident that the Palas had practically lost all power in South Bihar. Being ousted from South Bihar they tried to retrieve this patrimony in North Bihar, which came under the Pala hegemony during the time of Mahipal if not earlier. Here we have to remember that while the inscriptions of Pala rules have been found in abundance in South Bihar, we had only one up to this period in North Bihar and Naulagarh is the second. It is quite likely that when the Palas were sufficiently weakened in Magadha, they tried to strengthen their position in Tirhut, Mahipala I had established his authority in Tirhut and it is quite likely that his successors either Nayapal or Vigrahpala III should have extended their authority in that area. They must have established their fort in Naulagarh for the preservation of their power. Naulagarh's close proximity to Gandak shows its importance. The report in the previous pages shows that in ancient time Ganges water also touched the rampart area in Naulagarh. Another important point to be noted is that Naulagarh is only at a distance of about 35 to 43 miles from Imadpur, where Mahipala's inscription was found. it seems probable that when during Vigrahpala III's reign the Palas in Magadha were reduced to mere name. They shifted their centre of activity to Naulagarh which was probably protected by river from both sides. Vigrahpala III's might have ruled for more than 24 years. This inscription if studied in the light of other epigraphic evidences in connection with the Pala chronology, may help us in ascertaining the exact date of Vigrahpala III's reign.

The motif and design of the image, in question, are also remarkable and may help us in ascertaining the age. The Pala period of our history ushered in a local school with its own characteristics known as the Eastern School of Medieval Art. The Pala kings were Buddhists and as such they patronised the Buddhist art. The Pala kings were Buddhists and as such they patronised the Buddhist art. But here we have to remember that Gupta tide and tradition persisted for a longer period in Bihar and the majority of people were within the fold of Brahmanism. The religious objects were generally translated into the objects of art. The stone is typically the Blask Gaya stone. By the middle of the 11th century the flying Gandharvas had been balanced between the two extremes of exuberance and sensuous developments. On the either side the attendant divinities and other accompanying figures are placed on separate lotus pedestal which shows the Vahanas of the deities represented. The vigour and strength of the body were transformed into one of gracefulness and elegant mannerism and the emphasis on decorative aspect is clear from the present image. Thus considered from the artistic and sculptural points of view, we cannot but place the present image in the latter half of the 11th century A.D. and on this basis also we can safely conclude that this particular image insrciption was inscribed during the reign of king Vigrahpala III.

The propagation of Hinduism was the marked feature of the age. We know that inspite of the existence of different religions there was no sectaraian jealousy during this period. The Buddhist Pala Kings maintained catholic attitude. Judged from the number of cultimages we learn that of the two great sects in Brahmani-cal religion, Vaisnavism seems to have been more popular than Saivism. In official records, Vigrahapala III is given credit for maintaining orthodox social orders of caste[11] Vigrahpala III must have bowed before the overwhelming majority of Hindu populace, because he was politically very weak and had to depend, more or less, on the support of his Hindu subjects. Not only this, but the script of the inscription bears testimony to the fact that it belonged to the latter half of the 11th century and the beginning of the 12th Century A.D. The script of the inscription is of early Bengali character of the 11th and 12th century A.D. As no other Vigrahapala execept the third one flourished during the latter half of the 11th century, we may safely ascribe this inscription to Vigrahpala III and fix the length of his reign at 24 years, if not more, pending the results of other excavations. It is, therefore suggested tentatively that the chronology since Vigrahpala III may be followed as such :-

1. Vigrahapala	III	1055 to 1079	instead of	1055 to 1070[12] A.D.
2. Mahipala	II	1079 to 1084	instead of	1070 to 1075 A.D.
3. Surpala	II	1084 to 1086	instead of	1075 to 1077 A.D.
4. Rampala		1086 to 1128	instead of	1077 to 1120 A.D.
5. Kumarpala		1128 to 1133	instead of	1120 to 1125 A.D.
6. Gopala	III	1133 to 1147	instead of	1125 to 1140 A.D.
7. Madanpala		1147 to 1161	instead of	1140 to 1154 A.D.
8. Govindpala		1161 to 1165	instead of	1155 to 1159 A.D.

References :

1. Name of places where important Vishnu images have been found :- Hankrail (Maldah), Laksmankati (Bakarganj), Chaitanpur (Burdwan), Baghaura (Tipperah), Burdwan, Surohor (Dinajpur), Sagardighi, Itahar (Dinajpur) Kalandarpur stone Image of Vishnu, Trivikram standing Vishnu at Rangpur, Sarangarh (Bankura), Deorat (Bogra), Sonarang (Dacca).
2. "The ancient city and district of krimita" by Dr. D.C. Sarkar in "Indian Historical Quarterly" Vol. 20 No.
2. (June 1950 P. 138-41.
3. It cannot be Vigrahpala II as the admitted date of Vigrahpala III is 1055 A.D. Dr. A. Banerjee, Sastri has taken 1058 A.D. as the year 3 of that Inscription (JBORS XXVI -Pt. 3 P. 237). Hence 1058-3 = 1055 and as such it cannot be date of Vigrahpala II.
4. R.D. Banerjee - Palas of Bengal P.81.
5. Ibid - P. 112.
6. Vide "History of Bengal" Vol I, P. 177 Ed. by Dr. R.C. Mazumdar, (Published by D.U.)
7. K.P.Jayswal, JBORS IX P to 3 and 4 P. 300.
8. S.N. Singh, History of Tirhut P. 56.
9. i.g. Commentar.
10. Mazumdar Opt. Cit. 146.
11. Amgachi C. P. the year 12.
12. As suggested in "Histroy of Bengal" (Mazumdar) Vol 1P. 177.

Courtesy :
*G.D.College Bulletin series No. 1, 1952
Editor : R.K.Choudhary

●●●

Further Report on Naulagarh

(Bulletin Series No. 2* G.D. College Begusarai)

Since the publication of our Bulletin No. 1 on behalf of the society, vast materials including inscriptions, seals, coins and terracotas have been added to our museum. These finds, from Naulagarh, are really very important from the historical point of view, on the basis of epigraphic and numismatic evidences, it can be said, with some amount of certainty that Naulagarh was, an important Pala administrative centre in North Bihar, it was the headquarter of Krmila Visaya. That, Naulagarh inscription is an important one, has been amply corroborated by scholars like Dr. R.C. Mazumdar, A.S.Altekar and D.C. Sarkar. D.C. Sarkar has already published an article on naulagrah Inscription in the Journal of the Bihar Research Society (Sep - December issue of 1951). Dr. Altekar is of opinion that the silver coin, published in our Bulletin No.1 belonged to Vigrahpala. Due to our consistent effort, the site has been thoroughly explored by an expert Archaeologist, Mr. Krishna Deva, Superintendent, Central Circle, Archaeological Survey, Government of India, on April 30, 1952.

Through the kind generosity of Sri Ramnath Singh, we acquired the inscribed image for our Museum in June, 1950. Since then, various other materials have come to light. On the basis of these materials, it can be tentatively said that Naulagarh had a continous history from the beginning of the Buddhist down to the Muslim period. We have also discovered some Muslim coins from that site. The exploration of Jaymanglagarh (report published elsewhere in this Bulletin) and other adjoining sites leads us to believe that all these sites taken together constitute a great area of historical importance. The black (Gaya) stone images, ranging from the Gandhar School down to the Eastern School of Medieval Sculpture, have been discovered from Bihat, Birpur, Naulagarh and Jaymangla-garh. Full pottery pieces and huge amount of cowries etc. point to the existence of a big ancient establishment in this part of the state, For a scientific study of the whole belt we have to connect the link between two important ancient Buddhist sites, viz, Naulagarh and Jaymanglagarh. In Bulletin No. 1, it was pointed out that Birpur was the place of residence of the administrative officers and Jay-manglagarh was the religious centre. Birpur and Jaymangalagarh finds show that these places were contemporaneous with the Pala administrative centre at Naula-garh. We shall discuss below, on the basis of new finds, the continuity of the history of Naulagarh.

Both at Naulagarh and Jaymanglagarh fortifications are still visible, Naulagarh seems to have been a well- planned fort in ancient time. The construction of this fort may be traced back to the Mauryan period. As the folk - tales corroborate, these defensive fortifications were constructed against the enemy. The ruined fort[1], as it exists today, was on the bank of river Bainti and there is said to have been a lake or tank inside the fort area. It was surrounded by an artificial canal of water on three sides and the bed of that old moat is still visible. Such construction of forts is described in Kautilya.[2] This is the case with Jaymangalagarh also. It was a very wellplanned fort. It appears that in the construction of the fort, mud - bricks and baked and burnt bricks were used. It was a thick rampart. Clay balls have been found in abundance. The fort seems to have been in good condition upto a very late period. Our explorations have convinced us that a greater portion of the rampart has been robbed off and huge pits have been created in those parts. On the south- western side of the rampart, clay mixed with cow-dung has been found and on all other sides, traces of broken and disturbed walls are visible. In the present state of our knowledge, it is very difficult to say how this site came to be destroyed.

From the surface finds of the rampart area, we have collected and a large number of N.B.P. (Northern Black Polish) pieces, near N.B.P. glazad pottery pieces, grey pottery pieces, and a fine piece of polished stone. Various kinds of beads and terracotas have been found. On the basis of these finds, it can be conjectured that this site had some affiniy with the Mauryan peeriod. Mauryan period was noted for its excellence, inpolished structures and wares. Such N.B.P. Wares have been found in different parts of our country and in large quantity at Vaishali and Kumrehrar (Pataliputra). Polished wares were followed by grey and glazed wares. Specimens of all such verities are in our museum. Though much of the stray pottery finds have been destroyd, we have in our possesion few pieces of N.B.P. grey and glazed pottery pieces. All these finds indicate that Naulagarh had acquired prominence during the Buddhist period. A rare Sunga[3] terracota figurine shows that it was an important seat during the Sunga period. A very brilliant Gupta terracota figure has also been discovered. Other terracotas are still unidentified. Clay coin-moulds of two different varities are there. In one of them, we find a horse on the obverse and a rider on the 'horse' on the reverse (vide - plate in Bulletin No. 1). Perhaps, this was a coin - mould of the "horseman type." A blackstone image of Bodhisattva (plate in Bulletin No. 1), probably in Gandhar style, has also been found, Some rare images have been noticed, but they are in possession of private individuals. Unfortunately for us, an inscribed clay ball has been lost. The inscription, on the clay ball, was "Harshavardhan Rajjan." In the absence of the exact inscribed piece, it is difficult to believe in its authenticity. Much reliance can not be placed on this lost inscribed clay ball.

We have now ample evidence to show that Naulagarh was an important centre of the Pala administration. We have already discussed the importance of Naulagarh Inscription (No. 1) of Vigrahapal III in Bulletin No. 1. It has been an established fact that Tirhut formed a part of the Pala Empire[4]. From the Monghyr Grant of Narayanpala, we learn that a part of Tirabhukti continued to be in his possession[5]. The Bhagalpur Grant of Narayanpala records, the grant of the village Makutika to the temple of Siva and Kalasapota Situated in the Kaksa Visya of Tirabhukti. Till the discovery of Naulagarh Inscription No.1, we had no knowledge about the existence of Krmila visaya in this region. Even the exact location of Kaksa Visaya has not yet been fixed. Controversy centres round the exact location of Krmila Visaya. The earliest mention of the word Krmila is found in the Monghyr copper-plate of Devapala, wherein it is stated that it was a part of Srinagarbhukti. Dr. Sircar[6], on the basis of new inscriptions discovered in the small village of valgudar or Varagujar in south Monghyr, concluded that the city of Krmila stood either on the very site of that village or on a site, parts of which are now occupied by the village. In the light of Naulagarh inscription No. 1 we can not preclude the possibility of one Krmila Visaya in Tirabhukti also. The mention of the word "Krmila" in Naulagarh inscription No. 1 can tentatively be taken to mean that there was one such Visaya in Tirabhukti. Further light on the Pala rule is thrown by the discovery of a big stone inscription, known henceforward as Naulagarh Inscription No. 2, published elsewhere in this Bulletin. Naulagarh's importance during the Pala period is established beyond doubt. From the muslim coins, found here, it appears that it continued to be an important centre during the Muslim rule. It is mentioned as an old village in Aini - Tirhut[7]. The causes of its destruction are not known.

From what we have seen above, it is clear that a scientific excavation will yield valuable results. On behalf of our society and the College, we have done our best to bring to light this ancient site. Now we hope that the Department of Archaeology will examine this site more thoroughly and carefully and take some trial trenches here and there to assess its archaelogical value and importance. The site has already been destroyed but now it is hoped that it will be declared a protected area. Unless that is done, no protection is possible.

References :

1. Vide - "Diagram" in Bulletin No. 1
2. Arthasastra - Bk 11, Chapters 3 and 4.
3. Sunga and Gupta Terracotas have been indentified by Mr. Krishna Deva, Superintendent, Archaeological Surrey, Govt. of India.
4. Form Tirhut, there are sufficient epigraphic sources to prove this - e.g.

(a) Naulagarh Inscrip tion No. 1 (Published in our Bulletin No. 1)

(b) Naulagarh inscription No. 2 (Published elsewhere in this Bulletin)

(c) Balirajgarh Inscription of Madanpala (in Darbhanga district. This inscription is still unnoticed. I have been informed about this inscripiton).

(d) Imadpur Inscription of Mahipal.

5. R. D. Banerjee - "Palas of Bengal" P. 59.
6. I. H.Q. - XXVI - No. 2 pp. 138 - 141
7. Bihari Lal - Aini - Tirhut P. 143

Courtesy :
*G.D.College Bulletin Series No. 2 , 1952
Editor : R.K.Choudhary

Naulagarh Inscription No. 2*

1st line - Namo Dharmay ....

2nd line - Sradham Karunya Sambheda Snanamastum

3rd line - (m) (ayi) Punyadharam. Bhiksam Bhujamatyi
(s) Samayadha tumaksha.

4th line - (vad) .... asray manvita. Yadabadha cha
Svaha (?or Sradha) Kau dwau chinta.

5th line- bha Vamada .... damal Vyavasthitah.

6th line - Sradhyam yava (cha ?) ...... yada Grhadhi (Dhai) yad.

7th line ... . daka .... Vihara.

8th line .... Indistinct.

9th line .... Indistinct.

1st line - नमो धर्माय ....

2nd line - श्रद्धा कारूण्य संभेद स्नानमस्तुम

3rd line - (मयि) पुण्यधारां। भिक्षां भुजामत्यि (स) मायधतुमक्ष।

4th line - (वाह या वाद) .... आश्रय मन्विता। यदवध। (च) स्वाहा (? या श्रद्धा) कौ द्वौ चिन्ता

5th line - .... भा वमद् .... दमल व्यवस्थिताह

6th line - श्रद्धाया याव (व) .... यद गृहाधि (धै) याद

7th line - .... दक .... विहार ....

8th & 9th - Indistinct -

This Naulagarh Inscription No. 2 is another brilliant discovery and adds a new list to the already existing Pala records. The discovery is unuique in the sense that it gives an idea about the existence of a Buddhist Vihara in North Bihar. Unfortunately, the whole piece of the inscribed stone is not available. Some letters and words of the inscription are not distinct and hence it has not been possible for us to decipher it successfully. A tentative reading of the inscription has been given above and it is hoped that the scholars will throw more light on the importance of this inscription. Like other Sanskrit inscription of the Pala period, the language of the inscription is incorrect Sanskrit. It appears that the record has been carelessly incised. It seems that the purpose of this inscription was to record the erection of a monastery. There is no doubt that the whole of Monghyr district was an ancient Buddhist site and we find its reference in the writings of the chinese travallers. Before discussing the importance of this inscription, it would be better to give a brief sketch of Buddhist monasteries in the district of Monghyr.

According to the Chinese traveller, Hieun Tsang, there were ten Buddhist monasteries and more than four hundred bretheren in Monghyr, most of whom were Hinayanists. Besides that there were twenty Deva Temples and the adherents of various religious lived pell - mell[1]. Various Buddhist sites in the district of Monghyr have been discovered. Rajaona (Lo-in-ni-lo of Hien- Tsang) possessed a monastery. Uren was an important Buddhist site[2]. All these Buddhist sites lay onthe southern side of the Ganges. As yet, we have practically no information about the existence of any such site on the northern side of the Ganges (i.e. in North Bihar). We know that in North Bihar there were some important religious centres where the Chinese travellers flocked to pay their homage. Of these centres 'Sin-Che temple'[3] was the most important centre, where four Chinese travellers had come and lived. As it has been pointed out elsewhere in this Bulletin, (vide Report on Jaymanglagarh) this Sin - Che temple lay somewhere between the Anguttarap region (Auguttarap Janapada) on the one hand and Kusi country on the other. It appears that Sin-Che temple was an important centre and it later on developed into a Vihara.

During the period of Pala rule, Bengal and Bihar remained the last stronghold of Buddhism. Mahayan Buddhism became a powerful international force during this period. The Pala kings were the patrons of learning and during this period various monasteris were established. Odandpuri, Somapur, Vikramsila and Nalanda were some of the important Viharas. The other famous Viharas were Traikutaka, Devikot, Pandita, Sannagara, Phullhari, Pattikeraka, Vikrampuri and Jagaddala[4]. It is accepted that there were many other smaller institutions whose names have been lost.[5] Phullhari and its hermitages are frequently referred to as a place where several Buddhist Acharyas lived and varieous Sanskrit texts were translated in to Tibetan in collaboration with Tibetan scholars. It is said to have been situated somewhere near Monghyr[6]. Naulagarh Inscription No. 2 belongs to the 11th - 12th century A.D. On paleographic grounds, it can be said that the inscription belonged to the regin of Vigrahpala III. An inscription of Vigrahpala III has already been discovered at Naulagarh. The name of the Vihara in Naulagarh Inscription No. 2 has not been deciphered. The script of the inscription, any how, helps us in ascertaining the age of this inscription No. 2. We have noted above that names of Various monastries are now not known to us. In Bulletin No. 1, it was pointed out that Vigrahpala III shifted his centre of activity to Naulagarh. It is quite likely that the establishment of the Pala political power in Naulagarh was followed by the establishemnt of a Vihara there. The exact location of the above mentioned Phullhari Vihara somewhere near Monghyr, has not yet been settled. But it is sure that our inscription does not refer to Phullhari Vihara. The letters are blurred. Various mounds at Naulagarh, besides the fortification area, point to the existence of Vihars and other establishments. It is now for the arcaeologists to see for themselves the Naulagarh site. Only by laying out trial trenches, the site of a Vihara can be located.

References :

1. Watters 11 - P. 178; 11, P. 186
2. Wadde LL - Discovery of Buddhist remains at Uren - JASB, Part 1 (1892)
3. Beal - "Life of Hieun -Tsang"- PPXXII - XXXVI.
4. History of Bengal - Ed. by Dr. R.C. Mazumar, Vol 1. PP. 416 - 418.
5. Ibid also 1. C., 1,227.
6. History of Bengal opt. Cit.

Courtesy :
*G.D.College Bulletin series No. 2 , 1952
Editor : R.K.Choudhary

●●●

The Chakwars of Begusarai
(Bulletin Series No. 3* G.D. College Begusarai)

Antiquity of Samho -

Samho is situated on the bank of the river Ganges. Samho seems to be a very ancient village. Its antiquities have now been washed by the Ganges. Some ancient Buddhist sites are at a distance of few miles from Samho. Uren, an ancient Buddhist site in the district of Monghyr, is at a distance of six miles from Samho. Lord Buddha is said to have spent one of his rainy seasons at Uren and is believed to have visited Samho also. Before the destruction of Samho by the Ganges, Various dihs and mounds were there and people used to find a large number of antiquities. During this period of destruction, an image of Buddha (in black stone) was discovered. This image is inscribed and represents various mudras. it is now preserved in a temple. This image can be placed between 9th and 10th century A.D. The inscription reads ***"Svasti ye Dhammo hetu Prabhaba hetun (= Tesan) Tathagato hyavadat = (Tesan) cha yo Nirodha evam vadi mahasramah*** "-Meaning -" Blessings - Those functions that are born of causes - The Tathagata indeed knew that causes and that restraint of these too, the great Sramana saying thus."

There was a sacred place known as Chandi Asthan. There was a very old well and even today the villagers say that the well was filled in by the Europeans in the 18th century. About thirty five years when the whole site was being destroyed by the Ganges a big incised brick was discovered near the well. The theme of the incised brick was that in fasli 760 (=1351-52 A.D.) the well was repaired by one Dhiraj Singh and thereby the latter incurred an expenditure of Rs. 485/10/- only on that account. That brick was preserved in the village. In 1925-26, Sir Ganesh Datta Singh and the Collector of Monghyr, visited Samho. The Collector took away the incised brick. Where that incised brick is kept, nobody knows.

Traditional history -

The Chakwars belong to high caste Hindu and they claim one Chirain Misra as their ancestor. He is said to have migrated from Tirhut as early as 10th - 11th century and settled in Begusarai Subdivison. The purpose of his coming over to this part was to take holy bath in the Ganges. On his arrival here he found the circumstances favourble. Chirain Misra established himself here and carved out a small kingdom. From that small kingdom, there arose a big kingdom of the Chakwars. They extended, their authority in different parts of the district and became a powerful force. They claim that Muhammad Ghori's army had to face a stiff opposition of the Chakwars at Chakwara (modern Chewara in P.S. Sheikh-pura, District Monghyr). It is said that a fakir accompanied Ghori's army and it was believed that so long fakir would remain alive no one could be able to defeat the Muslim. Ultimately the fakir was killed and his tomb is said to be there. It is a well known fact that the eastward expansion of the Muslim power in north Bihar was at that time barred by the powerful Hindu Kingdom of Mithila under the Karnat dynasty and as such the momentum of Muslim offensive acquired a driving force in south Bihar. They (Muslims) occupied Nalanda and Odantpur monastries in south Bihar. It is not yet definitely known what other portions of south Bihar were conquered by Muslims during the period. It is very difficult to ascertain the actual history of these folk-tales which are preserved till today as a piece of family tradition. Tradition asserts that the Chakwars had to wage a war aganist Malik Baya , a commander of Muhammad - bin- Tuglak and ultimately Malik Baya was defeated and killed. It is said that Malik Baya's tomb is in Biharshariff. Traditional sources are conflicting. The Chakwars had to fight aganist the Lodi army. A thorough search for records in Chakwar belt will certainly yield good results. It is said that the Chakwar records are spread over different parts of Bihar.

Chak and Samho were the two earliest villages inhabited by the Chakwars. From Chak, the Chakwars came to be divided into 12 villages and these twelve villages again came to be divided into two groups, one consisting of nine villages and other of three. These nine villages were again subdivided into six parts. These divisions took place in the 17th - 18th century. These persons had occasional tussle with the English East India company in the 18th century. According to the Chakwars, the Chakwar Kingdom extended from Rajmahal in the east to Tekari in the west and from Darbhanga in the north to the borders of Orissa in the south. It is said that Tekari was under the contol of the Chakwar Raja Bakhtawar Singh and Raja Sunder Singh was one of his commanders. After the defeat of Bakhtawar Singh, Sunder Singh established a separate kingdom of Tekari. Tradition asserts that Bakhtawar Singh had contest with one Kamdar Kha, a general of Allivardi and in this contest with one Kamdar Khan, a general of Allivardi and in this contest the Chakwar Raja came out successful. The same tradition asserts that Allivardi called a conference of ten Chakwar princes for the settlement of rent but treacherously murdered them and sent back their heads to Samho by a special boat.

History of the Chakwars based on Records

Before passing on to the actual history of the Chakwars, as described in the Muslim and the Company records, it is better to throw some light on the acutal extent of the Chakwar kingdom and also on such Chakwar kings about whom incidental reference is made here and there. We have seen above that the Chakwar Kingdom extended to Rajmahal in the east and Darbhanga in the north. The traditional sources point out that their kingdom extended upto Pargana Chai in Thana Bihpur.[1] This particular fact is corroborated by the Muslim and other sources. It is stated that Raja of Purnea and other inhabitants of that part of the Chakwar tribe were refractory. As a protection against these chiefs the fort of Jalalgarh was erected and a commandant was posted there. Saif Khan was deputed to chastise the Raja of Birnagar and other malcontents of that part of the courtry. Refractory conduct on the part of Birshah induced Saif Khan to cross the Kosi. He succeeded in chastising the Raja of Birnagar. After this exploit, Praganas of Dhaphar, Nathpur, Dharampur and Govari, formerly attached to Sarkar Monghyr, were transferred to the Purnea jurisdiction.[2] Nawab Zafar Khan conferred the office of Zilla Purnea and that of Commandant of Jalalgarh upon him and also settled on him the pargana of Birnagar alias Dharampur Gond-wana, and also the mahals and jagirs forming an appendage to the office of the commandant of the above fort. The aforesaid Khan expelled Durjan Singh, son of Birshah, the Raja of Birnagar and brought the aforesaid Paragana under his subjection and having thoroughly chastised the other malcontents freed the road from all perils.[3]

In the first half of the 18th century, the distintegration of Delhi Empire had set in. The drama of Mughal history moved with extraodinary rapidity. The provinces had begun to raise their heads and within every province local chieftains took advantage of the chaotic political situation. Various kings and jagirdars ceased to pay taxes and attempted to extend their territory. By that time the chak-wars had become strong enough. That they had asserted independence is evident from the fact that they issued various land grants to various persons under their signatures and seals. Some such grants have been disecovered by us. Out of the five grants, discovered so far, it appears that Raja Bakhtawar Singh of Samho granted 100 (hundred) bighas of land to one Harnath Tewari of Keonta near Dalsinghsarai (N.E.R.) in fasli 1135 (1726 - 27 A.D.). This shows that Bakhtawar Singh's sway extended at least upto Dalsinghsarai. We have the following grants of Raja Bakhtawar Singh :-

i) Land - grant issued in the fasli year 1127 (1718-1719 A.D.). It bears the signature of Raja Bakhtawar Singh and the official seal is in Urdu. It records the grant of ten bighas of land to a particular person in village Salha.

ii) Land - grant issued in the fasli year 1131 (1722-1723 A.D.) - Other things same as in the previous grant.

iii) Land - grant issued in the fasli year 1133 (1724-25 A.D.) two land - grants of that year have been discovered.

-- These two have the seal (in Urdu) and signature of Raja Bakhtawar Singh - Raja Bakhtawar Singh's signature is generally in kaithi script in all the land grants.

iv) Land- grant issued in the fasli year 1135 (1726- 27 A.D.)- records the grant of 100 bighas of land to one in Keonta near Dalsinghsarai (N.E.R.)

v) There is one more land - grant, but its date is missing. In all these grants Raja Bakhtawar Singh is called "Maharaja Bakhtawar Singh Deva Devanam." The title indicates that he was not merely a feudal cheif of a particular area but a real ruler of a territory, how ever small it may be. On the basis of these five grants we can say that Raja Bakhtawar Singh was ruling between 1718 and 1727. If the year mentioned in the land-grants be taken as the Muslim Era, then there may be some difference in the fixation of equivalent English dates. He might have advantage of the chaotic political condition and asserted his independence. The company records mention Bakhtawar Singh was the king of the Chakwars.[4] Thus it is evident that the Chakawar kings granted land to various classes of people for their maintenance. We have one more record of another Chakwar king[5] of granting land to a Muslim Fakir. From a grant, still preserved in a family, we learn that one Hajrat Makhdum Saiyed Sah Alauddin Bokhari came to Ballia in hirjri 900. There flourished in his family one Hajrat Saiyed Sah Mohinddin Bokhari in the 1st half of the 18th century. He was a great saint and teacher. Raja Shivadatta Singh Chakwar was very much influenced by his personality. He was so much attached to this saint that he (Raja Shivadatta Singh) granted him 5229 bighas of land in village Ballia. The descendants of that fakir are still there. Raja Shivadatta Singh made this grant in the fasli year 1126 (1719 -20 A.D.) This grant was respected by Allivardi and his successors and later on confirmed by the East India Company in 1828. His descendants enjoy this privilege even now.[6] This confirmation of the grant by the later rulers shows that Raja Shivadatta Singh also enjoyed the Independent status otherwise his grant would not have been honoured by the later rulers. We are told that Allivardi and his successors respected the charters granted by Bakhtawar Singh. We further learn that one Ruko Singh Chakwar, uncle of Raja Bakhtwar Singh, took advantage of the chaotic condition in Pargana Pharkiya. Pharkiya was inhabited by Dusadhs. In the 15th century, a Rajput named Bishwanath Rai was sent from Delhi to restore order in this part and ultimately the Zemindari devolved on his posterity. In the year 1730 Raja Kunjal Singh was a prominent Zemindar of that area. Taking advantage of his weakness, Ruko Singh plundered the country and treacherously murdered Raja Kunjal Singh.[7] The Chakwars had become sufficiently strong in this part of Monghyr by 1730.

The Company records are also full of materials relating to the Chakwars of Samho. Muhammad Shah ascended the throne of Delhi in 1719 - 20 A.D. By that time the strength of the Mughal empire had already become a thing of the past. The Britisheres had started their trade vigorously in Bihar. In 1719 Edward Stephenson was appointed the chief of Patna with Thomas Falconer as his second. The Chakwars of Begusarai Sub-division had become very powerful and had asserted their independence. They defied the authority of the Subadar of Bengal and the Emperor of Delhi. They stopped payment of rent to the Goverment.[8] Their strength lay in the fact that they controlled the river-route (Ganges) from Monghyr to Patna, In those days river was the best trade route. They laid every thing, that passed on the river Ganges by Monghyr, under heavy contributions and thereby extorted a huge amount from the European traders. They did this simply to assert their independent status. They put to the

European traders to annual heavy expense of a large armament to ascort their boats carrying merchandise from and to Patna.[9] In 1718 the Calcutta Council noted that they would require a strong party of a hundred men to send with their boats carrying treasure for the settlement of their factory there as the Chakwars had grown extremely powerful at couna and other places during the vacancy of Subadarship.[10] This also shows that as early as 1718 the Chakwars had asserted their independence and had become powerful enough to levy taxes on the European traders. The place, Conna, has not yet been rightly identified. Most probably it was Khanua near Warsaliganj police-station in Gaya district. On 27th August, 1719, Messrs Stephenson and Falconer of Patna wrote to the Calcutta Council from Chandi (?) on their way from Calcutta to Patna that they were twice attacked by the Chakwars who were very strong and had entrenched themeselves by the river side. Chandi was at a distance of about thirty miles south-east of Patna. There was a fierce engagement for sometime between the European traders and the Chakwars but at length the Chakwars were driven from their entrenchments, many of them were killed and some were carried prisoners to Patna. On the Side of the Company a sergeant was killed and a drummer and a soldier wounded.[11] The Chakwars claim that they defeated the European traders on various occasions. Only July 11, 1720, Stephenson and Falconer worte from Patna that the Chakwars "continue very strong" and requested for a strong party of soldiers.[12] On August 2, 1720, the Calcutta Council sent 200 European soldiers to guard the way to Patna as the Chakwars had 'come to a great head' and that could at a little notice, double their numbers. By September 22, they succeeded in gathering together about 2500 horses and a great number of infantry, recruited from Buxar, and were "resolved to make an attempt" on the boats of the company.[13] From a study of the reports, it appears that the situation was very tense and the Europeans were certainly very anxious over the problem. The contingent was sent under the command of Major Richard Hunt. On October 14, the safe arrival of the boats was reported.[14]

In December, 1720, Nasiat (Yar) Khan was appointed Governor of Bihar. He could not subdue the Chakwars. From the Chakwars records, it is evident that Chakwars were independent during his governorship, Bakhtawar had his own official seal. Had he been under the Nawab, he would not have used his own official seal. In the month of March, 1721, the Patna authority reported that the Chakwars had defeated a party of the horse sent by the Nawab. Upon this defeat, the Nawab had ordered 4000 horses against the Chakwars. The Chakwars, thereupon, evaded an engagement.[15] The Chakwars continued to be sufficiently strong and the Company's boat had to be carried with sufficient convoy. The company thought it better to augment the party of soldiers.[16] By 1721 Bakhtawar Singh had come to be recognised as the Raja of the Chakwars. Conna Raja was also very strong. Jungalsaw, a great leader, joined Conla Raja and bordered upon the Chakwar country and joined his force with the Raja of the Chakwars, Bakhtawar Singh. This alliance alarmed the European traders and they prayed for more soldiers.[17] In the month of October, Conna Raja was driven away by his own Kinsmen. What happened afterwards is not actually known. From the Company records, it appears that the old brave Raja of the Chakwars died in 1730 and was succeeded by his son, a youth of seventeen years.[18] Unfortunately the records do not give us the name of the king who died, and the name of the prince who succeeded him. Until further evidence is forthcoming, it is difficult to arrive at any conclusion on this particular point. This young prince, being influenced by the examples made of several Bihar Rajas, submitted to Allivardi.[19] The Raja acknowleged the sway of the Delhi Emperor and subjection to the Subadar of Bengal. Here the tradition gives us a clue to the cause of the defeat of the Chakwars by Allivardi. It is Said that an offical (most probably his Rajpandita) of Bakhtawar Singh betrayed him and gave out the secret to Allivardi on a promise of Rs. 30/- per month by the latter to the former. After his victory, Allivardi granted a Sanad to that man confirming his promise of the said amount and that Sanad was honoured by Company later on. a frantic search is being made to find out that document, because that will show how treacherously Allivardi defeated the Chakwar Raja. It is known to all that treachery was one of the main traits of Allivardi's character. After the defeat of the Chakwars, an annual tribute was stipulated and was regularly paid for four years. A spot was fixed on thirty miles from the capital of the Chakwars (Samho) where the prince met every year Nawab's officer on a certain day and it was agreed upon that they should have only thirty attendants on each side.[20] Holwell writes that heads of thirty Chak-wars, who had gone to pay tribute to Allivadi, were severed and were sent back home and at the same time their capital was sacked and burnt.[21] This particular point is also preserved in the traditional history. Allivardi is said to have granted Sanad to many Chakwar chiefs for various purposes.

The brave old Raja who died in 1730 must have been some other man than Bakhtawar Singh because we find that Allvardi after having subdued the refractory Chiefs of Bihar, secured adhesion of a large number of Hindu - Muslim generals including one Bakhtawar Singh.[22] It seems probable that after being subdued by Allivardi, Bakhtawar Singh entered into friendship with Allivardi Khan and helped him in his consolidation of power. One Bakht Singh is mentioned as an ally of the Nawab[23] who led an expedition against the Raja of Tirhut. No last word can be said on the subject as materials are daily coming to light. A through search for the Chakwars manuscript is necessary.

References :

1. Narayan Shahi had established a Chakwar kingdom in Pargana Chai.
2. Heenter' Statistical Account of Bengal vol. XV P. 222.
3. A Salam - "Riyaz-us- salatin" P.36.
4. Wilson - Early Annals of English in Bengal vol. III P. 371
5. I am greateful to my Student Sahdeo Singh (IV year Arts) for this piece of information about Raja Shivadatta Singh Chakwar.

6. Of - Safarnama Mazhari by Md. Halim Ansari P. 188.
7. Hunter opt, cit. P. 18; Monghyr Gazetteer P. 243.
8. Riyaz -P. 36 and P. 296; of. Gladwin "A narrative of the transactions in Bengal" (1906) P. 79.
9. Holwell - Intereasting Historical events P. 68-70. cf. Dr. K.K. Datta. "Allivardi and his times" P.P. 14-15.
10. Wilson - opt. cit. P. 50.
11. Wilson - P. 153.
12. Wilson - p. 255.
13. Wilson - 275
14. Ibid - 283
15. Ibid - 325
16. Ibid - 353
17. Ibid - P. 371
18. Holwell Opt. Cit 69- 70
19. Riyaz - P . 296; Holwell 68-70
20. Holwell, 69-70.
21 Holwell - 70- 71.
22 Riyaz - P. 311.
23. Lalkavi's description of the battle of Kandarpi Ghat (in Maithili)

Courtesy :
G.D.College Bulletin series No.3 , 1952
Editor : R.K.Choudhary

●●●

A Report on The exploration of Rani Godhna

Nothing tangible is known to us about the antiquity of Rani - Godhna. In that village there is a mound known as "Majous Dih." Brick -bats and pottery pieces are found in aboundance. It is said that a few hundred of years ago, river Ganges used to touch that point. To great extent that mound has now been destroyed and various hutments have been constructed on it. Folk -tales about the antiquity of Rani- Godhna are given below.

It is said that Akbar stayed here for sometime along with his two wives - one Hindu and one Muslim. He had come here in connection with the conquest of Bihar. His arrival was commemorated by the establishment of two villages, viz, Akbarpur Rani in commemoration of his Hindu wife and Beghamsarai of his Muslim wife. While Akbar was staying here some Brahmanas of Tirhut had come to take a bath in the Ganges. At that time Akbar was anxiously waiting for the return of his son from battle. Having learnt about the arrival of the Brahmanas from Tirhut, he asked them to forecast about the return of his son on the promise that he would grant them Jagir if their prophecy came true. The prophecy came true and Akbar granted them Jagir. The area of Pargana Akbarpur Rani, 8935 bighas in all, was granted to them as jagir in recognition of their loyal services to the Emperor. At present there are five tolas, viz, Narepur, Shivatola, Sravanatola, Ranitola & Begamsarai. Godhna is a separate village attached to pargana Imadpur.

These folk-tales are of no help practically when we have no other evidences of this area. Muslim coins have been found in most of the villages but even these are now not available. What we know from history is this that Akbar conquered Hajipur in 1574. Before Akbar's campaign several Pathan families had settled in Tirhut. Akbar made Hajipur the base of all imperial occupation. Tirhut was made a separate Sarkar and was put in charge of Khan- i- Azam, Governor of Bengal. Sometime an iota of truth is there in the folk - tales. It is likely that Akbar's army might have come upto this region to suppress the enemy and in commemoration of victory might have named a village Akbarpur Rani and Begamsarai.

* This archaeological site has been reported to KPJRI, Patna under 'documentations of archaeological sites in Bihar' in 2007.

Published in "Archaeological sites of Begusarai" written by Dr. Shailesh Kr. Sinha and Dr. Amiya Krishna. P – 19 (Editor.)

Courtesy :
G.D.College Bulletin series No.3 , 1952
Editor : R.K.Choudhary

●●●

The Chakwars of Begusarai

(Bulletin Series No. 4* G.D. College Begusarai)

Arun Kr. Sinha*

Chak and Samho were the two earliest villages inhabited by the Chakwars of Begusarai in Monghyr District. From Chak, the Chakwars soon came to be divided into twelve villages. The latter again were divided into two groups. One consisted of nine villages and other of three. These nine villages were once again sub-divided into six parts. These divisions are said to have taken place in the 17th- 18th century. The Chakwars of these different villages are reported to have frequently clashed with the East India Company in the 18th century.[1]

The village of Samho is situated on the bank of the Ganga, and appears to be a very ancient village. some ancient Buddhist sites have also been discovered at a distance of few miles from Samho. Urena, an ancient Buddhist site in the district, is situated at a distance of only six miles from Samho, where lord Buddha is said to have spent one of his rainy seasons, and is believed to have now been completely destroyed by the Ganga.[2] An image of Buddha[3] of 9th -10th century A.D. was also discovered there. Besides, there was also a sacred place known as chandi- Asthana where a big incised brick was discovered about forty years ago near a very old well which is said to have been filled in by the Europeans in the 18th century. The theme on the incised brick was that "in Fasli 760 (=1351 - 52 A.D.) the well was repaired by one Dhiraj Sinha and there by the latter incurred an expenditure of Rs. 485/10/- only on that account."[4] The whole site has now been thoroughly destroyed by the Ganga.

According to the traditional history, the Chakwars belong to high caste and they claim one Chirain Misra as their ancestor. He is said to have migrated from Tirhut as early as the 10th-11th century and settled in Begusarai sub-division. He went there to take a holy bath in the Ganga. On his arrival there he found the circumstances favourable, settled there and carved out a small kingdom. From that small kingdom, there arose a big Kingdom of the Chakwars who extended their authority in different parts of the districts and thus became powerful force. It is said that Muhammad Ghori's army had to face a stiff opposition of the Chakwars at Chakwara.[5] According to them, the Chakwar Kingdom extended form Rajmahal in the East to Tekari in the West and from Darbhanga in the North to the borders of Orissa in the South. It is a well known fact that the eastward expansion of the Muslim power in North Bihar was at that time barred by the powerful Hindu Kingdom of Mithila under the Karnatas and as such the momentum of Muslim offensive acquired a driving force in South Bihar.

Tradition asserts that the Chakwars also waged a war against Malik Baya, a commander of Muhammad-bin-Tuglak, in which Malik Baya was defeated and killed. His tomb is said to be in Bihar Sarif. The Chakwars are traditionally also said to have fought against the Lodi army.

It is said that Tekari was under the control of Chakwar Raja Bakhtawar Sinha, and Raja Sundara Sinha was one of his commanders. It was after the defeat of Bakhtawar Sinha that Sundara Sinha established a separate kingdom of Tekari. According to tradition Bakhtawar Sinha had also fought against one Kamdar Khan, a general of Alivardi, in which the Chakwar Raja came out victorious. The same tradition also asserts that Alivardi called a conference of the Chakwar princes for the settlement of rent but treacherously murdered them and sent back their heads to Samho by a special boat.[6] All told, it is very difficult to ascertain the actual history out of these folk-tales which are preserved till today as a piece of family traditon.

Let us now turn to the history of the Chakwars based on Muslim and East India Company records. The traditional sources point out that their kingdom extended up to Pargana Chai in Thana Bihpur, where Narayana Sahi had established a Chakwar Kingdom. It is also said that the Raja of Purnea and other inhabitants of that part of the Chakwar tribe were refractory. The Fort of Jalalgarh under a commandant was erected as a protection against these chiefs. Saif Khan was deputed to chastise the Raja of Birnagar and other malcontents of that part of the country. Refractory conduct on the part of Bir Sah induced Saif Khan to cross the Kosi. He succeeded the Raja of Birnagar, and as a result the Paraganas of Dhaphad, Nathpur, Dharampur and Gorari, formerly attached to Sarkar Monghyr, were transferred to the Purnea Jurisdiction.[7] Nawab Jafar Khan conferred the office of Zillah Purnea and that of commandant of Jalalgarh upon him and also settled on him the Pargana of Birnagar alias Dharampur, Gondwana, and also the Mahals and Jagirs forming an appendage to the office of the commandant of above fort. Saif Khan expelled Durjana Sinha, son of Bir Sah, the Raja of Birnagar and brought the aforesaid Pargana under his subjection, and having thoroughly chastised the other malcontents freed the road from all perils.[8]

The first half of the 18th century witnessed the process of disintegration of the Delhi Empire. Things moved with extra-ordinary rapidity. The chaotic political situation in the country emboldened the petty provincial chieftains to raise their heads. Most of the Rajas, Zamindars and Jagirdars ceased to pay taxes to the Imperial exchequer. They also attempted at extending their territory. The Chakwars had by this time become quite strong. They had already asserted independence and issued various land-grants to various persons under their signatures and seals. Five grants have been discovered so far by Prof. R.K. Chaudhary.[9] They clearly show that Raja Bhaktawar Sinha of Samho granted 100 (hundred) bighas of Land to one Harnatha

Tiwari of Keonta near Dalsinghsarai (in Samastipur sub-division of Darbhanga district) in Fasli 1135 (=1726-27 A. D.). This shows that his sway extended atleast up to Dalsinghsarai. We have the following Land-grants of Raja Bakhtawar Sinha[10] :-

1) Land grant issued in the Fasli year 1127 (= 1718-1719 A. D.). It bears the signature of Raja Bakhtawar Sinha and the official seal is in Urdu. It records the grant of ten bighas of Land to a paritcular person in village Salha in Darbhanga Sadar.

2) Land-grant issued in the Fasli year 1131 (= 1722-23 A. D.) other things same as in the previous grant.

3) Land - grant issued in the Fasli year 1133 (=1724-25 A. D.)[11], Two Land-grants of that year have been discovered which bear the seal in Urdu and signature of Raja Bakhtawar Sinha. His signature is generally in Kaithi script in all the Land-grants.

4) Land-grant issued in the Fasli year 1135 (=1726-27 A. D.) records the grants of 100 bighas of Land to one in Keonta village near Dalsinghsarai in Samasti-pur Sub-division.

5) There is one more Land-grant. Its date is missing. All these grants refer to Raja Bakhtawar Sinha as "Maharaja Bakhtawar Sinha Deva Devanam." The title indicates that he was not a mere feudal chief of a particular area, but a powerful ruler of a territory however small it may be. On the basis of the above Land- grants.[12] It can safely be concluded that Raja Bakhtawar Sinha was ruling between 1718 and 1727 A. D. A feudal chief in the beginning, he probably took advantage of the chaotic political condition and assumed Independece. The East India Company records refer to him as the kings of the Chakwars.[13] This is also corroborated by the fact that the Chakwar kings granted Land to various classes of people for their maintenance. Another Chakwar king Raja Sivadatta Sinha Chakwar granted 5229 bighas of Land to a Muslim Fakir, Hajrat Syed Sah Mohiuddin Bokhari, in village Ballia, in the Fasli year 1126 (1719-20 A.D.).[14] This grant was respected by Alivardi and his successors and later on confirmed by the East India Company in 1828 A. D. The confirmation of this grant by later rulers conclusively proves the Raja Sivadatta Sinha also enjoyed independent status as otherswise, his grant would not have been so honoured. Alivardi and his successors are also said to have respected the charters granted by Raja Bakhtawar Sinha.[15]

It is said that one Ruko Sinha, uncle of Raja Bakhtawar Sinha took advantage of the chaotic condition in Pargana Pharkiya which was inhabited by Dusadhs. In the 15th century a Rajput named Bishwanatha Rai wa sent from Delhi to restore peace and order there, and ultimately the Zamindari devolved on his posterity. In the year 1730 Raja Kunjala Sinha was a prominent Zamindar of that area. Taking advantage of his weakness, Ruko Sinha plundered the country and treacheroulsy murdered Raja Kunjala Sinha plundered the country and treacherously murdered Raja Kunjala Sinha.[16] Thus, the Chakwara had become sufficiently strong in this part of Monghyr by 1730 A.D.

Muhammad Shah ascended the throne of Delhi in 1719-20 A.D. By this time the status of the Mughal had been reduced to nonentity. The English had started their trade vigorously in Bihar. Independent as they were, the Chakwars of Begusarai defied the authority of the Subadar of Bengal and the Emperor of Delhi. They stopped payment of rent to the government.[17] They also controlled the river-route (Ganga) from Monghyr to Patna and exacted heavy amount from the European traders to annual heavy expense of a large armament to escort their boats carrying merchandise to and from Patna.[18] In 1718 the Calcutta council noted that they would required a strong party of a hundred men to send with their boats carrying treasure for the settlement of their factory there "as the Chakwars had grown extremely powerful at Conna[19] and other places during the vacancy of subedarship."[20] They had grown so powerful that they often attacked the English Traders on their way from Calcutta to Patna. There was also a fierce engagement for sometime between the European traders and the Chakwars but atlength the Latter were driven from their entrenchments, many of them were killed and some were carried prisoners to Patna.[21] On the side of the company a sergeant was killed and a drummer and a soldier wounded.[22] The Chakwars, however, claim that they defeated the European traders on several occasions. On July 11, 1720 Stephenson and Falconer wrote from Patna that the Chakwars "continue very strong", and requested for a strong party of soldiers.[23] On August 2, 1720, the Calcutta Council sent 200 European soldiers to guard the way to Patna as the Chakwars had "come to a great head" and that could at a little notice double their numbers. By September 22, they succeeded in gathering together about 2500 horses and a great number of infantry, recruited from Buxar, and were "resolved to make an attempt" on the boats of the company.[24] The situation being tense, the contingent was sent under the command of Major Richard Hunt, and on October 14, the safe arrival of the boats was reported.[25]

In December, 1720, Nasrat Khan was appointed governor of Bihar. But he could not subdue the Chakwars. From the Chakwar records it is clear that they were quite independent during his governorship. That Raja Bakhtawar Sinha had his own official seal proves beyond doubt that he held an independent status and was not under the Nawab. In March 1721 the Patna authority reported that the Chakwars had defeated a party of the horse sent by the Nawab.[26] Thereafter the Nawab had ordered 4,000 horses to be sent against the Chakwars. They evaded an engagement, and continued to be sufficiently strong, and the company's boat had to be carried with sufficient convoy. The company thought it better to augment the party of soldiers.[27] By 1721 Bakhtawar Sinha had come to be recognised as Raja of the Chakwars. Conna Raja was also very strong. Jangal shaw, a great leader, joined with the Conna Raja, bordered upon the Chakwar country, and gained. his force with the Raja of Chakwars, i.e. Bakhtawar Sinha. This formidable alliance alarmed the European traders, and they prayed for more soldiers.[28] In October, however, the Conna Raja was driven away by his own kinsmen. What happened afterwards is not known. From the Company records it appears that the old brave Raja of the Chakwars died in 1730 and was succeeded by his son, a youth of 17 years[29], whose name is not given. The young prince, like several Bihar Rajas, submitted to Ali Vardi[30], acknowledged the sway of the Delhi Emperor and paid allegiance to the Subadar of Bengal. According to tradition, an official of Bakhtawar Sinha (Probably his Raja-Pandita) betrayed him and gave out the secret to Alivardi on a promise of Rs. 30/- per month by the latter to the former. After his victory, Alivardi granted a sanad to the man to that effect which was later honoured by the company. There is nothing strange in it as treachery was one of the main traits of Alivardi's character. After the defeat of the Chakwars, it said, an annual tribute was fixed and regularly paid to the Nawab for four years. A spot was fixed at thirty miles from the capital of the Chakwars (Samho) where the Prince met the Nawab's officer every year on a fixed day. It was also agreed upon that they should have only thirty attendants on each side.[31] According to Holwell,[32] the heads of thirty Chakwars who had gone to pay tribute to Alivardi on the appointed day were severed and sent back home, and at the same time their capital was sacked and burnt. This fact is also corroborated by tradition current there. Alivardi, then granted sanad to many Chakwar chiefs for various purposes to pacify them.

The brave old Raja must have been some other man than Bakhtawar Sinha as we find that Alivardi, after having subdued the refractory chiefs of Bihar, secured adhesion of a large number of Hindu-Muslim generals including one Bakhtawar Sinha.[33] It is also probable that after having been subdued by Alivardi, Bakhtawar Sinha entered into friendship with Alivardi and helped him in his consolidation of power. One Bakhtawar Sinha is referred to as an ally of the Nawab[34] who led an expeditin against the Raja of Tirhut that is Raja Narendra Sinha.[35] No last word can be said on the subject in the present state of our knowledge.[36]

References :

1. Cf. G. D. College Bulletin Series No. 3, 1952, pp 2 to 16.
2. For details see Ibid 1.
3. For the inscription on the image see Ibid.
4. Ibid.
5. Modern Chewara in P. S. Shekhpura, Dist. Monghyr. It is Said that a Fakir accompanied Ghori's army and it was believed that so long as the Fakir would remain alive no one could be able to defeat the Muslims. The Fakir was ultimetely killed and his tomb is still said to be there (Ibid P. 2.)
6. For 3 details Ibid 1-2, 16.
7. Hunter XV 222.
8. Rs. 36.
9. Edited and Published by him in G. D. College Bulletin Series No. 3, pp. 4-5.
10. Ibid 4-5.
11. For Plate See Ibid facing page 4.
12. For other grants and Sanad cf. Report of the ad hoc Records Survey Commttee, Bihar, 1951-52 pp.2-4 ff.

13. Wilson, Early Annals of English in Bengal, Vol. III, p. 371.
14. G. D. College Bulletin series No. 3, p. 5. The descendents of that Fakir are still there, and enjoy this privilege even now (c. f. Safarnama Mazhari by Md. Halim Ansarai p. 188.)
15. For other nine Land grants of Raja Bakhtawar Singh and Raja Jangal Singh Chakwar discovered by Prof. R. K. Chaudhary, See Report of the Records Regional Survey Committee, Bihar, 1952-53 pp 11-12 (These Land grants were issued mostly to the Brahmanas).
16. Hunter XV p. 18; Monghyr Gazettier, p. 243.
17. Rs. 36, 296; also cf. Gladwin, A Narrative of the transaction in Bengal (1906). p. 79.
18. Holwell, Interesting Historical events. pp 68-70; K. K. Dutta, Alivardi and His Times, pp. 14-15.
19. This place may probably be identified with Khanna near Warsaliganj P. S. in Gaya District.
20. Wilson, Early Annals of English in Bengal Vol. III p. 50.
21. Cf. the letter by Messrs. Stefenson and Falconer of Patna, dated 27 Aug. 1719 to the calcutta Council.
22. Wilson III 153.
23. Ibid 255.
24. Ibid 275.
25. Ibid 283.
26. Ibid 325.
27. Ibid 353.

Note :- I do not agree with the identification Conna, with Khanna in Gaya District. See my view in G. D. College Bulletin No. 3 (Editor - JAHSM- Bulletin No. 4).

28. Ibid 371.
29. Holwell 69-70.
30. Ibid 69-720; Rs. 296.
31. Holwell 69-70.
32. Ibid 70-71.
33. Rs. 311.
34. Cf. Lal Kabi's description of the Battle of Kandarpi Ghat in R. B. -Das, 84:

    " फौजदार महथा भये, संग सलावति राय, बखत सिंह कुल उद्धररग, रोड़मल्ल
    दिलपूर, चौभाग भानू भानू सुकुल एक एकतैं सूर".................

35. Cf. Thakur, History of Mithila (1556- 1947) Chap. III (unpublished).
36. For details cf. G. D. College Bulletin Series, No. 3 pp. 1-9.

Dept. of History and A.I.H & Culture
G.D. College, Begusarai

Courtesy :
G.D.College Bulletin series No.4, 1959
ON BIHAR
Editor : R.K.Choudhary

●●●

New Finds From Jaimanglagarh

(On Bihar Bulletin Series 4 G.D. College Begusarai)

R . C. Prasad Singh*

Jaimanglagarh is a site which has escaped the detective eyes of archaeologists. It is situated at a distance of twelve miles north or Begusarai. Its short history alongwith some finds has been published in the Bulletine No. 2 of the G. D. College, Begusarai, by Prof. R. K. Choudhary.

An excursion to the site was arranged under the joint leadership of Principal S. N. Sinha and Prof. R. K. Choudhary in honour of Maharaj Kumar Dr. Raghubir Singh, M. P. and Dr. R. S. Sharma of the Patna University who came to preside over the annual function and to inaugurate the Bulletin No. 4 of the Jayaswal Archaeological and Historical Society and Museum of the College respectively.

After our arrival we were taken round the settlement site and reached a point where people were sinking well. Prof. Choudhary was fortunate enough to find the rim of a broken vessel which probably came from a depth of 20'. From the appearance of the rim it can be guessed that the vessel is wheel-thrown and baked under proper heat.

Proceeding further we came across the moat where local authorities were excavating tank for public use. The tank is something like 300' long and 100' wide. The western bank of the tank cuts through the outer wall of the settlement site. Three rows of wooden posts - five posts in each row and each at a distance of 7 1/2' are to be seen approximately in the middle of the tank. In addition to this two outer posts one in the left and other in the rear - are also visible.

After a brief survey of the area Dr. R. S. Sharma observed that these posts are remains of ancient bridge constructed probably to connect the settlement site with Stupas in the north-east. If so, it would prove an unique discovery in the history of Indian Archaeology. So far no remains of ancient bridge have been found through out the sub-continent. Hence we would request the Archaeological Department, Government of India to take every possible measure to preserve and clear the monument.

Our exploration of the site yeilded one terra-cotta, one worship-cup, N. B. P., glazed ware, few jar rims and an iron sickle. All of them very probably come from a depth of 15.' Potteries are wheel-thrown and fired udner proper heat. In absence of necessary equipment it is not posible to produce the drawing of our finds.

DESCRIPTION OF THE FINDS :-

1. Terra - cotta, ram shaped, mouth and legs broken, hair dressed on the face, protrusion on the head probably meant for horns, right ear fairly big, left one is broken, straight tail, appears to have been added later in course of its making.

2. Rim of the cooking vessel, flat edge and all round depression on the rim, mark of red polish on the outer portion of the rim.

3. Rim of the vessel, flat with bavelled inner edge, chain design on the rim.

4. Rim of the butter vessel, flat edge and double bands all round the neck.

5. Rim of the water jar, straight edge and double bands all round the neck.

6. Rim of the water jar, straight edge and single band all round the neck.

7. Worship - cup, narrow base, protruding wall with straight edge.

8. Earthern lamp with flat band all round the neck, straight edge with four depressions to put wicks. The straight edge bears the mark of red polish.

9. N. B. P., base of a small pot, inner wall retains the polish in degraded form while polish on outer wall has worn out.

10. Glazed ware with stroke like design on the outer wall.

11. Part of iron sickle with thin and sharp working edge.

So far no scientific excavation has been done, therefore, it is extremely difflcult to assign any particular date but on the evidence of our finds it would not be unreasonable to suggest that the site belongs to the Post - Sunga Age.

*Dept. of History and AIH & Culture,
G.D.College, Begusarai

Courtesy :
G.D.College Bulletin Series No.4, 1959
ON BIHAR
Editor : R.K.Choudhary

●●●

A Short Report on the New Acquisition to JAHS Museum

R. K. Choudhary*

I

Surya image from Barauni.

Various Surya images have been noticed in this subdivision. Three of them are extant and well-preserved - (i) One at Jaimangalagarh (Vide our Bulletin No. 2, where it was described as an image of Badri Narayana),* (ii) One in Baraipura (Teghra) and (iii) the Barauni Surya image now preserved in our museum (for details, see PIHC - Agra session - 1956). The Barauni image is remarkable in various ways. Almost all iconographic representations are perceptible in our image. Standing on a lotus pedestal, the image is highly ornamented and holding full blown lotus. All the peculiarities of a Surya image are there. The two legs are booted and naturally the foreign influence is perceptible. The image is wearing a sacred thread too. Various items in the structure of the image weigh more in favour of its being placed in between the Gupta and the Pala period. The body is carefully modelled with considerable regard to realism and the same commendations may be bestowed on the attendant. The prominent Kirtimukha conveys supreme reality. (Cf. My article in the Journal of the Bihar University - March - 1959).

II

OTHER FINDS

(A) The Figure of an Apsara (Sanghoul)

This image was procured from village Sanghoul, P.O. Ulao (Begusarai). The image is unique in the sense that it is of the same type as that of Khajuraho and Bhubneshwara. The image is partially damaged but it does not detract us from assessing its artistic value. The present image tallies with some of the important sculptural designs of Khajuraho. It is in black stone and can be tentatively placed between 900 and 1100 A.D. She is steeped in the consciousness of her young, full and perishable body. It would not be an exaggeration to observe with Stella Kramrisch that "here Indian 'naturalism' has made an image of Sakti as 'naturanaturans' knowing her work and accepting her shape as its result." (Hindu Temple - Vol II - P. 380). Swaying with the onrush of its sap, the celestial damsel looks deep and her head droops towards its reflection on the curved surface held up and resting on her shoulder. The wave of her triply bent shape, rises, falls and rests on her stance. The hip surges into roundness, restrained by chains of jewellery. As a whole, the image in itself is a harmonious shape.

(B) - A broken female figure in black stone

This was also procured from Sanghoul. In this case, the ripples of movement are in chains, tress, crown and scarf, powerful in build and impact. It is deep in its volume and vibrant in its surface. The present image may be compared with Salabhanjika of the Khajuraho sculpture and also with the fragment from Harsiddhi temple, Chandrawati (Jhalawar, Malwa, 9th Century A. D.). Hair dressing is the most prominent part of this sculpture. It seems to be a part of the eastern school of medieval sculpture, the influence of the suava eastern Indian School extended as far as Sarnath. The present image is more akin to the Tara image of the Sarnath Museum (11th Century). The high strong allegiance of the Chandella sculpture is absent in the Sanghoul image and as such we can place it in the category of eastern school, whose influence here is all pervading. Rhythmic intricacy is in the modelled forms. Its structure is enriched emotionally and lessened in its sculptural compactness. The decoration of hair and mode of dressing are remarkable.

(C) - A broken inscribed image of Buddha (Sanghaul)

The broken image is in Bhumisparasamudra. The inscription is not legible clearly and a close examination of the image shows that the letters were inscribed by some persons who were not adept in the art of writing. It seems to have been a later interpolation on the image, which can be tentatively placed between 800 and 1000 A.D. The tentative reading of the Script is as follows :-

विरूपा

In the present state of our knowledge, it is very difficult to say anything about the actual identification of this name, though we know a Siddha writer of this name flourished in Bihar. Virupa was a contemporary of the famous Pala king, Devapala (C. 809 - 849 A. D.).[1] He was born at "Triur". Rahulji ascribes 18 works to Virupa. Since our reading of the inscription is tentative, we need not go into the details of this image.

(D) - Three broken and inscribed images of Buddha[2]

(From Rampur, Dist. Monghyr)

These three images are partially damaged and inscriptions on one of them are totally blurred. On one of the images, the famous Buddhist formulae is there. Tentatively we can assign these images to the Pala period. They are all in black stones, though the original colour is now vanishing. These images were collected from the village mentioned above. A thorough search for inscription in those regions will enable us to discover a good deal relating to the Pala history. Needless to point out that Monghyr was one of the important centres of the Pala kingdom and it continued to be so till the last, the last quarter of the 12th. century A. D.

(E) Miscellaneous

Various other broken images from Sanghoul and Naulagharh have been procured for our museum. The lower portions of various Surya images are there in the museum and on the basis of this evidence we can say that Surya image was not a rarity in this part. An image of the Surya is already in our museum, there is one at Jayamanglagarh and various broken pieces are there in our own museum. The lower portion of a flying Gandharva (in black stone) was procured for the museum. A very fine picture of 'kalasa' carved on a terracotta piece was observed by me at Naula-garh. During the last few years (since the publication of our Bulletin No. 3), hoards of coins and a very unique inscription of the time of Ruknuddin Kaikans[3] were discovered in Manjhoul area. This inscription is dated 1291-92 AD. and is unique and is one of the earliest muslim inscriptions of Bihar. Only few coins of the Jaimanglagarh hoard (of 1955) could be procured and a short study of the same is presented below. About 15 years ago, a hoard of muslim coins was discovered at Pabraghat but only a few of them could be available for study. The details of those coins are given below.

(F) Jaymanglagarh Hoard

In December 1955, news reached me about the discovery of a hoard of coins at Jaimanglagarh. Inspite of my best efforts, the hoard could not be procured and only a very few coins could be examined. My thanks are due to Sri T. D. Mehta, the then S.D.O, Begusarai, who personally went to Jaimanglagarh to find out those coins at my request and brought three silver coins which are published here. All these coins were returned to Mr. Mehta after examination. Most of these coins (of the hoard) belonged to the Tugluq period.

The continuance of Tugluq rule in Tirhut was till now supported by the two coins, discovered from Tirhut and preserved in the Indian Museum. The important Tugluq mints were at Daulatabad, Agra, Tuglaqpura (Tirhut), Darul -Islam, Sonargaon and Satgaon.[4] Out of the two copper coins, discovered from Tirhut, one is dated 731 A. H.with the inscription "province of Tirhut or Tugluqpur."[5] Of the coins recently discoverd from Jayamanlagarh, one bears the name of one more mint town, *Darul-Khilafat*. Darul Islam mint was, no doubt, well- known.[6] One coin, from the *Darul khilafat* mint, is one of our finds referred to above. The contents are as follows - "**Sultanul Azam Alauddin wald Abu zafar Muhammad Tuglaq Sultan** Reverse- "**Sikandara Zamane Darul Khilafat Nasir Amirul Momim**".

Sultan Alauddin Mahammad moved to his new city which was also entitled Darul-khilafat, a continuation of the city of old Delhi.[7] The city of Delhi, so described, is more probably Siri known as Darul-khilafat, a city which fulfilled the conditions laid down for Darul Islam.[8] Siri is also identifid with Darul-khilafat. According to Lanepool, Siri stood nearby old

Delhi and it was afterwards named Darul-khilafat.[9] Two more Tugluq coins in our finds read as follows :-

a) Ghazi Ghiyasuddin duniya waldun Abu Muzzaffar.

Reverse - Tuglaq Shah Sultan Nasir Amirul Momini.

b) La- ilaha- ill- illah Mohammad Ur Rasoolah

Reverse - Al Mojahid fee Sabibel Mohammadbin Tuglaq Shah[10]

Sharqui Copper Coins were discovered from Sanghaul. One such Copper Coin was discovered from Vaishali.

Pabraghat Hoard[11]

A Pot containing about 250 silver coins,was discovered in a field about 15 years ago. The people of that locality tried their best to procure the entire lot but to no purpose. Only 4 or 5 coins were procured and preserved Most of these coins, as reported, belonged to the muslim period

These coins belong to different Mughal rulers. One coin belongs to Shahjehan and that is the earliest coin in our find. The other belongs to Shahgar. Two coins of Muhammad Shah, dated in the 18th and 19th years, of his reign, are in our finds. There is one coin of Shah Alam, dated in the 19th year, of Murshidabad mint. Few of Shahjehan's coins are of any artistic merit. The confusion into which the coin of India fell on the breakup of the Mughal power may be gathered from the fact that there were about 994 mints in the early part of the 19th century.

The discovery of all these coins from the time of Muhammad Tuglaq down to Shah Alam indicates that the muslim sway over these regions were an established fact even as early as the 14th century. This is supported by an inscription of the last decade of the 13th century. An exploration of all these sites may yield valuable results that will throw an illuminating light on the history of North Bihar.

References :

1. Cf. Rahul Sankritayana- Purattatva Nibandhavali , Page 148 and 1 78 - there was another named Vinapa of Gauda.
2. These three images were collected from village Rampur, P.O Lakhisari (Monghyr) by my student, B.A. (Hon.) Sri Rambalak Singh Rampuri. These are now in our museum. I have sent photographs of these images to Dr. DC.Sircar for examination.
3. Published by me in the *Annals of the Bhandarkar Oriental Research Institute of 1955* The inscribed stone is now kept in the Patna museum. Dr. KK.Datta in his Presidential speech at the 21st session of the Indian History Congress at Trivendram in December, 1955, made a special mention of this inscription.

4. For details,Cf. my forthcoming book "*History of Muslim Rule in Tirhut*" (1200-1765)
5. S.Lanepool "*Catalogue of the Indian coins of the Sulians of Delhi*" -P.64
6. R.B.Whitehead- "*Catalogue of the coins in the Punjab Museum*"-Vol. II P.47
7. Elliot and Dawson-*History of India* -111 , 589
8. H.Nelson Wright- *The coinage and the metereology of the Sultans of Delhi*-P.106 *Cf. JASB XVII*-119 (N.S. 1921)
9. Lanepool-op. cit-91. In our Jaimanglagarh finds, there is another Secunderabad darul khilafat coins
10. My thanks are due to Professor S.A.F.Alam, M.A. Head of the department of Urdu and Persian, who has very kindly deciphered these coins.
11. I am very grateful to Sri Sudhir Kumar Singh of vill. Pabra (Manjhaul) who procured these coins of the Pabra hoard. My thanks are also due to Sri Krishnanandan Singh. Coins of Shahjehan have been noticed in other parts of this area.

* My attention to this discrepancy was drawn by my friend Dr. Bhagwati Verma. I am very much thankful to him.

* Dept. of History and A.I.H. & Culture
G.D. College, Begusarai

Courtesy :
G.D.College Bulletin Series No. 4, 1959
On Bihar

●●●

Epigraphic Records of Begusarai

Radhakrishna Chaudhary*

With a rich and glorious past, the present district of Begusarai is yet a virgin soil for archaeological explorers and a terra incognita for the historians. Due to our negligence coupled with ignorance, the precious treasures of history and valuable antiquarian remains have receded into the dirge of oblivion. The cruel agents of nature too had their own share. The ruins at Naulagarh and Jaimanglagarh speak volumes about the past and the records, discovered over here, throw a welcome light on the forgotten rather little known aspects of the history of our state.[1]

Hence I propose to give a short account of epigraphic records in their proper historical setting so that the people of this area might feel inspired to find out more and more of such valuable records in years ahead.

Naulagarh finds enable us to present a connected and coherent history of the area from the 6th century B.C. to the Mughal period and in spite of its despicable destruction it promises to be a rich site. An important seal of the Gupta Period (discovered 1972) gives an account of the fact that the area around Naulagarh was one of the main centres of economic activities, trade and administration[2] in those days. The seal under review, has two lines and there is a big sign of tree above the inscribed portion on the seal. It might have been an insignia of the administrative centre or a common administrative insignia prevalent in this part of the state. We find a similar tree on a seal discovered from Kumhrar in 1951. The letters on the Naulagarh seal under study have got box- head of the Gupta character and the letters resemble the Gupta script. The seal reads as follows :-

1. R (L) AKSAMUKTA VIS (J) AYA
2. ADHIKARANASYA

The text, if translated, will mean office of the Adhikarana of the Visaya of RAKSAMUKTA or LAKSAMUKTA or also a camp of victory. The seal seems to have belonged to an officer of the district administration and the district was possibly known as RAKSAMUKTA. Whether this Visaya was under Tirbhukti or not, we can not definitely say but I donot preclude the possibility of its being under Tirbhukti region. The administrative centre seems to have been located in and around Naulagarh. Adhikaran, indicating a district or a Visaya is at times synonymous with Mandala.[3] VISAYADHI KARANASYA indicates that the seal belonged to the district administrative officer.

Another Guptan seal[4] from Naulagarh was discovered by me in 1963 and was edited and published. The seal has a Trisula as its emblem on the obverse and legend *Sri Samudra* on the reverse. It is difficult to hazard any objective regarding the identification of "*Samudra.*" Obviously he can not be identified with the Gupta Emperor Samudragupta, who was a Vaishnava and not a Saiva. Naturally the irresistible conclusion is that this Samudra was a private individual, most probably a trader or an influential person holding Saiva faith. He used this seal in his private capacity. Such individual sealings have been found in abundance at Vaisali and other places. The two above-mentioned seals of the Gupta period and in Gupta character prove beyond any shadow of doubt that Naulagarh was decidedly an important centre of activities during the Gupta period.

Another important inscription[5] from Naulagarh belongs to be eleventh century A.D. and is attributed to the reigin of Vigrahapaladeva III of the Pala dynasty. This inscription belongs to the twentyfourth reginal year of that king. It records the construction of the image on behalf of a woman ASOKA, wife of Dhammji and the daughter of a Vintner of Krimila named Mahamati. The insrciption has two lines -

Line 1. (Siddhain II) S(R) i Vigrahapaldeva-rajye Samvata 24 Krimiliya - Sau.

Line 2. Ndikc-Mahamati -duhita Dhammji -Patnaya Asoka (ya) ka (ri) ta-

The rule of Vigrahapala III in north Bihar about the third quarter of the eleventh century A.D. has now to be reconciled with the Kalachuri expansion in Bihar. The Tibetan life of Atis'a Dipankara refers to an invasion of Magadha under Nayapala, father of Vigrahapala III. Magadha was[6] invaded by the Kalachuris and Karna is said to have defeated the forces of Nayapala. The Kalachuri army had advanced upto the capital. Atisa intervened and took an active part in bringing about a conciliation between the two parties. According to the *Ramacharita* of Sandhyakar Nandi, Vigrahapala III is said to have defeated the Kalachuris and a treaty that was signed between the two has been described as Kapalasandhi' by the author.[7] As a result of this treaty, the Palas, otherwise pressed on all sides, brought north Bihar or Mithila under their exclusive sway and made it one of their *Skandhakaras* in Bihar. Since. Naulagarh was the administrative centre from the days of the Guptas or even earlier, the Palas utilised this centre for their own administrative purposes. Both the Palas and the Kalachuris were struggling for supremacy in north Bihar and we see that Karna's son, Yasahkarna (1072-1125) was busy devastating Champaranya - a fact that is further supported by a verse in the Prakitpainglam.[8]

The Naulagarh inscription refers to Krmila Visaya, that is, the district of Krmila whether the donar belonged to Krimila Visaya or Naulagarh itself formed a part of the said Visaya is a debatable point. Under the circumstances, it may be suggested that Naulagarh formed a part of the said Visaya is a debatable point. Under the circumstances, it may be suggested that Naulagarh formed a part of the Krmila Vissya in the age of the Palas like Begusarai forming part of the district of Monghyr till recently. Krmila formed a part of Srinagarabhukti and naturally Naulagarh was a part of that administrative set up. The Palas might have made it so becuase of its proximity to the Ganges and also to its Skandhavara at Kanchanpur of the Bangaon copper plate.[9] There is yet another inscription from Naulagarh[10] having nine lines. The inscription was noticed and published by me in 1952. The importance of this inscription lies in the fact that it gives us an idea about the existence of a Vihar or monastery in the vicinity of Naulagarh. There are references to a number of monasteries in North Bihar but not even one of them has yet been located and hence the reference to a Vihara in this inscription is important. This inscription begins with '*Namo Dharmaiya*' and contains Buddhist benedictions.

An image (from sanghoul) of the seated Buddha contained a short inscription which could be read as *Virupa* or *Vinapa*. Amongst the list of eightyfour *Siddhas*, we come across the name of Virupa- as one of the Siddha poets but it would be too much to identify this Virupa with that well-known *Siddha* on the basis of this solitary evidence, though it is a fact that most of the *Siddhas* belonged to the state of Bihar. *Virupa* was a contemporary of Devapala and was born at Triur and Rahul Sankritayana ascribes 18 works to Virpua. It is difficult to say anything about the actual identification since the reading is tentative. Various Inscriptions have been noticed but lost and one at Rajaura on a boar image is yet undeciphered. Buddhist formulae "*Ye Hetu Dhamma Prabhava*" have been found inscribed on a number of images discovered from Bhairwar, Samho and Begusarai (at the residence of the late Shri Bisheshwar Narayan Sinha, Honorary Magistrate, Begusarai). A Village to Village survey and search may yield some valuable epigraphic records of the district.

Another important epigraphic record of the district of Begusarai is the discovery of a terracotta plaque containing five lines on the obverse and two on the reverse. The character of the inscription resembles Maithili or Bengali alphabets of the early period. The date quoted appears to have been the last quarter of the twelth century A.D. The record was issued on the day of a solar month of Pausha in the sixtyseventh year of an unspecified era. Since the inscription is in Maithili character the unspecified era is to be referred to the Lakshaman Samvata, which is believed to have originated between 1108 and 1119 A.D. The record under study may be placed between 1175 and 1187 A.D. The sealing possibly belonged to a man named *Suhmaka*. The object of the inscription appears to be that three persons named Sodhl, Echi, and Aka made gift of a lotus at the feet of Kesava at Nagaladamaka - the identification of which is doubtful in the present state of our knowledge. It further appears that Suhmaka was the chief priest of the temple of the deity or a royal official whose seal was believed to impart the required authenticity to the deed or gift. It should be noted here that the terra cotta plaques for recording donations were used by poor people who had no means of recording them in copper or gold. Offering of a louts was regarded important enough to be recorded. The inscription on the obverse reads as follows[11]-

Obverse :- **1. Sa 67 Dhau (Paus) Shadi (n) e........**
2. Naga (Ida) maka da (Ham pa)
3. dmam Sadhya- Echy- Akai (h)
4. Kesa (va) - pa(da)
5. Iti ....

Reverse :- **Suhmakasya.**
Suhamakasya.

Another important, say rather unique and the earliest, Arabic inscription was discovered and edited by me in 1955 and that inscripiton throws an interesitng sidelight on the early Muslim invasion of Bihar in general and Begusarai in particular.[12] Sultan Ruknuddin Kaikaus (1291-1301) was the son of Prince Nasiruddin of Bengal and was the acknowledged suzerain of Bengal and a portaion of Bihar. Bihar, which then formed a part of Bengal, again attained a separate status and was placed under a governor whose history is known to us from the inscriptions discovered from the old district of Monghyr (north & south - *Lakhisarai* & *Maheshwara* inscriptions). The inscription contains the names of the great Khans, Ikhtiyaruddin Firuz Aitigin -as- Sultani as governor and Ziauddin Ulugh Khan as Deputy Governor of Bihar. The epigraphic record ignores the Delhi Sultan, Alauddin Khalji, but records the allegiance of Bihar to Sultan Ruknuddin Kaikaus of Bengal. The assumption of lofty titles by the Bihar governor shows the attitude of Balbani lines towards the Khaljis, The *Maheshwara Inscription* confirms the claims of Firuz Aitigin. It appears from this inscription that there was an impregnable fortress at Maheshwara in the district of Begusarai. The high sounding titles of Firuz Aitigin (the governor of Bihar) indicate that the relation between Delhi and Bengal was sufficiently strained. Firuz's authority was unquestionable in Bihar. He seems to have attained independent status after the demise of Balban and made Bihar an independent unit and consequently made himself the master of Bengal.

Another important inscription of the district was discovered from Matihani in the late forties of our century and was shifted to Patna. The inscription belongs to Nasrat Shah (1520-32) the illustrious son of Alauddin Hussain Shah of Bengal. The Matihani inscription of Nasrat Shah records the erection of a mosque. Nasrat Shah brought a major portion of north Bihar under his control and made Hajipur his seat of power. After strengthening his authority in north Bihar, he took possession of the fort and district of Monghyr. The Bhagirathpur[13] inscription is explicit on the point that the ruling king was a terror in Tirhut to the king of the Yavanas (line-6). This assertion nails down the suggestion of Mulla Taqia that Nasrat Shah killed Kamsanarayan of Tirhut. That they were contemporaries is evident from the literary sources. Kamsanarayana attempted at independence and this attitude invited the invasion of

Nasrat Shah who could not tolerate a subordinate flouting his authority. Who killed Kamsanarayan yet remains a mystery. The Tugluqs did away with the independence of Tirhut and Nasrat Shah finally routed the Oinwaras of Mithila and brought the entire area of north Bihar under his control.

Abbreviations :-

El - Epigraphic Indica

JBRS - Journal of the Bihar Research Society

PIHC - Proceedings of the Indian History Congress.

References :

1. Being a member of the Dept. of History for more than 24 years at G.D. College, Begusarai, I, in my own humble way, did to resurrect the past of that region and published four Bulletins, under the auspices of the Jayaswal Arcaheological Historical Society & Museum, containing records of our achievements. Besides these, an account of the history of Begusarai was also published by me in the Ramcharita Abhinandan Granth (1957) and Begusarai Abhigyan Granth (1973).
2. PIHC - 1974 (Jadavpur) - p. 453 ff.
3. EI - XXIII; D. C. Sircar - Indian Epigraphical Glossary - p. 6
4. PIHC - 1964 (Ranchi)
5. G.D. College Bulletin Series No. 1; R. K. Chaudhary -Select - Inscriptions of Bihar; JBRS- 1952.
6. S.C. Das - Indian Pandits in the Land of Snow- p. 54; of R.K Chaudhary- The University of Vikramasila (Patna- 1976)
7. R.K. Chaudhary-Kapalasandhi-published in the Journal of the Oriental Institute, Baroda.
8. R.K. Chaudhary- Prakitpainglam-an important source for the study of Mithila's history.
9. cf. R. K. Chaudhary - select Inscriptions of Bihar.
10. G.D. College Bulletin series No.-2 Also - Inscriptions of Bihar.
11. R. K. Chaudhary- Select Inscriptions of Bihar.
12. Annals of the Bhandarkar Oriental Research Institute (Poona) 1955- cf. R.K. Chaudhary - History of Muslim Rule in Tirhut (1970)-p. 42 ff; &- Ahmad - Arabic and Persian Inscription of Bihar; Also see - Inscriptions of Bengal- Vol IV.
13. PIHC- 1955 (Calcutta) - my Paper on the Bhagirathpur Inscription.

Head,
Dept. of History and A.I.H. & Culture
G.D. College, Begusarai

Courtesy:
Souvenir of Bihar Itihas Parishad
II session, May 1978

●●●

Begusarai from early Medieval Period to the Revolt of 1857

A. Kumar*

The present district of Begusarai is bounded on north and west by the district of Samastipur, in south by Monghyr and in east by Khagaria Sub-division. It has an area of 1889. 14 square kilometer. The district of Begusarai was once the stronghold of the Palas. The ruined forts of Naulagarh and Jaimanglagarh still bear testimony to the rule of the Palas over Begusarai. Both Naulagarh and Jaimanglagarh were important administrative centres of the Palas. The Palas lost their ground in the 12th century and the Karnatas of Mithila and Senas of Bengal entered into conflict for the mastery of Tirhut. Who established his supremacy over the tract of Begusarai is still a matter of controversy and further research. The sources for the study of the history of Begusarai are very meagre, particularly in the medieval period. However, on the basis of inscriptions, coins, land grants and family records found here and there at Begusarai, a connecting link could be established with the history of Bihar in particular and that of the history of India in general.

At the outset I would like to disscuss the nomenclature of the word Begusarai. The two words Begu and Sarai indicate that it was an inn. The establishment of an inn in the medieval period was very common practice. Shershah in his short rule founded several Sarais on the road-side. Prof. R.K. Chaudhary believes that Shershah founded an inn at Begusarai. One finds a series of Sarais form Laheriasarai onwards and most of them are situated on the roadside. Among such Sarais mention may be made of Dalsingsarai, Begumsarai (Bachhwara), Begusarai and Lakshisarai etc. These Sarais were halting stations for the travellers. But it is strange that the word Begusarai is not mentioned in any contemporary Persian work. To begin with Aine-Akbari, we find 'Balia' as an important Mahal of Sarkar Monghyr having an annual revenue of 3,287,320 dams and Teghra, Saresa, Naipur and Imadpur were Mahals of Sarkar Hajipur.[1] It is self evident that either during the reign of Akbar or that of his successors, Begusarai had not even the status of a Mahal. In between the end of the Mughal rule and the establishement of the rule of the East India Company Begusarai came into prominence. The early English people preferred to stay in inns. Buchanan Hamilton has mentioned the roadside inns of North Bihar. These inns were run by the Bhatiyaras and they provided lodgings and food was served by damsels to the travellers.[2] The establishment of Indigo plantation further incrreased the importance of Begusarai and it became one of the famous carvan sarais as it was situated on the old Tirhut road which linked it up with the Ganges-Darjeeling road.

The last Pala ruler of Begusarai was Rampal. Rampal died by throwing himself into the Ganges. There is evidence that Indradyumanpal ruled over Monghyr and he built a fort near Indpai village (Jamui subdivision). The last Pala ruler Indradyuman fled away from Monghyr and he settled in Orissa. The absence of the Pala rule created a void and there arose two powerful kingdoms, one in Mithila and the other in Bengal. Mithila was ruled by the Karnatas and Bengal by the Senas. Who established their hold over Begusarai is not clear for want of historical evidences. Prof. R.K. Chaudhary is of opinion that the Karnatas of Mithila ruled over Begusarai. On the other hand the Senas also claim to rule over a portion of Bihar. In fact the entire country was divided into petty estates. This condition gave rise to foreign invasion. The first Muslim invader on Bihar was Bakhtiyar Khalji. It is said that he overran South Bihar and extended his sway over North Monghyr, Bhagalpur and Purnea. Prof. R.K. Chaudhary admits that "the reverine tracts on the north bank of the Ganges from the mouth of Gandak river to that of the Kosi was occupied by Bakhtiyar Khalji.[3] Thus the claim of the Karnata's rule over Begusarai becomes doubtful by the two contradictory statements of Prof. R.K. Chaudhary himself.

Bakhtiyar Khalji was killed by Ali Mardan in 1206 A.D. His son Ikhtiyaruddin Muhammad held the fiefs between the Ganges and the Sone and raided Bihar and Tirhut.[4] Ikhtiyaruddin submitted before Qutubuddin's authority and Ali Mardan was appointed governor of Bengal in 1208 A.D. The control of Delhi Sultan over Bengal and north-estern India never remained firm. The absence of means of communication gave rise to ambitious states and both the Hindus and the Muslims wanted to establish their own holds.

As to the area of Begusarai, the descendents of Chakwaras claim to have established their hold over Begusarai during the reign of Qutubuddin Aibak, A book, "Chakwar Chandrika" written by Gangotri Singh states that the founder of the Chakwar empire was one Chirayu Mishra, who came from village Susari in Darbhanga district. Chirayu Mishra was a renowned astrologer and a tantric. He settled near village Chak and ousted the aboriginals. There is no doubt that the state established by Chirayu Mishra was a very small one but later on it became a powerful one. Chirayu Mishra had two sons-Santosh and Paritosh. It was Santosh who extended the Chakawara territory both in North and in South Bihar.[5] The south portion of the Chakawara territory was named as 'Chakwara' (Chiwara).[6] The place Chakwara or Chiwara lies between Sheikhpura and Sarari railway station. There was no external danger on the Chakawara State up to the time of Santosh. The facts stated in the book Chakwara Chandrika are based on family traditions and it is difficult to believe its historicity.

However, the Muslims invaded both Tirhut and Bangal Several times. The impact of Muslim invasion was felt even the area of Begusarai. There is a mosque in village Brahmapura under Bachhwara Block which is said to be a gift of Sultan Illtutmish. But it is difficult to draw a conclusion on the basis of a single mosque that the entire area of Begusarai came under the influence of the Turks. The early muslims attempted to conquer Mithila but they could not establish their stronghold very easily. The conquest of Darbhanga, Tirhut and Bihar by Illtutmish did not destroy the independent status of the ruling dynasty and they followed the policy of 'vetasivritti' with regard to the Muslim rulers. Illtutmish made Bihar a separate unit and appointed Tughril Tughan as governor of Bihar. The Sultan left for Delhi and Iwaz, the governor of Bengal asserted his independence and extended his territory upto the Gandak in North Bihar. He expelled Malik Jani, the governor of Bihar. Malik Jani invited Prince Nasiruddin Mahmud to teach a lesson to Iwaz. The combined forces defeated and killed Iwaz. The victory was followed by the appointment of Malik Saifuddin Aibak as governor of Bihar.

Iltutmish died and his successors became victim of the powerful Turk nobility. But it was Balban who asserted Independence. and restored the prestige of the crown. Nasiruddin was governor of Bihar and Bengal. The death of Balban in 1287 was followed by the appointment of Qaiqubad to the throne of Delhi. Qaiqubad's appointment was resented by Nasiruddin and he left Lakhnauti for Oudh. It is said that he followed the North Bihar route and met with his son at Gogra in Sarkar Saran. The rupture between the father and the son was settled amicably and Nasiruddin was permitted to retain both Bengal and Bihar.

Nasiruddin was succeeded by Sultan Ruknuddin Kaikas (1291-1301)[7]. Ruknudin had been acknowleged as the Suzerain of Bengal and a portion of Bihar. Bihar had a separate status and both the Lakhisarai and Maheshwara inscriptions speak high of him. The date of the Maheshwara inscription is 1292 A.D. From Maheshwara inscription it is evident that both sides of the Ganges in the Monghyr district and the vicinity of the Burhi Gandak formed a part of Kaikas dominion. The inscription further contains the names of the great Khans, Ikhtiyaruddin Firuz Aitegin-as-sultani as governor and Ziauddin Ulugh Khan as the deputy governor of Bihar. The Bihar governors owed their allegiance to Ruknuddin Kaikas and not to the Delhi sovereign. The relationship between Delhi and Bengal was restrained and Firuz Aitigin assumed high sounding titles. These two inscriptions make it clear that the authority of the Bengal Sultan extended upto the Gandak in Begusarai Sub division.

Alauddin Khalji conquered the whole of Bihar. The Tirhut ruler had to fight and court friendship with Alauddin Khalji. In fact Bihar was the stepping stone for the mastery over Bengal and almost all rulers from Bakhtiyar Khalji to Ghiyasuddin Tughluq attempted to conquer one or the other portion of Bihar for conquering Bengal. Ghiyasuddin Tughluq defeated the last ruler of the Karnataka dynasty named Harasimhadeva. Harasimhadeva left for Nepal and the Independent kingdom ofTirhut came to an end.

Three coins disvovered at Jaymanglagarh in 1955-56 point out the influence of the Muslim rule in Bihar. In one of the coins the name of mint town is mentioned as Darul Khilafat. Lanepool has identified Darul Khilafat with Siri, a town near the old Delhi built by Alauddin. The content of the coin are as follows- "Sultanul Azam Alauddin Wald Abu Zafar Muhammad Tughluq Sultan"; Reverse- "Sikandara Zamane Darul Khilafat Nasir Amirul Momim."[8] The rest two coins belong to the Tughluq period, Similarly, a pot containing 250 silver coins were discovered in village Pabraghat. But only four or five coins could be preserved. These coins were of Muslim period. On the basis of Jaymanglagarh and pabraghat coins it can be safely admitted that the muslims had established their hold over Begusarai in the 14th century.

The death of Muhammad Tughluq emboldened Shamsuddin Haji Ilyas (1342-1357), the ruler of Bengal to invade Tirhut. The old municipal records confirm the foundation of a town by Haji Ilyas which is popularly known as Samastipur at present. Haji Ilyas controlled the area from Nepal Terai to Begusarai.[9] He divided Tirhut into two parts with Gandak as the dividing line and he founded the town of Hajipur. Mulla Taqia also confirms the occupation of a large portion of Bihar by Haji Ilyas. From Hajipur to Samastipur Haji Ilyas built several forts. But most of them were destroyed by the infidels according to Al Badoni.

The rise of Haji Ilyas opened the eyes of Firuz Tughluq. Haji Ilyas was nominated by Muhammad Tughluq to supervise the territory of Tirhut but he asserted independence and was ruling like an independent ruler. Firuz attacked on Haji Ilyas but the latter fled away and firuz moved upto Kosi river. It is said that Firuz was helped by the local Rajas in his war against Haji Ilyas. Firuz's occupation of Bihar is confirmed by a Jain stone inscription which refers Malik Vayu as the governor and Nasiruddin as Shahna or the Kotwal.

Sikandar Shah, the son of Haji Ilyas wanted to revive his paternal kingdom and therefore Firuz marched against him in 761 A.H. Sikandar Shah was no match for Firuz. Firuz established his authority and gave the fief of Bihar to Malik Bir Afghan. Malik Bir Afghan committed atrocities on the people and the Tirhut ruler had to approach the Sharqis of Jaunpur for help. Since then the Sharqis entered into the political affairs of Bihar and in course of time they established their hold over both north and south Bihar. The founder of the Sharqi dynasty was Malik Sarvar Khwaja Jehan and according to Faristha he subjugated both north and south Bihar. Ibrahim Shah was the third ruler fo the Sharqi line and one of his copper coins was found in village Sanghaul under Begusarai district. A coin bearing the name of Hussain Shah Sharqi was also discovered in the same village. On the basis of these two coins it can be asserted that the Sharqis held sway over Begusarai also. The Chakwar Raja Anand fought withone Ibrahim Khan and the Turk general had to sign a treaty with Anand and bestowed the title of 'Khan' to him. Who was Ibrahim Khan of the Sharqi line is not ascertained by any other source.

Nasrat Shah, Son of Alauddin Hussain Shah, erected a mosque in village Matihani under Begusarai district. It is proved by an inscription found at Matihani and preserved in Patna Museum. Nasrat Shah made Hajipur his seat of power. He routed the Oinwaras of Mithila and brought the entire area of North Bihar under his control. The Afahans of Bihar played an important role. In the 15th and 16 the centuries.

The political condition of India on the eve of the 16th century was a divided one and Babar having defeated Ibrahim Lodi come in conflict with Afgans in Bihar and Bengal. The defeat of the Afghans in the battle of Ghagra broke their power. But the Afghans raised their heads and they formed two groups. one was under the leadership of Nasrat Shah and the other under Sher Khan. The Lohani chief Jalal Khan joined hands with Nasrat Shah. But the plan of both the groups to secure control over Bihar failed and Babar succeeded in capturing Bihar.

The sudden death of Babar and the weak and vacillating policy of Humayun encouraged the Bihar Afghans to reorganise themselves under the leadership of Sher Khan. Humayun in course of his conquest of Bengal came upto Gogri which falls in Pargana Pharkiya. The Afghans were not united and Sher Khan had to fight with both the Afghans and the Mughals. As to the history of Begusarai, the battle of Nurpura is an important one. Sher Khan defeated Qutub Khan, the governor of Monghyr at Nurpura, an important settlement "not far from the tongue of the river." The defeat of Qutub Khan established the superiority of Sher Khan and the success in the battle of Suryagarha made him the master of Bihar. The materials that Sher Shah collected at Monghyr and Hajipur enabled him to consolidate his strength and he became the emperor of India.

The revival of Afghans under Sher Shah was Short-lived. The death of Sher Shah was followed by the dismemberment of the Afghan empire. The successor of Sher Shah was Islam Shah. Islam Shah was a weak ruler. He was succeeded by his son Firoz and Taj Khan Karrani was made his Wazir. But Firoz was killed within a few days of his accession and Adil Shah was appointed the new Sultan in his place. Adil Shah was killed by Sulaiman and Sulaiman became an independent ruler of Bengal and Bihar in 1563.

The Afghans had established a strong belt in North Bihar. Taj Khan Panwar became the new leader of the Afghans. Taj Khan collected a large number of Afghans and killed Mir Muhammad Shaukat, in charge of Hajipur. But the Hajipur rising of the Afghans was quelled by the Timely action of Muzaffer Khan Turbati. The defeat at Hajipur did not dishearten the Afghans. Satri and Catri, the two Afghans took possession of Teghra in Begusarai. Teghra was a cultivated area on the north bank of the Ganges and covered thirty kos long and twenty kos broad area. It was a Mahal under Sarkar Hajipur. Muzaffar Khan set out to quell the Afghan commotion at Teghra. A great fight took place and Fatah Khan fell together with 79 leading men and the territory came into possession.[10] As a reward Muzaffar Khan was appointed as governor of Bihar from Chausa to Garhi.

The Afghan rebellion between 1576 to 1580 virtually put Bihar under the command of a number of military chiefs. Akbar had to fight with several Afghan rebels from Hajipur to Monghyr. The rebellion of Azab Bahadur was put down and the victorious army passed from Serai Rani to Bihar to settle the affairs of Masum Kabuli and to clear the land of rebellion.[11] Was Sarai Rani Ranigodhna of Begusarai sub-division ? The location of Sarai Rani was six kos from the town of Bihar and also 6 kos from the south bank of the Ganges. Local tradition confirms that Akbar founded two sarais, one is known as Begumsarai and the other as Ranigodhna. However, the historicity of the foundation of this Sarai is doubtful.

Akbar appointed several Governors for Bihar like Azam Khan, Mansingh and others but there was lack of stability in arrangement for Bihar. A change in Governorship would always give rise to rebellion. Pargana Balia (Begusarai) was occupied by Chand and Alauddin. Chand had four sons out of whom, his second son named Hamid got the title of Khan. He was given the Tappas of Pharkiya, Simri and Hamidpur by a grant dated 1574 AD.[12] The rebellious attitude of the people made Teghra and Balia important centres of administration since the days of Akbar. Teghra was an important Mahal of Sarkar Hajipur and it included various villages of Begusarai execpt that of Pargana Balia. Several judicial headquarters were established in Begusarai belt. Among them mention may be made of Qazi Rasulpur, Rashidpur, Ranigodhna, Begamsarai, Berhampur etc. The family of Qazi Rasulpur still exists and they have in their possession the list of Qazis since the time of the Mughals down to the rule of the East India company.

Both Jehangir and Shah Jahan held their grip over Bihar. Shah Jahan's son Shuja was a very popular figure and in the civil war he got the support of the people of Begusarai subdivision. The village Shuja in Begusarai is said to be named after him. It is a fact that most of the villages in Begusarai are named after Muslim Newabs and the ruins of their buildings are found in abundance.

With the death of Aurangzeb, the central goverment became weak and several nobles, both Hindus and Muslims, asserted their independence. The confusion and chaotic state of affairs of the Delhi rulers gave rise to rebellion in Begusarai as well. The Chakwar Raja Bakhtawar Singh of Samho refused to pay tribute and assumed the title of 'Deva devanam'. The records of the early East India Company also confirm Bakhtawar Singh as Raja of the Chakwaras. He extended his territory upto Dalsingh-sarai as is evident from his land grant. One Ruko Singh son of Raja Manohar Singh of Samho and uncle of Raja Bakhtawar Singh occupied the turbulent area of Pharkiya Pargana in 1730. The Chakwaras proved menace for the English traders and they usedto plunder the goods passing through the Ganges. Raja Bakhtawar Singh fought with Kamdar Khan and humiliated him in the battle field. Similarly one Jayamangal Singh established his estate in village Manjhul. The Manjhaul Sardar was on friendly terms with the Chakwar Rajas. The commander of the Chakwara army was Sunder Singh Who later on founded an independent estate in Tekari under Gaya district. Raja Bakhtawar

Singh died in 1730 and was succeeded by his son Bahadur Singh.[13] He justified his name by fighting with the English.

Alivardi Khan was appointed deputy Governor of Bihar in 1734 and he suppressed the Chakwar Raja Bahadur Singh. Bahadur Singh agreed to pay the annual tribute to the Nawab of Bengal. A palce named Konan about thirty miles south form Samho was fixed to pay the annual tribute. Alivardi Khan treacherously murdered the Chakawar Raja. With the death of Bahadur Singh the influence of the Chakwars declined and they could not assert their independence in the face of double attack both from the Nawabs of Bengal and from the English. One of the leaders of the Chakwaras Raja Dalail Singh was the chief officer of Raja Mitrajit Singh of Tekari.

The independence of the Chakwaras was destroyed by Alivardi Khan. But since then Alivardi Khan got active support of the Chakwaras. It is said that the Chakwaras helped Alivardi Khan in his war for the Nawabship of Bengal subah. Alivardi Khan granted several sanads to the Chakwaras. Some of the sanads are still in the possession of their descendents.

Gradually the English took control of the area and with the defeat of Sirajuddaulah, they started loot of Bengal and Bihar. Mir Jafar was a helpless spectator. It was Mir Kasim who wanted to assert his independence but all his attempt proved futile and the company got the Dewani of Bangal and Bihar in 1765.

The English settlement at Begusarai dates back in 1730. An English factory was opened at Begusarai in 1730. Teghra and Dalsingsarai were imprtant centres of trade. The fertility of the soil of Begusarai attracted the English traders and the cultivation of indigo was starred in Manjhaul, Begusarai, Bhagwanpur, Begamsarai and Daulatpur. The cultivation of indigo was a profitable business and the high handedness of the English cultivators knew no bounds. Mir Kasim wanted to stop this abuse and he wanted to save the Indian traders. But he was defeated in hte battle of Buxar in 1764 and since then the English became the *de facto* ruler of Bengal and Bihar.

The permanent settlement of Cornwalis gave rise to Zamindari system and the entire village of Samho was settled in the name of Digbijaya Singh. In most of the villages the new zamindars came in and they became the active supporters of the early East India Company's rule. The English brought about some fundamental change in the administrative set up. Monghyr was created a separate district in 1812. In 1832 Monghyr was made a centre for revenue collection. In the same year some parganas of Tirhut like Malki, Masjidpur, Akbarpur Rani, Musri, Badafusri, Naipur, Imadpur, Kabkhand, Uttarkhand and Balia were merged with Monghyr. The early records of the Company confirm Balia as the subdivision but the office was at Begusarai. A separate subdivision for Begusarai was created in 1870. In the early part of the English rule Balia and Teghra were the two thanas of Begusarai sub-division. But later on Bariarpur, Bakhri and Bachhwara were made new thanas of Begusarai.

The people of Begusarai accepted the rule of the English but the Renaissance and the national movement inspired them to rise against the English rule and several youths offered their life for the independence of the country. Nothing is recorded in history about the role of Begusarai in the movement of 1857, the first war of independence.

References :

1. Ain e-Akbari : Vol. II, P, 167.

2. R. Balchand : "Romance of Bihar's ancident and modern highways" Indian Nation 22nd July 1973.

3. R. K. C. : History of Bihar, p.129.

4. R. K. C. : H. M. T. P. 33.

5. G. S : Chakwara Chandrika, p. 5.

6. Ibid.

7 R. K. C. - H. M. T. p. 42.

8. G. D. C. Bulletin No. 4. Appendix III p. 4.

9. R. K. C : H. M. T. P. 60,

10. R. K. C. : HMT. P. 135

11. Ibid. p. 138.

12. Ibid. p. 145.

13.G. S :- Chakwar Chandrika', p. 57.

* Dept. of History
G.D.College, Begusarai

Courtesy:
Souvenir of Bihar Itihash Parishad,
1978, Begusarai

●●●

Vegavati and Bagmati : Important rivers of Anguttarapa

A. C. Verma*

Rivers have always played an important part in the life of Aryans from the very ancient. times. Here the subject matter of my study is two important ancient rivers which played an enormous role in the life of the people of Anguttarapa. These rivers are Vegavati & Bagmati. Now I shall discuss them one by one.

Vegavati : The Jain Literature[1] mentions a river Vegavai which seems to be the Sanskrit Vegavati. The river is said to have been flowing near the village of Attigama.[2] Martin[3] identified it with the Gandaka. But in Muzaffarpur district, there is small river called Baya[4] and Vegavati is probably the ancient name of the Baya. The modern name of the river seems to have been derived from the Prakrit word Veyavai.

The Baya is a spill channel, which leaves the Gandak in the district of Champaran. It enters Muzaffarpur disrict at Karnaul and flows in a south-easterly direction passing through Duria, Sarya, Bhataulia, Chitwara, and Shahpur Patauri. As it flows on it sinks deeper into the ground, it ultimately falls into the Ganga, near old Simaria Steameraghat near Barauni in the district of Begusarai.[5]

Bagmati : The Bahumati or Bagmati is a sacred river of the Buddhists in Nepal.[6] Gokarana has been identified with the river Bagmati.[7] The Bagmati rises in the Mahabharata range[8] of the lesser Himalayas. It flows to the south through Darbhanga District. It formerly joined the little Gandak at Rosera but now it joins the river a little lower at Tilkeshwar together with the Tiljuga river. Thus it falls into the Ganga through the Burhi Gandaka. In the Mithila Khanda of the **Brihad Vishnu Purana**, the river has been mentioned as Bagvati.[9] But this book was probably written in later centuries.[10] **The Svayambhu**[11] and **the Varaha Puranas**[12] call it Vagmati. In the **Purshaparkisha**,[13] a Fourteenth Century work, Vidyapati names the river Baghvati. The **Majjhima Nikaya**[14] refers to the river Bahumati. The Bahumati is probably the Vagmati of Sanskrit, since the names are similar. It is called the Bachamati.[15]

also in Buddhist literatures beacuse it was created by the word uttered by the Buddha Krakuchhanda when the latter visited Nepal with his disciples from Gaudadesa. The Buddhist legend and the **Brihadvishnupurana** show agreement over the traditional origin of the name of the river.[16] The Udana[17] mentions a river Vaggumuda which flowed to the east of the Vajji territory. This Vaggumuda seems to be the Bagmati of present times. The name Baghavati given to the river by Vidyapati seems to have some connection with the word Vyaghra (tiger); and tigers are found in abundance on its banks in the Nepalese Terai.[18]

Once Buddha was staying in the Kutagarsala of Mahavana. He told the Bhikhus about some evil stories and decried evil thoughts.[19] Afterwards Buddha receded and spent half a month in loneliness. Only the person who brought him food could meet him during this period. In the meantime it so happened that some of the Bhikhus misconstrued his preaching and thought their life to be useless. They went to Miglandik Saman - Kuttaka and requested him to kill them and take their belongings. Miglandik did accordingly. In this context we find him cleaning the blood of his sword in the river Vaggumuda.[20]

Again once it so happened that Buddha was staying in the Kutagarsala of Mahavana. At that time a good number of Bhikhus went to spend the rainy season on the banks of Vaggumuda,[21] but there was a famine. Finding it hard to spend the rainy season without ado and to solve the food problem, they devised that they should glorify each other and thus people would come under their influence and there would be an end to their hardship. They practised the device which brought them rich dividends. People were turned to hold them high and offer them all facilities. The Bhikhus became healthy and handsome. After the rainy season was over, they came to Buddha. It was customary for Buddha to meet the Bhikhus on such occasions and enquire about them. When these Bhikhus met Buddha, Buddha also enquired about them and they narrated the truth. Buddha chastised them for misleading the people.[22]

The above two incidents clearly indicate the nearness of Vaggumuda with Vaisali, Therefore, this river has been identified with modern river Bagmati in Muzaffarpur district.[23]

References :

1. Life in ancient India as depicted in Jain Canons, p. 257
2. Ibid p. 257
3. Eastern India, Vol. II., p. 9
4. M.s Pandey; Historical Geography and Topography of Bihar, Patna, 1963 p. 61
5. SAB; Vol. XIII, PP. 21-22
6. Law, B.C. Historical Geography of Ancient India, p. 32
7. R.L. Mitra, N. B. Lit, p. 253, Law, Geographical Essays, p.46
8. Himalaya Mountains and Tibet, Part- III p. 148

9. Singh, S. N; History of Tirhut from the Earliest Times to the End of the Nineteenth Century, Calcutta - 1922 p.2 (footnote)
10. Ibid p. 2
11. Svayambhu; Purana, p. Ch. V
12. Varaha Purana; Ch . 215
13. Labdhasiddhi Katha- Verse., I
14. Majjhima Nikaya. Vol. I., p. 39
15. Geographical Dictionary of Ancient & Mediaeval India.p. 15
16. M.S. Pandey; op.cit, p. 62
17. Udana; III. 3
18. M.S. Pandey; pp.cit, p. 62
19. Vinaya Pitaka,, Parajlka. 3
20. R. Sankrtyayana; Buddhachkaryya, Banaras, 1931, p. 298 ff.
21. Ibid. 298 ff.
22. Vinaya Pitaka, Parajika, 3
23. M.S. Pandey; op. cit, p. 64

Head,
Dept. of A.I.H. & Culture
A.P.S.M. College, Barauni

Courtesy:
Souvenir of
Bihar Itihas Parishad , 2nd session
(21 and 22 may, 1978, Begusarai)

●●●

Archaeology of Begusarai

Phuleshwar Singh*

Begusarai is a newly formed district, comprising areas of Bachhwara in the west and Sahebpur-Kamala and Monghyr-Ghata in the east, Bakhari and Garhapura in the north and Samho across the Ganges in the South. The land of the area is made of alluvial soil of the Ganges and the Gandaka. Besides the two main rivers, the Ganges in the south and the Gandaka in the middle, there are four small and seasonal rivers namely Baya, Balan, Baiti and Dewaki. The major parts of the area is of plain - land and there are a few low - lands called Chaura and Kawar. The whole land is of high fertility and of rich crops.

With this geological and geographical situation, Begusarai is full of archaeological and historical mounds, sites and places. It is misfortune that a proper archaeological survey has not yet been done. It is under the auspices of the Jayaswal Archaeological Historical Society and Museum, G.D. College, Begusarai that a number of antiquities have been collected and were reported through four successive bulletins called "On Bihar". Due to lack of funds and disinterestedness of the authority concerned, further reportings of the findings remained unfulfilled.

The site of Naulagarha has yielded more antiquities and gives more informations. The present writer has collected sherds of plain and painted variety of Grey-wares, which are lying in the Museum of the department of Ancient Indian History & Archaeology, Patna University. Innumerable shereds of N.B.P. Ware, similar to those of Rajagrih and Vaishali, have been found. Same is the case with Jaimangalagarh, another important site of the locality. At Naulagarha, there is a rich deposit of the Gupta period. Sherds of a variety of redsliped ware are collected. A seal bearing insciption in the Guptan Kharosthi is in the possession of late Dhruva Narayan Singh of village Bhitha. It has already been deciphered by Prof. R.K. Chaudhary. A number of Pala arts, particularly Nandi-bull and Shiva- linga and door frames have been unearthed by the farmers of the village and are in their possessions, Fire-bricked -Fort is being destroyed by the farmers and its ghostwall with shed light on its fortification. Thus Naulagarha gives information of human setlements from the later-Vedic period up to the Pala period. It awaits further exploration and extensive excavation.

Another important site and widely known in the locality is Jaimangala Garh. It is amidst the Kawar lake near Manjhaul. It is of the same nature of as that of Naulagarha, but of a bit different nature. While Naulagarha was all round fortified with thick- burnt- brick wall, Jaimanglagarha is of mud-rampart. There were four stair cases in the four - sides of the Mahi-durga. We have references of Mahi-durga. (mud-rampart) in the Kautilya's Arthashastra. Both Naulagarha and Jaimanglagarha were fortified during the Mauryas and the Pala ruler, probably Vigrahapala III who made Naulagarh as one of his capital encircled with burntbrick fort. The architectural remains of an outer-post for river-route between Naulagarh and Jaimangala-Garha is being destroyed by the farmers. Prof. Chandradeo Pd. Singh of Manjhaul, found a bust of femal terrracotta from here and now it is in the possession of the Museum, of G. D. College Like Naulagarha, Jaimangalgarha has no setlement site in the vicinity. At both the sites of Naulagarha and Jaimangalagarha, there is no trace of Muslim-pottery.

Besides these two improtant and archaeologically rich sites, there are several mounds and places of archaeological and historical importance. Of these mounds Garhapura in the Bakhari Block, Khanjhapur (Soniyadiha) in the Cheriya - Bariyarpur Block, Sanghaul and Ulao in the Begusarai Block, Sanghaul and Ulao in the Begusarai Block are of much importance. From here, we have no N.B.P. wares, Sherds or terracottas prior to the period of the Guptas. These sites yield varitties of red-sliped wares. In some cases yellow and orange colour sliped ware were used. These are variteties of incised wares having no red-slip. There are sherds of totidar-water -pots and surahi having round base and high neck. Sherds of storage-jars having thick-section are found abundantly.

These sites also yield terracotta beads, bone- beads and semi precious stone beads of different varieties. There are found terracotta ball, mace and terracotta.

As from the deposited red-slipped wares at Naulagarha an inscribed Guptan seal is found, and these sites start with the redslipped wares, so there is high probability that at these sites human settlements must have been started in the Gupta period, Prof. R. K. Chaudhary in his article in the magazine "Begusarai Abhigyan" (Locally published on the occasion of the first anniversary of the establishment of Begusarai Disrrict) has mentioned the rule of the Bharas, who were ousted from South Bihar (Magadha) by Samudragupta in the beginning of the second quarter of the 4th cent. A. D. It is therefore highly probable that the red-slipped ware ceramic technology was carried from South Bihar by the Bharas in the 4th cent. A. D. It is also plausible that after the fall of the Maurya power in Magadha, Anguttarapa (the flooded area north to Anga, as it is called in the early Buddhist Text remained out of the Sunga power.

The third category of archaeological sites and historical places are Kaith-Baraita, Sugharan in the north-eastern part of Begusarai Block, Kankaul and Pachamba in the north of Begusarai town, Diha and Birpur in the north part of Barauni Block, Dahiya and Bhagawanpur in Bhagawanpur Block, Samsa and Mansura Chaka in Bachhwara Block and few other mounds like Badurwasthan (Bachhwara). etc. Along with the sites mentioned above, these sites yield only the art objects, and architectural remains of the Pala period. Fragments of icons on black-stone are scattered all over the sites. A number of icons of the Eastern image school, both Brahmins and Buddhist are being worshipped in the temples of the locality. There are few Pala icons in the possession of the local people. Of such icons, one Barah image at Rajaura (East), Vishnu image at Kankaula, Vishnu at Kaith Baraitha, Kali image at Pachamba, one Dhyani Buddha at Bagawara, Kali image at Birpur, and a female image at Ulao are of special importance.

It appears that during the Pala period this area was thickly populated and the Pala king most probably Vigrahapala III, whose inscription, mentioning "Krimala-Visaya" found from Naulagarha, paid much attenttion to establish his rule in the locality.

Besides the mounds and places, we have a number of villages, associated with events of the mediaeval history of our nation. The villages like Rani- Godhana, Begusarai, Maharathpur, Suzalehara, Maheswara, Amoliya-sarai etc. bear some legends connected with the time of the Mugals. We have also a number of villages connected with the history of the later Mughals.

Thus, the area north to the Begusarai town is important from both archaeological and historical purposes. A thorough survey of mounds, places and villages and folk-lores prevailing in the locality enable a historian to write down a comprehensive history of Begusarai.

*Head, Deptt.of AIH and Archaeology
G.D. College, Begusarai

Courtesy:
Souvenir of Bihar Itihas Parishad
II Session, May 1978

●●●

Anguttarapa : An ancient region of North Bihar

Kiran Bala Sinha*

The river Ganga has divided Bihar physically into two broad divisions : North Bihar and South Bihar. North Bihar is bounded on the north by the Nepalese Terai, on the east by the state of West Bengal, and on the south by the river Ganga. North Bihar, at present consists of several districts. But the case in ancient India was altogether different. There were a large number of states. Most of them were originally known by the names of the Tribes inhabiting them. In those days North Bihar comprised the state of Mithila (Videha), Vaisali and portions of the state of Mallas, Allakappa, part of Kosala, Anguttarapa and portions of Vanga.[1] Now it will be a Herculean task to fit in the ancient states, showing their proper territories in modern existing districts. Here, the subject of our study is Anguttarapa only and I shall give a short account of it.

Northern portions of Ganga comprised this area. The Kausikaiksetra, which lies to the north of Anga across the river Ganga, was probably known as Anguttarapa.[2] According to the Samyutta Nikaya,[3] it was in the kingdom of Anga, near the water, across the Ganga. The term Anguttarapa indicate "Ang-uttar-apa"[4] meaning thereby "the waters to the north of Anga." Lord Buddha had visited Apan Nigama of Anguttarapa.[5] Loard Buddha is said to have visited Anguttaarpa, a flourishing Janapada and an important centre of trade.[6] Not only this, in the Sutta-nipata,[7] it has been also. mentioned. From Vaisali Buddha, with 1250 followers, proceeded to Vaddiya and stayed in Jativana. From Jativana, Buddha[8] went to Apan Nigama and Anguttarapa.[9] Here Pottaliya met with Buddha.[10] Mahavagga[11] further tells us that Buddha, with his 1250 followers, returned towards Kusinara. Apan[12] is mentioned as a township in Anguttarapa, tract which lay north of the river Mahi, evidently a part of Anga on the other side of that river.[13] Thre area from Bhaddiya to Apana lay through Anguttarapa.[14] The Jalodbhava of the Mahabharata[15] may be identified with the area of Anguttarapa.[16] Raychaudhuri[17] idenitifies Jalodbhava with Videha.

In Sankrit Buddhist texts,[18] mention is made of a dvipa called Purvavdehad-vipa along with other three dvipas, namely the aparagodaniya, the Uttarakuru, and the Jambudvipa. Dvipa is obviously used here in the sense of a country, but it is difficult to ascertain which country is meant by Purvavidehadvipa. The Lalita-vistara refers to the script or alphabet of the Puravavidehadvipa, which the Lord is said to have mastered in his boyhood.[19] The same text further refers to the extent of the four respective dvipas, the Purvavidehadvipa is credited to have been nine thousand Yojanas in extent. Its exact location admits of no verification at this stage.

Again Anguttarapa is said to have been situated to the north of the river Mahi.[20] The river Mahi has been identified with a small rivulet of the same name in the district of Saran.[21] All the rivers of this area flow from the north to the south, thus Anguttarapa cannot be to the north of any river other than Ganga.M. S. Pandey[22] thinks that here Mahi seems to be used as an adjective of the mighty Ganga which flows from west to east.

Further we have seen that the Anga territory extended on both banks of the Ganga. From the Ramayana[23] we gather that at some time the Anga Kings either ruled the Kausiki Kshetra or had overwhelming influence in this region. Magadha originally was vassal of Anga but some time in the first half of the Sixth Century B. C. it became independent. Later on Magadha under Bimbisara invaded Anga[24] and the Anga territory was permanently annexed, and a prince from Magadha ruled over Anga with its capital at Champa.[25] Though Anga lost its separate existence after Sixth Century B.C; still the later literary works very often refer to the kings of Anga. This is probably because the early rulers of Anga[26] had once wielded a great deal of influence.[27]

References :

1. Havaldar Tripathi, Baudha Dharam & Bihar, p.5
2. M.S. Pandey; Historical Geography and Topography of Bihar, Patna, 1963 p. 97
3. Samyutta Nikaya; Vol II. pp. 437, 439
4. R. Sankrtyayana; Buddhacharyya, Banaras, 1931.p. 144; footnote; cf M.S. Pandey; op. cit., p. 97
5. Mahavagga; 6.5.1.21.
6. R. K. Chaudhary, History of Bihar, p.15
7. Sutta - nipata. 33
8 R. Sankrtyayana, op cit., p.141 cf. Mahavagga.6
9. H. Tripathi, op. cit., p. 90; cf. Attakattha 2:1:4
10. Majjhim Nikaya 2:1.4
11 Mahavagga 6.5.3.1
12. B.C. Law; Historical Geography of Ancient India, Parts; 1954- Also Calcutta, 1954 p.43 Samyutta Nikaya, V. pp. 225-26.

13. Parmatthajotika, II, 437; cf. Malalsekhera, Dict of Pai Proper Names, p.22
14. Vinaya, I, 243 ff; cf. Dhammapada Commentary, III. 363.
15. Mahabharata, II. 304
16. M.S. Pandey. op. cit. p. 97
17. Political History of Ancient India p. 55 (footnote)
18. Lalitavistara, pp.19, 125, 149 etc.
19 Ibid, p. 126
20. Sutta Nipat Attaktha, II. pp. 437, 439
21. M.S. Panday, op. cit. p. 59
22. Ibid . p. 97
23. Bal; ch. 10
24. Sacred Books of the East XVII, cf. Parisistaparav VII. 22
25. Nirvavali Sutra, p. 3; cf. Journal of Asiatic Society of Bengal. p. 1914 p. 321
26. Aitareya Brahman, VIII.2,
27. M.S. Pandey. op. cit. p. 99

* Begusarai

Courtesy:
Souvenir of Bihar Itihas Parishad
II session, May 1978

●●●

Iconography of Some Buddhist Images Discovered From Tirabhukti

Jayadeva Mishra*

Excavations have been made at the sites of Chirand Basarh (Vaisali) Svetapura, Naulagarha, Katra, and Balirajgarh. Some valuable pieces of pottery, Buddhist images have been found in these places. Some excavation reports have come to definite conclusions. Numerous images of the Buddha and some beautiful fragments of Buddhist art and other objects throw light on the spread of Buddhist culture in this region of Bihar[1] during early medieval period. The following Buddhist sites deserve special mention.

Kolhua, Ponjha (Vaisali), Chougama, Pandaul, Jarahatiya and Andhradhari (Madhubani district), Jaymangalagarh, Bihat, Samho in the Begusarai district. Of these Naulagarh and Jayamanglagarh are most important and second only to Vaisali, Mathali, Mehisi, Birpur, Srinagara in the district of Saharsa and Gorodiha in the district of Purnea.

On the basis of the material discovered from the Naulagarh,[2] it can be said that Naulagarh (Begusarai district) had a continuous history of Buddhism from the beginning of the Buddhist age down to the Muslim period.

The exploration of Jayamangalagarh, situated very close to the other ancient fort, Mangalagarh in the Samastipur district and other adjoining sites has furnished valuable things discovery of the black Pala stone images, ranging from the Gandhara School to the Eastern Pala School of early medieval sculptures from Bihat, Birpur, Naulagarh and Jayamanglagarh indicate the existence of big ancient establishments in this part.[2] A black stone image of Bodhisattva in Gandhara style has also been discovered there.

A small black stone image belonging to the Gandhara school has been found in Bihat village. It is evident from its headdress which represents the Buddhist art of the Gupta period.[3]

We have another very fine image of standing Buddha surrounded other images of Buddha in various mudras. The pedestal of the image bears an inscription which is the famous Buddhist mantra[4] as found on other similar Buddhist images of the period. Palaeographically it can be placed in the ninth century A.D. This image is now in possession of Sri Bisheshwar Naryan Singh of Begusarai.[5] A similar image in black stone with the same inscription is preserved in village Samho in Begusarai district and is now preserved by the villagers.[6]

A rare image of Avalokitesvara Buddha in black stone bearing an inscription was discovered in Lakhisarai (Munger district). It is now preserved in the Sri Ashutosh Museum, Calcutta University, Calcutta.[7] Different images of the Buddha in different mudras have been found in Mathiahi (Madhepura District). Several Buddhist images have been found in Mehisi village, an old seat of the Maithila Brahmanas (Saharsa district). Recently an unique image of Namsangiti Manjusri has been discovered from Ramchaura Ghat near Hazipur. Iconographically it is unique and not discovered in India before this[8]. In Sultanganj (Bhagalpur district), Buddhist remains were discovered as far back as 1864. The most important image was the colossal figure of Buddha (Now preserved in the Birmingham museum). The statue weighing nearly one ton is of copper. The figure bears a close resemblance to the sand stone statue largely found at Saranatha. It stands in abhayamudra.

The pieces of Buddhist art were discovered in course of a trial exacavation conducted in the Chaugama village in Bahera (Darbhanga district). Some execptionally beautiful relics of metal images have also been unearthed.[9]

A red stone image of the Buddha, weighing about 30 pounds belonging to the Gupta period has been discovered in a village near Pandaul in madhubani district. A big image of the Dhyani Buddha was unearthed in a field to the west of the tank, said to have been dug by order of Maharaja Bhairava Sinha of the Oinavara dynasty of Mithila in village Jarahatiya[10] in Madhubani district. The image also bore an inscription on the pedestal, but it was too blurred to be deciphered.

Saptari, Bhala pargana Buddhama (Buddhagrama), Ratnapura, Brah-mapura Visala, Vethadiya or Betia, Radhia and Mathia (in Champaran district) and other place were strongholds of Buddhism in Tirabhukti as described in Mithilamahatmya.[11]

Brahmanism and Buddhism flourished side by side in Tirabhukti though Buddhism gradually lost its hold among the followers. However, the process of borrowing and intermingling never stopped. The Hindus borrowed art ideals from the images of the Buddhist goddesses like Tara, Manasa, Chhinnamasta, all symbolising the Sakti cult. The Buddhists, on the other hand absorbed the art ideals of Hindu deities like Yaksesvara, Gandhari, Dhyans Aparajita and others.[12] It is true, the latest form of Vajrayana weakened Buddhist influence on every aspect of Indian life, but is also true that it has left a permanent mark on the culture of India.

Reference s:

1. G. D. College, Begusarai, Bulletin Series Nos. 1-2
2. G. D. College Begusarai, Bulletin No. 2, p. 1.
3. Ibid., 2. p. 20.
4. Ibid., p., 20-21.
5. Ibid., pp. 20-22. N. K. Bhattasali, Iconography of Buddhist and Brahmanical Sculptures in the Dacca Museum, Dacca, PP. 16-29. (16-19)
6. G. D. College, Begusarai Bullentin Series No. 2, pp. 22.
7. Ashutosh Museum, Modern Review 1951, p. 377.
8. This image is preserved in the Tantrik Siva Temple of Ramchauraghat in th Department of History, Patna University and Sri Ram Bilash Jha, journalist.
9. R. K. Choudhary, "Discoveries i North Bihar" JBRS, vol, XLIII, pp 365 ff.
10. Upendra Thakur, History of Mithila, Mithila Research Institute, Darbhanga, 1956, Chap - VI
11. Prameshwar Jha, Mithila Mahatmya, Darbhanga, p. 92.
12. R. K. Chaudhary, Bihar, the homeland of Buddhism. Chap. V.

* Dept. of A.I.H. and Archaeology
Patna University, Patna

Courtesy :
The Journal of
The Bihar Research society
Vol.L XXI, LXXII, LXXIII -1985-86

A Rare Surya Image in G. D. College Museum

Parma Nand Singh*

The late Prof. R.K. Choudhary has put it that “Begusarai is historically rich, culturally important and industrially the focal point of North Bihar.”[1] It is almost a virgin soil from exploration point of view. It has a rich past, every mound, every stone, every heap of ruins has a history of its own to tell only if they could speak. In this context, several examples of the iconographic evidence have been brought to light of which a rare Surya image is one.

The famous Surya image was found at Phulbaria near Barauni indigging from a well and collected by late Prof. R.K. Choudhary and A. Kumar (present principal of G. D. College, Begusarai). Now it preserved in K. P. Jayaswal Historical and Archaeological Society and museum of G. D. College, Begusarai. The antiquity no. of this icon is 301. It is made of black basalt stone, generally available from Rajamahal hill. The stele is pointed on the upper portion. The stele of the image, under review, is 78.5 cm in length and 42 cm in width. The main figure ofthe Surya from crown to boot is 57 cm. in length and 24 cm in width.

The main figure is of the Sun God who is in standing posture. The standing Surya icon of black stone have been found from various parts of Mithila during the Pala and Karnata period[2]. The Karnata artist followed the artistic model of the Pala. The land of modern Begusarai district was part and parcel of both the rulers i.e. the Palas and Karnatas. Therefore, this image may be dated either to Pala or to Karnata period.

Almost all iconographic representations are perceptible in our image, standing on a lotus pedestal. There is halo behind the head of the figure, carved on the stone. It is not circular but oblong. The presentation of Sun - dise begins from Gupta period[3] and continued all Pala and the Karnata period, because almost all Surya icons found from different parts of North Bihar are adorned with halo.[4] Our image wears Kirita-Mukuta. Pointed probably with Kirita Mukuta is seen in every medieval Surya figure of Eastern India[5]. Long hair has been shown on his head. A circular ear-ring in each earlobe is found on both of the shoulders. He is seen bearing a beautiful necklace over his chest and Yajnopavita, which we do not find in early icons. The Yajnopavita is shown by three minuted threads hanging down from the left shoulder upto the right thigh. There is no cloth above his waist while below his waist transparent cloth is seen. Foldings and curves may be seen on it. The two legs are booted and naturally the foreign infuluence is perceptible.[6] There are a few images of Surya, belonging to the Pala and Sena period, have been found in Bengal. Here we find that the boot is absent from the feet of the Surya icons. The fingers of the feet of the Surya images have been easily shown but the image under review bears long boots in his feet. This is a Kusanian affinity, traditionally carried down upto the Palas and Karnats period. It is said that originally the worship of the sun image was done in Iran-Magi or Saka Brahmana, brought this cult from Iran to India. There was a belief prevalent in Iran that there would be a disaster if the finger of the sun image would be shown. That is why, artist of Iran showed boots in the feet of the sun images. The same belief was passed on from Iran to India and it continued up to Pala and Karnata period at least western part of Magadha but the artist belonging to the Pala and Sena period of Bengal made some innovation. They were not very influenced by artist of the western part of Magadha.

The Surya has got two hands. He wears armlet in each arm and breacelet on his wrists. His both hands are holding a long stem of double patalled lotus flowers. All these attributes can be seen in several Surya icons of North Bihar belonging to this period.

Near his knee, there is a figure of goddess, depicted up to the thigh of the main deity. She is holding Mukuta on her head. There are ear-rings in her both earlobs. She wears necklace on her chest. She is touching her both breasts with her right hand holding a Kamandala is losely hanging down. She is manasveta, one of the consorts of Surya. The appearance of such a deity with sun god is the special feature of the image under consideration. Just in front of her thigh, there is depiction of a male figure which is mutilated. He has got two hands but his legs are not prominent. He is in sitting position. Perhaps, he is Arun, the chariot driver of the God. The driver Arun is essentially seen in every image of the Surya from beginning up to the mediaeval period.[7] He is driving chariot by seven horses. One is in the centre and three horses are depicted on each side.

On the left side of the main figure is a female figurine which is highly decked with ornaments. She appears in standing pose. She has got two hands. Both hands are loosely hung down resting on her thighs. She is perhaps a queen of the main deity.

On the right side of the female figure, there is a bearded male figure with a Mukuta on his head. He is wearing several ornaments, like necklace, armlets, bracelets etc. He is wearing dhoti below his navel. He has got two hands. He is holding an inkpot in his left hand and a pen in his right hand. He is Pingal. The figure of Pingal with inkopt has been seem in the Gupta period[8] also but appearance of a pen is unique feature of the image. Just near the knee of the male figure, there is a female figure in sitting posture. She is looking left and shooting arrow.

She is holding a bow in her right hand and her left hand is near her left ear. She is perhaps Usha.

On the left side of the main figure ,there is highly decorated ornamented a female figure.She is holding a Chammar in her right hand and the left hand is resting on her left thigh.She perhaps Rajani,a queen of the Surya.She also may be seen holding chamara in the Surya image of Madhubani district.[9]

Just near his knee ,there is a female figure .She is in shooting position. She is holding a bow, in her left hand and her right hand is resting up to her ear. She is Pratyusa. Both figures, namely Usa and pratyusa may be seen engaged in chasing darkness with their bows and arrows in several mediaeval images of the Surya, found in different parts of Eastern India.[10]

On the upper portion of the stele, flying Vidyadharas are depicted in each side. The Manasara describes the flying posture of Vidyadhara.[11] On the right side, he is holding a graland in his both hands. He wears crown on her head, ear-rings , armlets and bracelets. There is a lower garland with lining on it. Same is the case with other side of Vidyadhara.

Just near the right hand of the main figure, there is a depiction of male, figure riding on a lion. He is in standing position. The back two legs and front two legs of the lion are folding. There is a depiction of seated elephant with a male rider on his back. The same figure is also depicted on the left side of the figure.

On the extreme left of the main figure, Revanta, the son of the Surya is depicted in standing position. He wears Mukuta on his head. He is wearing ear-rings. necklace, bracelets and armlets. His yajnopavita is hanging from his left shoulder down to his right thigh, lower garment (dhoti) is shown below his waist with lining on it. The deity is holding a wine cup in his half bent right hand. A long sword is in his left hand. Dandi usually holds a sword in his left hand. The edges of the sword have been finally depicted. We know from the iconographic text that Revanta usually holds a sword and a wine cup in his hands. The depiction of Revanta, the son of the Surya is a very peculiar in his sculpture, under consideration.

After a careful analysis of the figure of the Sun mentioned above, it may be concluded that there are some rare features in image. Firstly the son of the Surya, Revanta has been clearly depicted along with other supporting deities, Secondly, it may be pointed our that the sun image presevred in the G. D. College Museum is rare one as it contains both foregin and Indian concepts mixed in one.

References :

1. Bihar Itihas Parishada - Presidential address, (Second session 21 - 22 May 1978, Begusarai) p.1.

2. P.N. Singh - Cultural History of Mithila during the Karnata and Oinwar period (Unpublished) p. 379.

3. J. N. Banerjea - The Development of Hindu iconography p. 434.

4. V. Mishra- The Cultural Heritgage of Mithila, P. 261

5. J. N. banerjea - Op.cit.p. 439.

6. G. D. College Bulletin series, No. 4, Appendix - III, p. 1.

7. J. N. Banerjea - Op. cit. p. 436 - 39; V. Mishra- Op. cit., p. 261- 262.

8. Ibid.

9. V. Mishra- Op.cit., p. 261.

10. J. N. Banerjea - Op. cit., p. 439; V. Mishra - p 261.

11. Manasara - p. 370, vv 7.9.

* Dept of A.I.H.& Culture
R.B.S. College, Teyay

Courtesy :
The Journal of
The Bihar Research society
Vol.L XXVI, LXXVIII -1990-92

●●●

Sanghaul (Begusarai) :

The Second Largest Buddhist Site in North Bihar

Phuleshwar Singh*

After Vaishali, Sanghaul, in the district of Begusarai appears to be the second largest Buddhist site in north Bihar. It is situated in between NH-31 and NE Railway line, two and half kilometres west to Begusarai district Head quarter. The mound is 1 to 3 metre in height and it is extended in a area of approx. 125 metre X 58 metre. At present the eastern portion of the mound is under inhabitation and rest portion of the mound is under cultivation, where there is a state tubewell. Late Prof. R. K. Chaudhary collected some broken pieces of icons of black stone, a few of which is of Buddhist deities. The author of this article has also collected few more broken pieces of icons of the same nature. The villagers have also collected broken icons of black stone at a local temple. These collections clearly indicate that the mound is of the Pala period (800 A.D. to 1000 A.D.)

It was in the year of 1989 that an owner of a piece of land. nearby the state tubewell, started digging a ditch for earth, which yielded remains of structure. The mukhiya of the village, who had been a student of A.I.H. & Archaeology reported the author about the remains of structure at Sanghaul. The author of the article, with the help of his P.G. students of A.I.H. & Archaeology took a trial trench to know about the structure.

A five metre trench was taken. The trench yielded four circular structures adjacent to each other, built on different plateforms in different subsequent times. The structures are made of burnt bricks of 5 x 15x30 cm. with the help of mud-mortar. The diameter of the structures are slightly different to each other. It is 194 cm. to 205 cm. The upper portion of the structure was ruined during digging of the state tubewell in 1956, as reported by an old woman of the village and is also evident from the section of the trench. The plinth of the structure is slightly different in height. It is 103 to 105cm. in height. The structure was plastered with sand and lime. Above the plinth, the circular structure remained 50 cm. to

55cm. in height. The lower portion of the circular structure is carved with cutting of bricks projecting outside.

The circular structure appears to be the votive stupa. The structure resembles with the votive stupas found at Vikramshila near Kahalgaon in the district of Bhagalpur. It also appears that this structure was built in the campus of a vihar whose remains is found by the cultivator nearly 50 metres from the circular structure. As the site is under cultivation since 1956, the site is badly robbed by the cultivators and bricks of the Vihar have been taken away. One farmer has erected a house from the bricks unearthed from this plot. It also appears that there had been a course of river Ganga in the southern side of the mound. Remains of such low land is yet called Gangiya by the local people. The present course of the Ganga is about 4 kilometer south to the mound. There is no doubt that during 800 to 1000 A.D. the Ganga use to flow by the southern side of the mound.There are a number of mounds in the district of Begusarai which yielded Pala icons of black stone. Among the mounds of the district Naulagarh and Jaimangalagarh are more important than the remains found at Sanghaul. Naulagarh yielded one inscribed image of a Buddhist deity. It has an inscription written during Vigraha Pala III, the later Pala king. From the same site, hundreds of silver coins of Vigraha Pala III were found in previous year. The author of the article has surveyed the mound and is of the opinion that in the time of Vigraha Pala III, Naulagarh might have been the head quarter of the Pala administration. From the record of Kalchuri king, it is apparent that Laxmikarn invaded Banga, Anga and Magadh and defeated the Pala king. The defeated Pala king was Nayapala. It is said that Deepankar Shrigyan Atish, the Vice-Chancellor of Vikramshila University, mediated in between the Pala king and the Kalchuri king, and the princess Yauvanshree was married with Vigraha Pala III, the son and successor of Nayapala.

The areas of the western portion of Begusarai district is called Nayapur Pargana. It clearly indicates that Nayapala, the later Pala king. might have shifted his seat of power in north Bihar and founded a village after his name which became centre of his revenue colleciton. It is also evident by the above fact that Naulagarh was also founded and named after Nayapala. In the troubled days. Nayapala and his son and successor Vigraha Pala III might have made Naulagarh his seat of power, as we have an inscription and thousands of silver coins of his name.

In the later Pala period, teachers of Vikramshila used to propagate Tantrayan out side India. From the Tibetan record, we know that Mahasthavir Deepankar Shreegyan went Tibet to propagate Tantrayan there. It is also learnt that the Tibetan, in larger number, use to come Vikramshila for tantric teaching. The excavation of Vikramshila has yielded a special Vihar meant for the Tibetan monks, awaiting for admission in Vikramshila. It is possible that Vigraha Pala III, for the convenience of the Tibetans, constructed a Vihar which was later on named Sanghaul. In the district of Begusarai there are a number of Buddhist icons found from different adjacent villages of Sanghaul. From these remains it appears that during the later

Pala period, the area of Begusarai was under the influence of the Buddhist tantra. It is, therefore, quite possible that in the time of later Pala king Vigraha Pala III, a Buddhist vihar at Sanghaul was constructed. There is no doubt that an extensive archaeological exacavation will bring the whole area in light and it will emerge as the second largest Buddhist site of North Bihar.

*Reader, Deptt. of AIH & Archaeology
G.D.College, Begusarai

Courtesy:
Art and Archaeology of Eastern India, 1997
Edited by Naseem Akhtar

●●●

A Glimpse Into The Sculpture Of Anguttarapa Janapada Area

P. Gupta,*
Dr. Prabal Gupta

A. Introduction

In our perliminary exploration of Saharsa. Khagaria. Begusarai and Samastipur to find out the identify of Anguttarapa- a Janapada referred to the Buddhist literature. We came across with a plethora of lithic sculpture belonging to early medieval period largely contemporaneous with the Pala dynasty and possibly in some cases associated with the Post-Pala chronology.

The tapestry of the Plastic art of the afore mentioned region is pretty vast and complex. In this short communication, it would be rather diffcult to elaborate the theoretical contour of the subject comprehensively precisely because time and facilities necessart to carry out such an investigative study were not available at our disposal. Preliminary being the nature of our exploration, this note on art should be considered as provisional one.

We shall refer to those icons which have been recovered in a relatively intact condition. They mainly belong to the Buddhist and the Bramanical Panthenos. So far not a single mage of the Jaina Pantheon has been recorded. Similarly we have not come across any metal specimen. The Terracotta plastic art along with seals and sealings has not been dealt with in this note. It needs a separate narration.

B. Tabulation of Specimen

Let us first tabulate the specimens along with their respective provesnances :

1. Saharsa District

a) Deonadih. Kabra block : 9km west of HQr.

i) Sivalinga with a round Argha 81 cm diameter/ 17 cm high.

ii) A damaged sivalinga

iii) A crocodile shaped water spout

iv) A Nandi- 14 cm high, 19cm long

v) Two others smaller nandis

vi) A broken figure of Visnu with face. Kirit Mukut, cakra in left hand.

vii) Two door jambs with several motifs

b) Kandaha : 13km west of thte district HQr.

i) Surya image = renovated with fives or more fragments. Beautifully curved stela.

ii) Door frame = ornamented

c) Mahisi

i) Icon of Tara

ii) Icon of Buddha in Parinirvana Posture

d) Okahi Village : 10 km N.W. of the district HQrs.

i) Borken figure of Vishnu found in the mound of the village. Now the icon is placed in a temple in the near by village known as Darma. The icon is badly repaired and worshipped as Deviji. The Priest refused to co-operate in the iconographic study of the image.

e) At the Kapileshwar Sthan of Baruari on Khardaha River

i) Varaha avatara with Prthvi.

ii) Damaged Surya with Aruna and lotus depicted on the left.

iii)Standing Surya with lotus in both hands and decorated with Vanamala. Divine attendants like Aruna, Dandi, Pingala, Usha, Pratyusa with flying Gandarbhas in the stela - are depicted.

iv) A damage icon of Kubera

2. Khagaria District

a) Alaoligarh

i) Icon of Sadyojata

3. Samastipur District

a) Keos : 10 miles east of Samastipur

i) Ganesh

ii) Camunda

iii) Mahisa mardini

iv) Visnu

v) Siva linga

4) Begusarai District

A) Buddhist Pantheon

a) Proper Buddha

i) Buddha- in Bhumisparsa mudra

Balia P.S.

ii) Padmasana Buddha

Balia P.S.

iii) Buddha in Bhumisparsa mudra

Sangaul

iv) Standing Buddha

Sanghaul

b) Misc Buddhist Icons

i) a small male specimen bering in legend 'Birupa' - Sanghaul Birupa was one of Siddha Charayas of early medieval period.

ii) Avalokitesvara - Birpur - Barepura

iii) Marici - Rajbara, near Barauni Junction.

B) Brahmanical Pantheon

a) Visnu Cult

i) anthropomorphic : Birpur- Barepura, Kankaul, Kaith (inscribed)

ii) Theriomorphic :

Varaha (inscribed) - Rajaura

Syncrestic Varaha and

Sivalinga - Itwa

Nr. Simha - Birpur Barepura (Stolen)

b) Saiva Cult

i) Siva linga - Birpur - Barepura. Ulao

ii) Uma Mahesvara - Birpur

iii) Bull - Birpur-Barepura

iv) Ganesa - Sanghaul

v) Dancing Ganesha- Birpur (Stolen)

c) Surya Cult

i) Surya- Birpur, Barepura, Kaith, Barauni

ii) Revanta Barepura

iii) Pingala in Door frame- Birpur- Barepura

iv) Navagraha- Barepura, Jaimangalgarh (Stolen)

d) Sakit Cult

i) Camunda - Barepura, Pachamabha, Birpur

ii) Mahish mardini- Barepura

C) Iconographic and stylistic Narration of Icons : Some General Observation :

At this stage it is not possible to present an elaborate descipition of all the icons and in some damaged but highly sculptured sevaeral architectural pieces. In fact temples in which these icons were once installed, were not seen. According to canoncial texts, Vastu-Brahma-Vada deals with the aesthetic aspect of Hindu architecture. According to this postulate sculpture and painting constitute the sub-ordinate disciplines of architecture. So icons without temples do not convey full aesthetic panorama of the plastic art. So we shall have to limit ourselves to Iconographic and stylistic parameters of the subject ot a certain extent.

As pointed above, we could not devote equal attention in our investigative study to the icons of all the districts. Fortunately time and facilities were available to study the plastic art of Begusarai relatively elaborately. Further descriptions by Professor R.K. Chaudhary and others has helped us immensely. So we shall mainly deal with them in this note.

It is a historical puzzle that the Brahmanical icons numerically over whelm the Buddhist pantheon in our region. So far, we have not noticed a single Jaina image. The problem can possibly be solved if a thorough archeological investigations are carried out of major archeological mounds like Mangal garh (Samastipur). Naula garh (Begusarai). Jaimangala Garh (Begusarai) Alaoli garh (Khagaria) etc. This will help us in the identification of the nature of polity of three major centres and hence the cultural elan.

Being on the northern side of Anga we may find seminal linkage with plastic art of Anga. Now shall briefly deal with the iconographic analysis of certain icons of Begusarai.

Buddhist Icon of Begusarai : Marici

In the earlier table, we have noted the icons of Budhist Pantheon exclusively from Begusarai and Saharsa. In Samastipur and Khagaria we have not come across any Buddhist icon. Let us now deal with the iconography of Marici of Begusarai.

This mutilated femal deity- Marici of Buddhist Pantheon is mistakenly worshipped as male deity as Moor Katoa Baba by the local people. It is 2 high and 19" wide. Its 3 heads are chopped off and arms are badly damaged. The image is decorated with necklace along neck chain, girdle and Payel. It is standing in Alidha Position with right leg bending and left leg straight. The sari is transparent and its folds are meticulously depicted. Though upper limbs are mutilated, the following features are discernible :

i) It is an eight armed deity

ii) One left arm is depicted in the act of touching left breast.

iii) Lowest left hand is broken but associated with left thigh.

iv) Third left hand is broken but depicted in relation to bow and arrow.

v) Right side upperlimbs are completely effaced.

In the lower corners of the stela, four female, attendants are depicted in low relief in the same alidha posture. One devotee with garland is fashioned on the right corner, where as the image of a devotee on the left corner is now missing. The image of the charioteer is extremely mutilated.

On the pedestal, we find an undeciphered inscription. Besides we find a chariot run by seven pigs- three on each side. In the middle the pig is depicted with open month and protruding teeth. Below the Central Pig we find the image of Rahu.

Both the Sadhan Mala and the Nispanna Yogavali deal with the iconographic features of Marici. Our specimen is comparable to the Maricipuva type of Sadhanmala with 8 arms. In case of Nispanna Yogavali Marici is provided with 6 arms. Benoytosh Bhattacharya notes that all images so far recovered are eight armed. No where of our area any other specimen of Marici inculding the Anga has been found. It was all the more strange, that Nispanna Yogavali which was composed in Vikram Shila (Anga) during the time of Rampal dealt with the Iconography of Marici was not responsible for producing the images of Marici in the entire region of Anga and north of Anga. From this one can deduce that there is no seminal linkage of our Marici with Anga Nispanna Yogavali was composed by Abhaykara Gupta.

Brahmanical Icons

Begusarai is a rich repository of Brahmanical icons we shall make only brief reference to Visnu, Surya, Revanta and Camunda.

Vishnu

As noted above, we came across with visnu images in Birpur-Barepura, Kankaul and Kaith. We shall describe first two specimens :

i) Barepura Vishnu

It is in standing posture (sthanak). The stela is cut along the boarder of the central diety giving a partial impression of figure in round. Two flying Gandharvas are shown at the top of stela. Thus the stela is sparsely decorated. The central deity is wearing crown, various ornaments, girdle along with vanamala.

Four arms are depicted with Ayudhs in the follwoing manner :

a) Rt. Upper limb = mace

b) Rt. Lower arm = wheel

c) Left Upper limb = Stalk of lotus

d) Left lower arm = conch.

Various folds of the Dhoti are artistically depicted. Two female attendants with chamara standing on two smaller lotuses are depicted in low relief. The central deity stands on a bigger lotus throne which bears the sculpture of Garuda.

ii) Kankaul Vishnu

It is maller in size in comparison to previous one. It is more or less undamaged except the mutilated crown. The main deity is profusely decorated with ornaments and vanumala. The stela is highly decorated Vishnu is flanked by two divine consortws. Laksmi and Saraswatii-depicted in low relief. The pedestal carries the image of Guruda.

Not a single sitting nor reclining Visnu has been recorded in this area. In Ajgaibinath (on the Southern side of the Ganges), we come across a Pre-Pala Visnu in reclined position stylistically all Visnu images are not similar. From this, one can presume that the orgin can be traced to different ateliers.

iii) Surya

We find several surya images in Birpur, Barepura, Barauni and Kaith villages of Begusarai.

Let us first describe Birpur Surya :

a) Birpur Surya

The image is 5ft X 3ft. Pointed stela resembling the final of a temple is obvious. It is sparsely decorated having 3 figures : two flying Gandharvas on both sides of the top portion and the face of a tiger in the middle of those two Celestial being. The central deity is standing on a big lotus throne bearing the relief of seven horse of the chariot. Two hands hold two stalk of full flown lotuses. The deity is decorated numerous ornaments like crown and waist girdle. Besides a thick sacred thread is also depicted. Folds of upper and lower garments are tastefully fashioned. Surya is flanked by several divine attendants like Mahesvata, Pingala, Dandi, Chhaya, Samjana, Usha, Pratyusa. The charioteer Aruna is depicted with lower limbs.

The central deity is not cuts along the boarder and hence it gives the two dimensional impression. All the deities including the femal ones wear boots.

b) Barepura Surya

It exhibits all the iconographic features mentioned above. At the same time stylistically both are a little different. In case Barepura specimen, stela is highly decorated in comparison to Birpur image. Besides the main deity of Barepura is partially separated from the stela at the leval of chest and waist thereby giving partial three dimensional impression.

According to Brhat samhita surya should be represented with udici (Northern dress) with boot. In these two cases udici dress disappears, particularly from the Pala period. Besides Dandi, Pingal, Chhaya, Samjna, Mahesvata, Usha, Pratyusa were added to the main Panel during the Pala period one can notice this transition in a Pre pala Surya image of Gaibinath. Stylistic differences in these two icons of the same village may be traced to their fashioning into two different workshops and possibly co-incidental to two different chronology.

c) Revanta : Barepura

The booted central deity Revanta (son of Surya) rides over a highly caparisoned horse, the head is entirely mutilated. Upper limbs are partially destroyed. The right one is slightly raised and probably holding a cup and the left one reins. Behind the horse, an attendant is depicted holding a very big shaft of a parasol lifted over the head of Revanta. Left forelimb of the horse is shown in relation to the body of pig, while the left hind limb is shown in moving posture. In the middle of stela above the leval of the horse, four female figures, two on each side, have been depicted. One of the figures on the left side is seen with a pitcher. The other three carry chamaras. On the left side, below the level of two famele attendants one can see a male figure holding a hunted animal over his shoulder. At the bottom two attendants are depicted in the front; the front one is holding sword while the hind one is playing musical instruments. A dog found running under the belly of the horse. On the pedestal there is a relief of figures dancing and playing with musical instruments.

According to Brihat Samhita Revanta should be depicted as riding on a horse back along with hunting party. According to Dr. B. Sahay, there are two varieties of hunting Revanta:

a) The first one actually in the act of hunting.

b) The second one in which hunting is over and the hunting party is in the act of returning with the booty.

From the above description, our image belongs to the second group. In this connection one can refer to a broken panel with three images of Revanta recovered fromm Rajaona, Luckisarai on the Southern bank of the Ganges i.e., Anga.

iv) Camunda of Barepura

We came across three specimens of Camunda - (a terrible deity belonging to Sakti cult) at Barepura. Birpur and Pachamba of Begusarai.

We shall describe Barepura icon which is relatively showing paractically all the iconographic features of the deity.

The female deity is depicted as a heinious one with Sunken eyes and belly. The chest is emaciated with visible ribes. She is dancing on a platform underneath is lying a male body (corpse). At the head of the body, a Jackal is looking upwards while near legs an eagle is sitting. She has eight upper limbs (astabhuja) The upper most hands on both sides holding an elephant. The right one the forepart while left one the hindpart of the animal.

The second upper limbs- the right one holds a Khadga while the opposite one touches the chin expressing the emotion of surprise. The third limb on the right side carries a cup and the left counterpart holds a trident on which a male figure is lying on a supine position. The 4th right limb plays Damaroo while the left one holds a chopped head.

Near the right leg a male figure is sitting while playing on a percussion instrument like Tabla. Whereas on the left side, another figure playing a Kartala. The most interesting feature of the icon is the intaglio of Vrischik i.e. Scorpion - the 8th sing of Zodias as conceived by astrology.

The icon follows the iconographic features of camunda as mentioned in Agni Purana and Viskarma Sastra which assign eight arms of the deity Regarding Vrischik, astrology contends it to be feminine sign denoting violence and sex also. Mythlogically speaking camunda belongs to the group of violent female deities. She is the destroyer of two Asura brothers canda and Munda.

D. Concluding Remarks : Plurality of Plastic Styles of the Region

The Pala sculpture of our area has not been studied as yet in its evolutionary lineage as per the allied parameters such as time, space, iconography and aesthetics which includes styles. Stella Kramrisch, the noted art historian observes that the continuity of the Indian Art is determined by the notion of time i.e., the Indian art every time begins from the very beginning. Co- incidentally there is practically no predecessor of lithic art of this area : hence there is no question of beginning from the beginning.

By the reckoning of the above mentioned perception the Pala art of Anguttarapa should be considered basically as an art of Diaspora. This can be deduced from the various land grants inscription issued by the Pala Kings. The royal decrees entrusted the donees the responsibility to manage cult objects installd in temples of various pantheons.

Frederiseh Asher, who questions the traditional divisions of the Indian art accoridng to ruling dynasties, proposes to trace out the root of the Pala Art from the interlude of the post - Gupta period to the emergence of the Palas. According to him, before the extension of the Pala rule in the Eastern Indian, the whole region was divided among several ruling houses with respective regional ethos. One can get the glimpses of "अनेक नरपति" (many kings) from the Bhagalpur copper plate inscription of Narayana Pala Deva. Incorporation of regional styles to the main trend of the Pala Art leads Asher to designate multiple Pala styles in palce of a single Pala Style. The correlation of the local styles associated with smaller centres of

Polity like Alaoli garh, Jaimangala garh, Naola garh, Mangl garh etc. with the main genre of the Pala art can be properly comprehended when proper archeological exploration of these mounds will be undertaken.

To understand the above hypothesis, let us refer to the icon of Sadyojata of Alaoligarh of Khagaria. This specimen depicts Parvati in reclining position with a new born baby near the breast. No other specimen of Sadyojata has been recovered from any other spot of our area of enquiry. On the other hand, we find this icon from Antichak Bhagalpur on the Southern bank of the Ganges. Kramrisch refers two beautiful images of Sadyojata of Manda and Chopra of Rajsahi of Bangladesh. From this one could presume that Alaoli specimen was imported from outside.

Similarly we come across Sadyojata Sculpture image belonging to Post-Gupta and Pre-Pala period at Ajgaibinath hill near Sultanganj at the southern bank of the Ganges (Anga). This may help us to trace out its root in the Pre pala interlude as mentioned by Asher indicating linkage between North and South Anga.

Susan Huntington has classified the Pala styles of Bihar asper regional parameters in the following way :-

SL. No.	**Type of Sculpture**	**Region**
1.	Primary Sculpture	Magadh (Old Patna Districts)
2.	Interface Sculpture	Anga (Old Bhagalpur Districts)
3.	Peripheral	I. Chhotanagpur
		II. North Bihar
		i) Muzaffarpur Old
		ii) Darbhanga Old
		iii) Begusarai
		iv) Khagaria
		v) Saharsa
		vi) Purnea

We know that the evolution of the Vajrayana Buddhism evolves as the resultant of the integration of Tantra with Mahyana Buddhism. Dr. Benoytosh Bhattacharya observes that Magadha is the ritual terrain of this transformation, sometime in the 8th century A.D. Contemporaneous with the Magadhan School, the Bengal School flourished from the 10th century A.D.

The 'Primary' nomenclature of Huntingtons indicates the origion of this new genre of the Pala art takes place at Magadha. At the same time we propose that the Anga art is not a mere regional expression as denoted by the nomenclature interface. In fact, Vikramshila of

Anga is another genetic area of the Pala art from where the later's dispersal to North Bihar, Nepal, Tibet etc. took place. One can refer to the migration of Dipankara to Tibet from this place. Besides. Nispanna Yogavali of Mahapandit Abhaykara Gupta - a Buddhist iconographic text was composed here. The historic nature of this international dispersal should be comparatively studied to understand the character of the sculpture of our area. Only then suitable nomenculature can be adduced to the art of our area.

The pluarity of styles can be approached from the concept of Desachara and Gramachara of Dr. B.N.S. Yadava. According to him, the medieval factor fo the Indian history has paved the way for the emergence of local units of economy. This gave rise to the evolution of local customs (Desachara/Gramachara). Man violating local customs were castigated as degraded (Patitah). The laws prescribed by Dharmasastras were not prevalent in all the regions uniformly. On the contrary, local customs (Desharma) were also rigidly enforced. Thus Asher's postulate of the emergence of local ruling units get further confirmation by Dr. B.N.S. Yadava's hypothesis. This will help us to understand the plurality of styles as per the compulsion of Desachara.

Before Concluding, One may refer to role of itenarent sculptors as elaborated by Dr. R.N. Mishra. In certain places of our areas say Birpur, we come across an unfinished sculpture. So apart from the art of diaspora, there is corrosponding evidence of fashioning icons by the itenarenat sculptors in the spot. Uptil now no major workshop catering the entire area has been found out. Most likely icons were imported from the different ataliers functioning outside our area possibly Anga.

*Medical Practitioner
and dedicated to Regional History and Archaeology,
Patna

Courtesy :
National Seminar on
Anguttarapa ka Kshetriya Puratatva
Aivum Itihas, 2004
G.D. College Begusarai

●●●

Vethadvipa

A.C. Verma*

Loard Buddha Passed into Mahaparinirvana under a grove of Sala trees in his eightieth year in the land of Mallas in Kusinagar. His last ceremony was celebrated in a royal manner. Ajatsataru from Rajagraha, the Licchavis of Vaisali, Sakyas of Kapilvastu, the Bulis of Allakappa, the Mallas of Pava, the Koliyas of Ramagrama and a Brahmana from Vethadvipa, all claimed their shares in the division of the relics. It appears that after the division had been made a messenger of the Mauryas of Pippalivana came for a portion of the relic. As there was nothng left, he took pieces of coal which the Mauryas began to revere and placed it in a stupa. Thus, originally there were eight stupas, in Rajgraha, Vaishali, Kapilvastu, Allakappa, Ramgram, Vethadvipa, Pava and Kusinagar.[1] In addition to these relics there are various stupas or places of Buddhist interest where hair, tooth etc. were shrined. Brahaman Drona who had distributed the relics took away the Vessel pot from which, he had distributed the relic and a Chaitya was also built on it.[2]

In this context, We find the name of Vethadvip. But in due course of time, we have forgotten its location and the name remained only preserved in the Buddhist literatures.

Vethadvipa is thus and important religious place for Buddhists. The Hindus believe Lord Buddha to be an incarnation of Lord Vishnu, hence the Hindus also attach importance to this site also. Vethadvipa, later on became a tantric seat for the Buddhists and it adopted many rituals and worship practices of the Hindus and after the downfall of Buddhism the Hindus prevailed there. It remained the seat of tantrism but converted this seat as shakt centre and it became a place for the worship of Bhagwati or Devi.

The location of Vethadvipa is shown in Anguttarapa according to Maha-parinibban sutta. Anguttarapa has been identified by Rahul Sankrityayana as consisting the area now belonging to Begusarai, Khagaria, Some south-western part of Saharsa and North Bhagalpur District. Rahul Sankrityayana says that the word Anguttarapa is coined by adding three words i.e. Anga + uttar + Aap, meaning therby the place on the northern side of Anga after Aap i.e. water-meaning the river Ganga. Thus, the Kausikiksetra, which lies to the north of Anga across the Ganga was known as Anguttarapa.[3] From Samyutta-nikaya,[4] it is presumed that Anguttarapa asseted its independence after the conquest of Anga by Bimbisara,[5] and joined the Vijji Republic. The Vaisali Republic is said to have extended up to the river Kosi in the east.[6] During the region of Mahaparinibbana, this area seems to have come under Magadh again.[7]

The Mahavagga and Majihima Nakaya[8] speak of some four visits of this land by Lord Buddha. R. Sankrityayana[9] clearly points out this area to be in Anguttarapa.It is also evident, according to the findings of Prof. Liang chi-chao, that as many as 162 out of the number of Chinese pilgrims who went out to India during the 5th, 6th, 7th and 8th centuries can be traced from the chinese sources of information. Dr. Chou Hisiang, Kusung has also described in detail about the Indo - chinese relation after lord Buddha. Prof. Liang Chi xhao's researches in chinese history, which remain untranslated still, are summarized in a paper, Chinese sources of Indian History, contributed by Dr. Lolia chuen to the Silver Jubliee session of the Indian Historical Records Commission in Dec, 1948; Dr. Lo, an eminent chinese scholar, now serving in the Govt. of Formosa was china's ambassador to India in 1945-50.[10]

Further, we know that there is only one island in this area i.e. it is only in presenet Begusarai District at Jaimanglagadh surrounded by Kabar Jheel. Thus this place may be definitely considered as vethadvipa.

Tradition asserts that a large number of Chinese and Siamese travellors visited this place.[11] as far as they know that the folowing travellors[12] besides Hiuen-Tsang visited north Bihar viz.

i) Hiuen chiu (Indian name Prakashmati) - spent his time in Sin-che temple.
ii) Tao Hi (Indian name- Srideva)- dwelt in Kusi country.
iii) Sin- chiu (Indian name- Charita Verma) - lived in Sin che temple.
iv) Chi-Hing (Indian name- Prajna Deva) - visited Sin-che, temple.
v) Tang- visited Vaisali and Kusi country.
vi) Hwui -Lun (Indian name- Prajna Verma) visited the Sin-che Temple.

We also know that several Korean monks had gone to India, but out of them several died in India of whom a few of them used to live in Sin-che Temple. Tsing the chinese traveller has confirmed this in his travel account.[13]

The exact location of Sin-che Temple has not yet been rightly identified. It can be conjecture that this temple was situated some where between vaisali and Kusi country and on this basis this sinche temple must have been situated somewhere in Anguttarapa region. This important Buddhist shrine may further be identified by the religious site near vethadvipa.

Even if we presume a bit further we can safely assume that the four mounds of daitadih are closely connected with Vethadvipa or i.e., present Jaimanglagadh. These mounds are about 1km. away on the side of Jaimanglagadh. They are about 1.5 km away on the northen side of the Jaimanglagadh- Gadhpura road in Sakra-Rajaur mauja. In those period this place was far from village and was completely in lone and isolated place.

People used to dispose of dead bodies far away from habitation and in a lonely place. In old literature, we get references about such place. In the Secred Book of East,[14] we come across the word samsana. This word is described as follows : Samsana is the name of the burial mound in which the bones of the dead man were laid to rest (cf. Anagniadadha). It is mentioned in the Atharvdeda[15] and often later.[16] The Satpatha Brahmana[17] prescribed a four corneded mound facing the south-east on ground inclined to the north, out of sight of the village in a peaceful spot amidst beautiful surroundings, or on barren ground. For an "Agnieit" builder or a fire alter, a funeralmound like a fire-alter is prescribed. The Easterneres (Prachya) made their mounds round.

In the above context, we can presume that out of these four mounds, the main stupa in the centre may have contained the relic of Lord Buddha and out of the remaining three stupas they are containing the relies of Taou-Hi (Indian name Srideva), Sin-Chiu (Indian name -Charita Verma) and that of some important Korean monk who died at Sin - che Temple respectively. This suggestion may not be palatable to all but now the responsibility of proving or disproving this claim lies mainly on the archaeologists and the Govt. may kindly be requested to move into the matter.

In this connection we must remember the visit of Dr. M. Dharmma Rakshita of Thailand to this place. In the year 1939-40 A.D. or Thai (Shyam Country) Buddhist piligrim Dr. M. Dharmarakshita (Ph.D California university) came over this place. He was on a piligrim trip of the important Buddhistsites of India. He came to Bihar.

This Thai pilgrim, after reading a column about Kabar Jheel in Searchlight news paper by Chakradhar Prasad, came to Begusarai and met the then civil S.D.O. and requested him to help him as he wanted to meet Chakradhar Prasad. Chakradhar Prasad was a Mokhtar (later on called advocate) in the Begusarai court. He was immediatedly summond and was introduced to the pilgrim. The pilgrim showed him the paper-cutting and wanted to visit the place. Chakradhar Prasad belonged to Cheria Bariyarpur. He received the pilgrim and took him to his village. The pilgrim stayed with him for a fortnight as his guest. The Kabar Jheel and Jaimanglagadh was situated at a distance of about three miles from Cheria Bariarpur. The pilgrim almost daily visited the site. He made a detailed inspection of the site of the fortrses and its environments. He took a great interest and studied the images and broken pieces of slabs and pillars. He took keen interest in all relevant matters concerning the place and the legand prevailing in connection with the fortress and the Temple. He took notes and always consulted the Palitext Books which were with him. One day, he became very excited and begen to worship that place. He begen to salute the place repeatedly in Sastang mudra by laying himself horizontally on the ground. The piligrim asserted that the relics of Lord Buddha was lated down here. He narrated that the Nivran of Lord Buddha, his body was cremated at Kusinara in a Royal like manner. his remains after cremation were collected and was distributed in eight divisions by a Brahmin named Drona. The vessel used for this purpose was a wooden Drona and all the above mentioned claiments, as stated in the beginning received their shares and erected stupas on them in their respective places and with devotion worshiped it.[18] The pilgrim further stressed that according to the Pali sacred books of his country one of such stupa erected at Vethadivpa was located on the left bank of the river Herna (Harnavati) and this river flowed on three sides of this stupa and the monastery which was situated near the stupa. Monks and nuns were imparted Buddhist teaching in this monastery. The monsatery had a fort like structure with one gate and there was a moat all around it, which had its water connection with the river. The various small and big stupas and Chaityas had likewise inter connected chain of moats all around them and canal breached off rom this area which joined them again at a downward place of flow. He further stated that there were four fortresses situated on different sides of this area, wherein military garrisons were stationed by the rulers for protection of the relics.

He expressed that it was during the region of one king Dhamma Ashoka that due to a breach in the river Hirnavati, the entire monastery was inundated and the stupas and Chaityas were demolished, dilapldated or otherwise washed away and a great lake was permanently formed around the monastery area.

The pilgrim also opined that four huge mounds of earth on the eastern side of Jaimanglagadh, were actually Chaityas and they are still expected to conain relies of monks and nuns. He even expressed doubt that one of them, possibly the largest of them which is in the centre may contained the relics of Lord Buddha. He asserted that this is a holy place for the Buddhists and this place was in the past constantly visited by the Chinese, Burmese, Tibetans, Simse, and other south-eastern Buddhist pilgrims. He was of the opinion that the place has become important place for study of Tantric Buddhism but later on with the decline of Buddhism, this place passed on to the Brahmanic people, who transformed the place into a seat of Sakti worship of the Brahmannical faith and installed an image of Goddess into the temple out of a disfigured idol of Lord Buddha.

Chakradhar Prasad had narreted this incident to Dr. A.S. Alteker and Prof. Radha Krishna Choudhary of G.D. College, Begusarai before Dr. A.C. Verma when Dr. A. S. Altekar has once visited G. D. College, Begusarai in connection with the Practical examination of B.A. (Hons) in the year 1960 A.D.? Chakradhar Prasads had also narreted that the Thai pilgrim Dr. Dharmarakshita had one unique pali book in his possession and that this book was inscribed on thin golden plates. The pilgrim narrated him that this book contains the details about the division of relices of Lord Buddha after his cremation.

The Buddhist records also testify that after the Mahaparinibbana of Lord Buddha, the details were prepared after Buddhist council and the book Mahaparinibbana Sutta was prepared on golden plates. Three such books were prepared and out of them one book was kept in India and out of the other two books one each was sent to Sri Lanka and Siam respectively. We had still no information about such Indian book. Some fragments of Sri Lankan golden book was found in central Asia and is kept in Russian Museum in Leningnarad in Moscow. A fragmentary Sanskrit version of this Sutta of Mahaparinibaanan has been discovered in central Asia deciphered and published by Prof. Waldschmidt[19] in 1950. The Siamese book was brought to India with Dr. M. Dharmarakshita.

After his identification of this site, Chakradhar Prasad now requested him to come back to Begusarai but he insisted that he would continue his journey to Kapilvastu on foot[20] as to the direction given in this book. At last Chakradhar Prasad left him at Manjhaul. The pilgrim proceeded on foot but he was arrested at Motihari. I (Dr. A.C. Verma) myself while preparing for my thesis in the year 1962 on the direction of my guide and supevisor for Ph. D Degree, Prof. R.K. Choudhary, visited Motihari to know personally about Dr. Dharmarakshita. In the S.P. office of Motihari no old record was found in this connection but a retired Muslim constable told me that in his presence, the pilgrim was arrested. He was suspected to be a spy as Thailand was with Japan in the second world war. The pilgrim was kept in the room of the Reader of the S.P., K.P. Ambastha. The muslim constable suggested me to meet K. P. Ambasta who was then D.S.P and the directed me to meet him. He told me that the D.S.P.'s home town was Gaya and his home was on the northen side of the Vishnupad temple. I went there and met him. K.P. Ambasta confirmed me about the arrest of the pilgrim and he said that the pilgrim was brought by him to Patna and was handed over to the I.G. Office. The pilgrim, as reported by him, was sent to Delhi and handed over to the Defence Department where he was Court Marshelled and shot to death. Thus, nothing could be known about the Golden book which was with him. The D.S.P., K.P. Ambasta is still live and this can be testified by him even.

If we assess critically the various issues introduced in it, we can certainly come to the conclusion which will support the theory of the above pilgrim. If the geographical and archaeological aspect of the place and its environments are examined, we find the following points in favour of our assumption that this place is the old Buddhist site of Vethadvipa.

i) The fortress which has been termed as a monsatry by this pilgrim is actually situated on the left bank of the Burhi Gandak.

ii) Burhi Gandak was formerly known as Hirnyawati and not Herna as stated by the pilgrim.

iii) Rahul Sankrityayan also names Burhi Gandak as Hirnyawati.

iv) This river has taken a circular turn at this place in such a way that it flows to north, west and south of this fortress area.

v) The four fortresses situated on different sides of this area, whrerin military garrisons were stationed by the rules for protection of the relics which can be still seen as they are the sites of old and ruined fortresses of Manglagadh, Nawalagadh, Ramgadh and Gadhpura. All of those gadhs lie on the four sides of this monastery area.

vi) From the beginning, there was a deep lake around the fortress is amply borne out by the fact that there is sill a deep wide moat all around gadh.

vii) The lake has dried up recently, many times and the entire lake area has been found studded with remanants of stupa like mounds with clear cut moats around them. The local people call them as 'Nasi' and the mound (moats) are called as 'Rahis.'

viii) Many times skeltons and bones were found inside the 'Rahis' as well as in round the Gadh itself. Some times in well laid graves made of brick plinths skeltons are found. Some such brick laid with skeltons were discovered by the panda during their process of bringing the northeren part of the Gadh under cultivation. On 27th october 2008 when I visited Jaimangla Gadh with Sri Alok Kumar Agrawal, Ex-chairman, Begusarai, Nagarpalika and Santosh kumar and Shristi Garg research scholar, we happended to trace a few mounds containing graves on the western side outside the main fort area of Jaimangla- gadh still intact.

ix) The marble beads and other finds in possession of the pandas also disclose their chinesee and Tibtan charater, there by indicating the content of such people with this place.

x) The north western part of the lake is called 'Goaban' and if closely inspected it discloses that this water course is a man made canal which connectes the moat partition of the Gadh with the Burhi Gandak. Chandrabhaga Water course to the southeast the lake is also man-made canal flowing down towards the east to join the river at its downward points.

xi) A number of broken Buddhist images and other slabs containing Buddhistic engravings and inscriptions can reasonably be constructed to mean that this place was originally a Buddhist site.

xii) T.N. Ramchandran, the then director General of Archaeology Govt. of India also supports that the entire lake area containes remains of graves as human skeltons clearly indicates that the entire lake area containes remains of graves as human skeltons clearly indicates that these mounds were Chaityas of the Buddhist period and not stupas as commonly called. As term stupa in analogous to Chaitya, as it also means a mound or something which is raised and that later, the term Chaitya came to mean a shrine an alter or a temple or as meaning a mound containing a relic e.g. ashes, bones hair or a tooth of the Buddha.

xiii) In the above context, it would not thus appear surprising to find that it was due to the entire lake area being studded with graves or relics of human being that during the Muslim period, this lake became generally known to be called by the name of 'Qabar', Jhael of later on Kabar Jheel. In persion qabar means a grave.

xiv) The enormous number of graves scatterd all over the Jheel proves that Jaimanglagadh was a famous Buddhist religious site and the Vihar which was attached to this religious place housed thousand and thousands of monks or pupils getting Buddhist spritual training and teachings. This place housed permanent monks also and perhaps even it was thought to be such a great religious place that even if one died at this spot, it was thought to incure some special religious favour for the person.

References :-

1. Sacred Book of the East XI.-135ff.

2. Buddha Dharma Aur Bihar - Tripathi, Havaldar,p.-133, Bihar Rastra Bhasa Parisad, Patna.

3. Historical Geography and Topography of Bihar, Pandey, M.s. - p.-97

4. Samukta Nikaya, vol II, pp. 437, 439

5. Sacred Book of East; XVII, p. - 1 of Parisistaparva, VII-22

6. History of Bihar, Choudhary; R.K. pp. 13-14 cf. Mahavagga, 65 cf Suttanipat 33 cf. Paramatthajyotika,II, 437, ef Dictionary of Pali Propernames, Malalsekram, p-22

7. Mahavagga VI; S.B.E. 17 pp. 127-134

8. Sutta Nos - 54,66,92

9. Op. cit, Sankrityana, p - 144, foot note

10. 2500 years of Buddhism; Ed prof. Bapat, p.v.page 185 foot note the Pub Div Minstry of infor and Broadcasting Govt. of India- 1956

11. A History of Chinese Buddhism, Dr. Kusung Chou Husiang.

12. Life of thin entsang. Beal, XXVI, XXXVI

13. 2500 years of Buddhism; Ed prof. Bapat, p.v.page 276-279 Publication Division Minstry of Informa tion and Broadcasting Govt. of India - 1956

14. S.B.E. Vol III p - 397

15. Altharvaveda V 31, 8, X, 1, 18

16. Taittriya Samhita V 2, 8, 5, 4 II 3
Kathaka Samhita XXI, 4
Maitrayani Samhita - III, 4,7,
Satapatha Brahman, IV, 5, 2, 15, etc.

17. Satapatha Brahmana, XIII , 8, let Seg. cf. Eggaling, SBE 44, 424 et seg.
cf. Zimmer, altindisches leben, 407
Hopkins. Journal of the American oriental society, 16, c- III

18. Bauddha Dharma and Bihar, "Tripathi Havaldar, p - 133 Bihar Rashtra Bhasa Parisad Patna

19. 2500 years of Buddhism, Ed by proj. Bapat P.V.P - 154 the publication Division Ministry of Information and Broadcasting, Govt. of India 1956.

20. Op. cit; Verma, A. C., p.- 133.

*Rtd. Principal and Univ. Prof.
Dept. of A.I.H.&Culture
A.P.S.M., College, Barauni

Courtesy :
Jaimanglagadh
Journal of Historical Studies
Volume - 1 , 2010

Sculptures from Jaymangalagarh, Begusarai

Umesh Chandra Dwivedi*
Ram Shekhar Singh*

Jaymangalagarh, an ancient mound, is at about 20 Kilo meters from Begusarai. This whole area is full of ancient mounds but due to negligence and ignorance, the villagers have destroyed certain portion of mounds. It is said that Jaymangalagarh was the religious centre of the ancient rules of Naulagarh. Even today, it is an important religious centre and people of this area assemble here on Tuesday and Saturday to worship the goddess Jaymangla.

The site on which the temple of Jaymangla is located is as Jaymangalagarh, though in revenue settlement record the village is known as Jaymangalpur. It is surrounded on all sides by a moat and then by a lake known as Kabar Tal. This lake is of about 13km. in length and 15km. in width. It is said that in ancient time, this lake was connected to river Ganga., Gandak and Kamala. According to local tradition, the mound of Jaymangalagarh was once a fort of king Jaymangal.

Jaymangalagarh is very close to another fort Mangalgarh in the Samastipur district. Mangalgarh is situated at a distance of about 23km. from Jaymangalagarh. The ruler of Mangalgarh is said to have been a powerful monarch and a contemporary of Askoka, the great. The king of Mangalgarh is said to have extended his sphere of influence up to Jaymangalagarh.[1]

Goddess Jaymangala is regarded as one of the important 'pithas' of India. However, there is no clear cut record to suggest when and how this 'pitha' come to be established. The site of Goddess Jaymangla is mentioned in Mithila-tattvavimarsa and Mithila Darpan. Jaymangla is mentioned in Mithila Mahatmya, Brahma Vaivarta Purana, Devi Bhagavata etc. It is believed that Lord Siva Killed demon Tripura and established this 'Pitha' here.[2]

According to Siamese Buddhist tradition, it was also a centre of Tantric Buddhism.

Jaymangalagarh is even today regarded as an important centre of Tantric cult and tantriks come here from far of places. However there is no literary source to confirm it.

Though, The antiquity of this place goes back to at least 5th Cent. B.C., most of the sculptures are either of Pala Period or later.

The image of Jaymangala Devi has a unique iconography. The original face of the deity was perhaps lost and is replaced by a rounded head with no significant characteristic. The deity is shown standing slightly cross-legged. In her right hand, she carries a straight sword which is placed on earth near a bird probably Saras or Hamsa who has long neck. The left hand of this deity catches the neck of the bird. Unfortunately, no iconographic tradition of this deity is known to us and there is no literary support to the iconography of this deity isknown so far. The material of the image is black stone but on the basis of its finsishing and art style, it is difficult to place this image in Pala- Sena period and it may be a letter product of Medieval period.

However we have so many images from this place which can be placed in Pala-Sena period.

One of the important image is that of Varaha incarnation of Lord Visnu. Here the four armed varaha is shown standing. While his right lower hand is placed on his thig, his another right hand carries a Gada. The god is known rescuing Goddess earth on his left shoulder and one hand perhaps carries a Sankh. The right leg of the God is placed on surface and the left is slightly upraised. The snake figurines are shown worshiping the god on either side. A kshatra has been provided to the God. The image can be dated 9th-10th century on the basis of art style of Pala period.

We have another image of this period that of Lord Surya. This was identified as Badri Narayan by R.K. Choudhary.[3] However this image on the basis of its iconography can be easily identified as that of Lord Surya. Here the deity is shown standing with lotus in both upraised hand and a boot can be noticed in his leg. He is being attended by Danda and Pingal and his consorts Surenu and Nikshukha on either side. The goddess Usha is placed in front of the Sun and before whom is placed his charioteer Aruna driving Sun's Chariot of one wheel and seven horses. Two vidyadharas on either side near the top of stele are also noticed. The image can be dated in 9th Century A.D. on the basis to its style.

We have another image of this period that of Uma- Mahesvara. Here Goddess Uma is shown seated in the left thig of Lord Siva as usual. Here the Lord is Shown seated on a lotus seat with the pendent right leg resting on his Vahna Bull. Uma's left leg hangs out and is placed on the back of her Vehicle lion. Of the four hands of Lord Siva, one is placed near the left basest. One is touching the chin of the goddess.

The Matsya Purana gives the best and the most detailed direction as to how these images should be made. According to the text, the God may have either two or four hands. He should have the lotus and the trident in his right hands and one of his left hands should hold the breast or the breasts of the goddess. The goddess embraced should sit on the left thigh of the god and should be grazing on his face. She may be depicted as supportively touching with her right hand the left shoulder of the god or his right shoulder or his right side. The left hand should hold either a lotus or a mirror.

The two maids, Jaya and Vijaya, the two sons of the couple, Kartikeya and Ganesa and various other ghosts and superantural being should be depicted at suitable places.[4]

However this image is more close to a description given by Pandit Bipin Chandra Kavyaratna in article on Uma-Mahesvara in the Journal of Rangpur Sahitya Parisad, 1316 B.S., P. 178 who quotes from another Purana (Which he does not name) to show that god may also be depicted in the following manner. "The upper left hand (of the god) should hold the trident, the lower one should be placed on the bosom of the goddess. The upper right hand should hold the nagapasa or the Khatvanga and the other right hand should supportively touch the chin of the goddess."

A beautiful image of a female deity identified as Ganga is also reported from this place. However an examination of the photograph of image indicates it as that of tapasacharya Parvati or Gauri. The goddess is shown standing with his one right hand in varadamudra and the other carrying rosary. In her left hand she has a trident and a water-pot. She has been provided a jatamukuta here. Gouri's vahan alligator may have been represented on the pedestal of this image also, which may have been identified as makar leading the identification with Ganga.

We have another sculpture from this place depicting the Navagrahas presently in Begusarai Museum, Begusarai. The image is important as this depict the vahan of these figures also. Here on the right side of these grahas is Ganesa, standing on lotus pedestal which depicts his vahan mushak on the front. The next figure is that of Sun or Surya carrying lotus in his both hands. He has been provided a horse as his vahan. The next figure that of Soma who carries a water pot in left hand and his right hand is in varada mudra. He has been provided a vahan who looks like a makara. The next figure Mangal's head is broken. His right hand placed near his naval carries some indistinct object and his hand carries a sword like object. He has been provided peacock as his vahan. The next figure Buddha carries an object which he holds with help of his both hands. He has been provided a dog as his vahan. The next standing figure in row is Brihaspati, more heavy than the other figures. Here Guru Brihaspati shown with a water pot in left hand and his right hand with abhaya mudra. He has a rosary also in this hand. he has been provided a swan as his vahan. The next figure of Sukra or Sukra-charya also carrying a water pot in left hand and abhaya mudra in right hand. He has a slim body. He has been provided a frog like animal as his vahan. The next figure is Shani whose right hand is in abhaya mudra and left hand carries dand like object. His vahan looks like a donkey or buffalo. The next figure is that of Rahu whose bust is only shown in the image. He is shown with his hands in tarpan mudra carrying probably crescent. He has been provided a rolling wheel as his vahan. The last figure is that of Ketu with serpent or fish like lower parts and a Serpenthood over head. His hands are in anjalimudra.

Another image of crown Visnu was also discovered from this place which was taken by late Dhiran Singh of Village Mohanpur in the Begusarai block. He installed this image in front of his house where a temple was also constructed, just by the western side of the embankment of river Budhi Gandaka. It is hardly 1/4 Km. from state higway no. 55.

All these images are important for the study of the art of this region.

References :

1. R. K. Choudhary, A Report on the Exploration of Jaymangalagarh and Mangalgarh, G. D. College Bulletin No. 2 Year 1952, P 12
2. Ibid, P. 13
3. Ibid.
4. Matsya Purana, Chapter 260, P. 898.

*Director
Patna Museum, Patna

Courtesy :
Jaimangalagadh
Journal of this torical studies
Volume - 1, January 2010

●●●

Searching Anguttarap & Aapan Nigam In Jayamanglagarh

Umesh Kr. Singh*

It is pathetically sad to note that written history on many events of our past is not available, many of the archeological and numismatic evidences too have been in due course of time, either washed away, due primarily to the continuous disastrous erosions of many turbulent rivers, or fell victims of cruelties of adverse situations, or prolonged negligence and were damaged by terrible earthquakes or disastrous volcanic eruptions, or intentionally ruined by the plunders, or cruelty of some orthodox and fanatic foreign invaders. Even the Vedas or subsequent writings were mostly with religious purposes, though historians were able to search out of them some political as well as socio-economic themes. But archaeologists' continuous efforts have enabled us with various valuable informations of our past and now we are able to know that Paleolithic, Neolithic, Chalcolithic sites also exist in various parts of Bihar besides the NBPW (Northern Black Polish Ware) culture. Now their reconstruction creates insurmountable and formidably impossible and intricate tasks to the Indian historians.

Like some other matters of ancient Indian history, unanimity of opinion among historians and archaeologists still awaits regarding fixation of the exact location of Anguttarap and Aapan Nigam and the visits and stays of Lord Buddha. Consequently, on the basis of availability of scanty materials to the historians, they have opined divergently. Hence, before arrriveing at a definite conclusion and to locate these palces at Jaimanglasthan, we have to keep in consideration the existing claims of other place also, about whom some historians have furnished some ground of claims.

Meaning of Anguttarap & Aapan-Nigam :-

It will be quite proper to explain the connotations of Anguttarap and Aapan-Nigam before mentioning the facts, which can establish one's legitimacy for such claims.

Buddhist religious books mention a region called Anguttarapa in north of Ganga, particularly in the north of Anga. The literal meaning of Anguttarapa is the area, which fall in the north (Uttar) of Anga and; fully surrounded with water (ap) i.e, habitation on the islands and so on. In Ancient/India, the term "Nigam" was used for traders committee also, but in Amarkosa "Nigam" has been described as a city.[1] Jain texts explain 'Nagar' as the city of traders, where trading activities and transactions used to be carried out chiefly.[2] On a seal, recovered from Basarh "Nik-Nigam" is engraved, which was interpreted by Dr. Bhandarkar[3] and Majumdar[4] as city. Many interpret it as a city of craftsmen or traders[5]. In Shilperatna[6] it is suggested that in ancietnt India traders had separate and independently exclusive trading cities. Now these ancient habitational sites are found mainly on the shallow slope of a deep lake, or in the centre of the shallow lakes (or Chaurs), which remain under water for at least three to six months in year.

Probable Sites :-

On the above featured parameters, there are more than one such sites, which deserve mention as the probable sites for them.

On the basis of geographical description of Anguttrap, such areas, falling straight north of Ang, having watery swamps and encircled territories are more than one. Such probable sites can be one among the following-(1) Kursela of Katihar, or (2) Gogri -Parbatta, or (3) Alauli of Khagaria, (4) bangaon-Mahisi of Saharsa district and (5) Jayamangalgarh-Nawalgarh of Begusarai district. All these five regions are among the areas, matching the defined criteria for Anguttarap. Many scholars like Prof. R.S. Sharma also concedes the idea that Anguttarapa was an independent Janapada, besides the sixteen Janapadas in 6th century B.C.[7] but he also kept mum on the point of furnishing any details about it, regarding its exact location and the territorial boundaries of Anguttarap. About its rulers also, he had made no mention. Similar is the case with other eminent scholars and historians. Hence, until its location is decided, Aapan Nigam can not be spotted out. But before reaching any final conclusion, we have to keep it own mind the number of ancient sites of antiquites, and so far recovered archaeological, numismatic and inscriptional evidences and only then, it will be possible to arrive at some decisions.

Findings of Historians :-

Prominent among eminent historians, who had written on Anguttarap, are Rahulsankrityana, Prof. R.K. Choudhary and Havaldar Tripathi. They are also not very specific to fix-up the location of it. Some others have simply made a cursory mention of it without giving any accounts worth mention. Contemporary texts like Jain and Buddhist also mention Anguttarap but they are also silent to furnish details All such writers agree on one point that Anguttarap was one of the janapada, surrounded with watery swamps. Since, it is in the north of Ang so it might be one among the five mentioned above.

Havaldar Tripathi in his book, Bauddha Dharma Aur Bihar[8] has narrated in details the accounts of travels of Lord Buddha with a detailed note on Anguttarap and Aapan Nigam. He has given in detail of happenings with Loard Buddha while staying in Anguttarap. Due to space constrainsts, it is not possible to mention in detail,but I will like to write about some interesting episodes.

It is learnt that after a stay of Lord Buddha in Kuttagarshala of Vaisali, went to Champa (Bhagalpur) and reached Bhaddiya (Bhadariya, near Bhagalpur) village along with his 1250 Vikshus, as also disclosed by Rahulsankrityayan, in his book Buddha- charya, as quoted by Havaldar Tripathi.[9] It has been mentioned that there lived a prosperous (trader) shresthi, namely Jetil Mendak. It is also said that he was one among the five prosperous and rich shresthis in the realm of Bimbisara. Other four were Jyotiya, Purnak and Kakvaliya, the five crorepati Shresthis. He was endowed with five greatly endowed talents, namely his wife Chanciraprabha, his son Dhananjaya, his daughter-in-law Sumana, his dasa Purnak. On the information of Buddha's arrival in Jativan-Vihara, he reached there to greet Lord Buddha.[10] He had sent his grand-daughter, Vishakha along with 500 bards to felicitate Lord Buddha. Vishakha's mother's name was Sumana and father was Dhananjaya. Grihpathi Mendak bore all the expenses of Buddha's stayal at Bhadiya and he and his family members were so much impressed with Buddha's principles that his entire family got converted to Buddhism as Buddha's disciples. It is said that ultimately Vishakha became a maid (dasi) of Lord Buddha.

In Apana Nigam, a very prominently famous Jatil, namely Keniya lived.[11] He decided to meet and pay respect to Lord Buddha, who had attained Buddhahood, but he was indecisive with regard to the presents to be offered to Buddha at the first stance meeting, and finally he decided to offer a kind of drink to Buddha and his Bhikshus, which used to be earlier consumed by the prominent Brahman Rishis like Attak, Vamak, Vamdeo, Vishwamitra, Yamdagni, Angiras, Bhardwaj, Basishtha, Kashyap, Vrigu, etc.[12] He carried a special drink, namely Marraiya, prepared by fruits and leaves of plants on hand loads of manual labours and offered, on arrival, that special drink to the Lord after offering respectable compliments. Earlier Bhikshus hesitated to drink, but on Buddha's approval, they drank to the full. Keniya invited Buddha for a feast, but Lord Buddha in the beginning hesitated to accept the plea that his companions were very large in number and he was a very kind hearted donor, with an intention to avoid burden on him. But on repeated persuasions, Lord Buddha consented, when requested thrice by Keniya and on his departure Buddha allowed this drink to Bhikshus for future also.

It is learnt that Lord Buddha started his journey along with his twelve hundred disciples for Anguttarap (north of Ang (Bhagalpur), a part of Saharsa), Mendak Grihpati had dispatched provisioning materials on bullock-carts, fully laiden with salt, oil, Madhu, rice and other eatables, besides a herd of 1250 milking cows and met him on way in a jungle;[13] and refreshed all the accompany Vikshus with the fresh cow's milk. It is learnt that on that very moment, Lord Budha presecribed for Vikshus "Panch Goras" in the menu of diet[14]. Through the forest (Jativan), Buddha had reached Aapan Nigam of A nguttarap. (Havaldar Tripathi fixed up to the probability of Bangaon and Mahishi in Saharsa district as the location of Aapan Nigam and Mahisi and due to their traditional rich culture, they were the centeres of religious activities, proven by recovery of many deitites of ancient period form this site. Mandan Mishra, a great scholar of philosophy belonged to Mahisi village, where Aadi Sankracharya came over to have a religious discourse with him in the second half of the ninth century. Due to Sankaracharya's visit, the village could have been named Mahishmati, which later on became

Mahisi in due course.[15] One Grihpati, namely Pottaliya had met Buddha there.[16] Potali, after handing over his entire assets to his sons, was spending a Vanprast life. Lord Buddha had enumerated and preached his eight fold precepts to him and soon after Potali accepted Buddhism on being convinced with Buddhist precepts.

Another story we learn that there lived; a great scholarly Brahman, namely Sail, in Aapan Nigam, who was imparting education in Vedas, Kalp, Nighantu, history, poetry, grammar, philosophy etc. Keniya Jetil was Prominetly respectful among Sail Brahmins and Sail had reached the place of feast and on seeing the on-going preparations for a great feast, asked him if the emperor, Bimbisar, would be visiting. But on getting information about Buddha, Sail rushed to Lord's place of stayal and at the very first meeting only, was so much impressed that he converted in to Buddhism along with his 500 pupils.[17] Keniya's joy knew no bounds to see Sail along with his 300 disciples with shaven heads, sitting at the site of arrival of Lord Buddha for feast. Buddha, after lunch, preached, "*Agnihotra* among Yajnas, *Surya* among lights, *king* among men, *sea* among rivers: *moon* among stars and *Savitri* among Chhands are prominent"[18] "Likewise Sang is important to them, who donate to earn 'Punya." (It resembles to Bhagvatgeeta's Sibhuti-yoga). Thereafter, Lord Buddha left the place of host.

After visiting some other places, Lord Buddha left Appan Nigam for" Kusinara."[19] It is an irony of facts that beyond the above-facts, other specific details, regarding exact location of Aappan Nigam or Anguttarapa Mr. Tripathi does not say anything.

No scholar has given any substantial arguments regarding its location in Kursela of Katihar, Gogri, Parbatta and Alouli-Beldaur of Khagaria So far, but they also deserve to be historically probed. Prof. R.K. Choudhary finds his historical logistics to fixup the probable site of Anguttarap in Jaymanglagrah of Begusarai and for that he advances his arguments on the ground of two main factors-one being its reach old history and other of its historical location with physical matching geography i.e. a presence of big Kabar Jhil around the mound and continuity of its recorded ancient history right from Lord Buddha's times to the Pala period.

Reasons of Claims of Jayamanglagarh :-

Entire district of Begusarai is having in abundance the sites of archaeological antiquities. Some of such sites of early historic period in the district, where shards of Buddha period have been collected, are Mansurchak, bangarha, Birpur, Chanan, Jogiadih, Masuriadih, Damdama, Kushmaut, Grahpura, Mortar, Sakarwasa, Chirainyadih besides Naulagarh and Jaimanglagarh, which have extensive mounds, spread over a very extensive area.[20] Small mounds are in Nurullahpur, Vikrampur, Rosanahadih, Auredih-Sonadih, Kamaledih, Pawaraghat, Maujhaul, Maheshwara, Harisandih, Aijaniparaura, Bhithasarai (Bhitha), Rasalpur, Basudevpur, Chandpura also.[21] Among the above, Jaymanglagarh is having the richest one. It lies to the north- of Begusarai at a distance of about 20 Kilo-miters. In the revenue settlement record, the site, on wihich the temple of Jayamanglagarh is located, is mentioned as village Jayamangalpur. Presently, it is called as Jayamanglagarh. It is enclosed from all sides with a moat and by a big lake of about 15 KM in lenght, 3 KM in breadth, known as Kabar Jhil/Tal. It is learnt that in ancient times, this gigantic lake had connections with rivers like the Ganges, Gandak and Kamla. There was an island of monkeys with jungles all around, but no such jungle exists now. most of the mounds are now leveled and are in agricultural use.

In the fifties of the 20th century, some explorative excavations were carried out under the guidance of late Prof. R.K. Choudhary, which resulted in unfolding valuable historical informations to us. By now, it is evidently established that Jayamanglagarh was the centre of historical importance sicne the Buddhist period, or even prior to that also. The whole area is dotted with mounds, but tragedically many of such sights got perished and destroyed due to the lack of awakening in the people, villagers' ignorance, lack of knowledge, carelessness and the most possibly due to some natural catastrophic happenings also, like flood deluges and earth-quakes. With its-reach historical continuity right from the Buddhist period and during the Mauryas, it was an important religious centre during the period of Pal rulers.

Some cast-coins have also been found and they are in possession of the G.D. College Museum. Prof. Choudhary held that copper coins were cast as early as fifth century BC Nearchus says that "the Indians used only cast bronze, but not hammered[22] The casting of coins was a very ancient practice in Indian. Those coins were for the most part anonymous and as such, it is difficult to assigh them to any particular regin or territories. Prof. R.K. Choudhary said that "these coins belonged to a period ranging from 5th century BC. to 2nd century BC. Such coins were found in abundance, but have been either lost or misused. some of them are in the possession of Panda, Sri Lura Jha. All such stray finds help us to ascertain at least the period of antiquity of Jayamanglaagarh. It continued to be a centre of Buddhism for a pretty long period. Tradition also asserts that a large number of Chinese and Siamese travelers visited this place.

Bricks of different dimensions and number fo clay balls (cf. Naulagarh) were found, along with the traces. of brick structures here and there and the stray finds confirmed Prof. R.K. Choudhary, an eminent historian, to have a strong conviciton that it was definitely a fort in ancient time. Some traditions confirm that it was a fort of king Jayamangal. It is also said that the ruler of Mangalgarh was said to have been a powerful monarch and a contemporary of King Asoka. Prof. R.K. Choudhary had mentioned its antiquity on the basis of revovery of some punch-marked and Gupta coins from Mangalgrah area. Prof. Chaudhary held the view that traditionally, Mangalgarh and Balrajgarh (Samastipur) were said to have some connections with each other in the past.[23] According to a legend there is a region on Nawalgarh mound, which is known as "Fansiyari," a palce where criminals were executed during the time of Asoka, the great, which suggestively speak of its being a centre fo administration in Asoka's rule.[24]

Chinese traveler, Hiuen-Tsang mentions about the existence ten Buddhist monasteries and more than four hundred bretheren in Mongher district, most of whom were Hinyanists. Besides them, there were twenty Deva temples and the adherents of various religious sects, living in those days.[25] Fine images of the Pala period have been discovered at

Jayamanglagarh of Varah, Badri-Narayan (Images of Surya) Ganga, Shiva-Parvati etc.[26] and most of them belonged to the Pala period. Jayamanglagarh was an important historical site during the Pala period also in its continuity with a very long past and after the Palas, it prominently assumed a prominent Sakti Cult centre, with continuation of Tantric Buddhism. Accordingly to some folk-tales about Jayamanglagarh, it is regarded as an important "Siddha Pitha of India." This site of Goddess Jayamangla finds a mention in Mithila-Tattvavimarsa and Mithila Darpan, besides Mithila Mahatmya, Brahma Vaivarta, Purana, Devi Bhagvata and Pran-Toshini. A legend says taht Lord Shiva had killed Tripura Raksas and established this Pitha here.[27] One of the other folk tales says that Raja Mangal established this "Pitha" and named the Goddess Jayamangla, after his name. But such folk tales do not find any other corroborative evidences.

It was also learnt by Prof. R.K. Chaudahry from a panda of Jayamanglasthan temple, Sri Luro Jha[28] that in 1936-37, a Siamese Buddhist traveler visited Jayamanglagarh and he disclosed that in ancient time, the Buddhist travelers from China and Siam (Thailand) used to flock there because in those days, it was a sacred Buddhist place. That traveler had also come over to visit to the sacred Buddhist shrine and according to him that centre was a Siddha Pitha of Tantric Buddhism. He stressed its being an important Buddhist site and in support of his argument, he quoted references from the Siamese Buddhist traditions. He also disclosed of some Chaityas and Stupas at Jayamanglagarh (vide-Daitahadih, very well-preserved mounds- in the plan of Jayamanglagarh). It is even now known as an important centre of Tantric cult and Tantricks from distant places visit it. The priest cited an example of Stayal of a 'Bengali and a Nepalese Tantrik, who lived here fc.r nearly three years for their attainment of Siddhi.[29]

On the basis of folk tales of Naulagarh, Jayamanglagarh was a religious centre of rulers of Naulagarh. During the reign of Hindu rulers; the priests of Jayamanglagarh have enjoyed rent free land and some emolument for the maintenance of the temple. Earlier, the priests possessed some copper plates also, but sorrowfully, they are lost now.[30] All the above evidences suggest adequately the antiquity aspect of Jayamanglagarh of its being of Buddhist period and its being an ancient site with peolonged continuity up to the Pala period without any dispute. It is said that in Anguttarap, Buddhism was a driving force in this part of Bihar. Prof. R.K. Choudhary, on the basis of recovery of stray coins and beads from Jayamanglagarh, confirms with conviction that it was an important Buddhist site even during the time of Buddha.

One scholar of history, citing Anguttaranikaya, says that the old name of', Begusarai is 'Anguttarap' and he also lays down that Gautam Buddha stayed in ? 'Aapan' a marketing place (a market encircled by water from all the sides) and Lord Buddha's preaching's eschewed animal sacrifices of the people of Begusarai.[31] He also says that by the time of Gautam's visit Begusarai was Aryanized without any substantiation."[32] It may be a reality, but to establish it more convincing evidences, in my opinion, are required. In his hypothesis, no instance has been cited from Anguttaranikaya on the point of entire Begusarai, being called Anguttarap in ancient times. Hence, it can be said that such conclusion is hasty and it can be regarded as a conjectural! contention. Cojectrual hypothesis and speculative ideas cann't over-ride the truths of history and the truth is so conspicuously transparent and powerful that is itself disseminates a vibrantly convincing message to all alike, without leaving behind any iota of doubt or dilemma.

Some specific observation has been made by some other historians also such as Vidyalankar & Mehta to quote them, "Though the Buddhist literature delineates the area of Anguttarapa straight to the North of Bhagalpur and Monghry, yet it was an observation of an eminent historian that this 'Janapada' was having a very small area and this area is even today repreented linguistically by the eastern variety of Maithili speaking people."[33] Long before the expansion of Aryans; these people had develped a non - Vedic and non-Aryan culture. Vedic culture was extended up to Mithila and progressed sufficiently during the days of Janaka dynasty. Subsequently, Videha was converted in to a-republic. Vaishali had grown in to prominence and Buddhism became a driving force in this part also of Bihar. On such criteria, Jaymangalgarh or Bangaon-Mahishi may have strong claims to have Anguttarap and Aapan Nigam in the past.

In the mid of ancient archaeological materials and writings of some eminent historians, I hold the view that probability of Lord Buddha's visit to Jaimanglagarh can not be over-ruled and even if we admit Bangaon and Mahisi or Mahismati as the probable sites of Aappan-Nigam and Anguttarap, because of their exact location towards north of Anga (Bhagalpur) and also because of a very big watery swamp in the immediate vicinity of Bangaon, Lord Buddha must have traveled back on way to Kusinara via Alouli to Jairnangalagarh, and through the lands of Naulagarh, Samastipur and Vaisali, for reaching Kusinara. On the basis of the above narrated antiquity sites and the very geographical locaiton of Jaimanglagarh, if some historians hold it to be a site of Aapan Nigam and Anguttarapa, there seems to have no excesses, but at the same time other probable sites like Bangaon and Mahishi can not be overlooked. Authentication of their exact location still awaits and requires some more specific historical evidences and investigative findings after deep probes to arrive at a definite conclusion. I also take it to be one of such probable sites, due primarily to its being at that time a probable good trading center of fishing due to the presence of big water reservoire there and some other businesses, because the term Nigam was used in ancient period for the city of traders also. Unless we succeed in reaching the truth and getting relibale evidences, we will be doing haste in concluding our judgment. Hence, with an open searching eye, we should make efforts to analyse all such evidences to resolve it.

References :

1. Amarkosh a, edited by Har-Dutt Sharma, P.74, cf. Udai Narain Roy, Prachin Bharat Men Nagar Tatha Nagar-Zivan, Lok Bharti Publication, 1997, P.36.
2. Havaldar Tripathi, Sarthavah P.163.
3. Bhandarkar, Karmaikel Lectures, PP. 44-45.

4. Majumdar, Corporate Life, PP. 44-45.
5. Mansar, Chapter -10, Line- 84- " बुहकर्मकरैर्युक्तं निगमं तदुदाहतम् ।"
6. Shilperatna, Chapter -5- "कर्म्मकारैनौकार्मोपजीचिः ।"
7. R.S. Sharma, Political Ideas and Institutions in Ancient India, PP.167-81.
8. Havaldar Tripathi, Bauddha Dharma Aur Bihar, Bihar Rashtra-Bhasha-Parishad, Patna, 1998 A.D., PP. 76-133.
9. Rahulsankrityayan, Buddha-chrarya, P.151, cf. Havaldar Tripathi, op.cit., P.89.
10. Mahabagga - 6,5,1,1.
11. Mahavagga - 6,7,5,5,15.
12. Havaldar Tripathi, op.cit. P; 91.
13. Havaldar Tripathi, op.cit,p.90.
14. Mahavagga, 35, 1, 11- अनुज्ञानामि भिक्खले पचत्र गोरसे–खीर, दधि, तक्कं, नवनीतं सध्यिं ।" and for intricate journeys "Patheya Sanchaya" provisioning. (Havaldar Tripathi, op.cit., P.90.
15. Havaldar Tripathi, op.cit, footnotes, P.90.
16. Majjhim Nikaya, 2,1,4
17. Suttanipat-33.
18. Suttanipata-33.
19. अथ खो भगवा आपणे यथाभिरन्तं बिहरत्वा येन कुसिनारा तेन चारिकं पक्कामि महता भिक्खुसद्धेन सिंद्धिं अड्ढतेसेहि भिक्सुसतेहि ।"– महावग्गो, 6, 5, 3, 1
20. D.P. Singh, Explorations of Archaeological Sites in Begusarai, Samastipur, The Journal of The Bihar Puravid Parisad, Vol-XIXXX, 1995-2000, chief Edt. Dr. Kameshwar Prasad, PP. 334-335
21. Ibid, P. 235.
22. Strabo, xv, c. P. 16.
23. Prof. R. K. Choudahry, G. D. College Bulletin Series, No.- 2, Archaeological Records of Begusarai 1952, P.12.
24. Fuleswar Singh, Begusarai Ka Itihas, Begusarai Smarika, 1995, Chapter- III, P.15.
25. Watters II-P.178; Beal, II, P.186.
26. Ibid, P.16.
27. Prof. R.K. Choudhary, op.cit, p.13.
28. cf., Prof. R.K. Choudhary, G.D. College Bulletin Series, No.-2, Archaeological Records of Begusarai, 1952, P.13, by Prof. R.K. Choudhary himself.
29. Ibid, P.14.
30. Ibid, P.14.
31. Prof. Fuleshwar Singh, Begusarai Ka Itih as, G. D. College, Smarkia, 1995, Chapter- VI, P.I5.
32. Ibid.
33. Vidyalankar & Mehta, Bihar, P.12.

*Retired I.G. of Police, Bihar

Courtesy :
Jaimangalagadh
Journal of Historical Studies -
Vol. 1, 2010

●●●

The Image of Mahakapalic

Manas Ranjan Manbansh*

The Image of Mahakapalic was procured from Sanghaul village, Ulaw Begusarai Now, the image is preserved in the museum of G D. College, Begusarai. The image is very interesting and rare for the art history of Bihar. The icon is mutilated but it does not detract us from artistic value. The present image is identified by late R. K. Choudhary as an Apsara and compared with the group of Khajuraho and Bhubneshwar style.[1]

In fact the image is very different to the Apsara. This sculpture is made of black stone in round relief. The image tallies with some of the important sculptural designs of tantric goddess of Buddhist cult.

She is stepped in the consciousness of her youngful and perishable body The image has slim body with voluptuous breasts. Her right hand is broken while left, one holding a Kapal. Her hair is raised like flame of fairs. Another female holds the stem which curves on the back of the fairs goddess The figure has been curved in tribhang posture.

The anatomical treatment of the body is superb. The proportion between the neck and the face, the bust and the lip, the navel and the pot bellied stomach, the thigh and the leg are.really eye catching. The face is somewhat oral. Eyes, nose, chin and depression around the lips are exact representation of female beauty in itself. The forehead is decorated with a beaded omament. Her bust is uncovered, but a closely filled torque has been shown round the neck.

Another beaded oranament hanging from the neck is touching her breasts. She bears a big size carrying, armlets and bangles. The lip surges its roundness, restrained by chains of Jewelry. As a whole, the image of Mahakapalic in itself is a harmonious shape.

On the basis of these features the image in not compared with Apsara, the representation of the Kapala, the most characteristic emblem of some of the fearful aspects of Siva and Parvati, a cup made out of a human skull, to drink wine from which is one of the various rights of a tantric Sadhaka[2] but the mundmal is not present in this female image. According to Banarjee,[3] animal and birds are rarely placed in the hands of the image of deities, like goat, ram, dear and dog etc. A horse is depicted between the curve tendrils of a stem show above the head of the image.

As we think that the image of Kapalic or may be Bhairavi was accepted by Buddhist, Instances are not unknown where Mahayana or Vajrayana goddess concepts seen to have influenced the iconography of some goddesses belonging to Hindu pantheon. The fierce Vajrayana deity Nairatma clearly resembles Kali in her iconography. In late mediaeval times the Tantric aspect of Shakti worship seems to have adopted much from the Mahayana cum Vajrayana cult, and there is much that is common between many of the deities associated with both cults.

In this way, we say strongly, that the image of Mahakapalic clearly resembles Bhairavi in her iconography the image proves that the Buddhists were worshipper of the tantric aspect of Sakti in late medieval times.

References :

1.On Bihar, G D. College, Bulletin series no. - 4, year 1956

2. Benerjee, J. N. DHE p. 304.

3. ibid

*Research Investigator
K.P.J.R.I.,
Patna

Courtesy :
Jaimangalgadh
Journal of Historical studies
Vol. - II, 2010, Begusarai

●●●

Anguttrapa : A Case Study of Begusarai District

Alongwith Cultural Aspects of the Kosi Area

Mukesh Kumar*

Begusarai an important district in North Bihar is situated on the northern bank of the river Ganga. It is a holy land in the middle part of the Gangetic basin which is surrounded by the district of Samastipur in the west and some parts of north: and Khagaria district in the North-East. Begusarai was separated as a full-fledged district on 2nd, October, 1972 from the old Munger district, which is located at 25.25' south Latitude and 25.48' N longituede.

Begusarai is made of river's deposits. Besides the Ganga there are rivers like Budi-Gundaka, Bainti, Balan, Koel etc. It seems that whole land of the district is made of the deposit of two rivers, mainly the Gandaka and Ganga,' where as its northern part seems to be older than the southern part made by two rivers such as the Gandaka and the Bagamati.

Begusarai has three famous lakes known as Kabar Lake, Nawla-Bhagawanpur chawar and third is Kola- Chawar. Among them, Kabar lake is 8 miles in length, 4.5 miles in width. In the middle of the lake, there is a famous mound known as Jaimanglagarh while Nawlagarh Bhagawanpur chawar is nearly four miles in length and two and half miles in width. The river Balan and Bainti flow in the north and south side respectively which comes out from Baraila-Chawar in Samastipur district. The third famous chawar is Kola. It is nearly 15 miles in length and 3 miles in width. These three famous lakes are evidence of the formation of the plains of the district. We have a number of mounds of the older inhabitation of the old course of the river Ganga.

We have literary information that the area north of Anga janpada (Area from Munger to Bhagalpur) was called Anguttarapa. (Area from north to Anga full of water). The Suttanikaya furnished a detailed description about Anguttarapa. From this Buddhist scripture, we come to know that Anguttarapa was an area between Mahi in the north and the Ganga in the south. ***(Anga eva so Janapad, Gangaya (Mahamhigangaya) pana ya Uttonena apo, tasam***

aviduratta Uttarapti Vuccati.)[1] The same script refers to a village named Apana in the Anguttarapa, where lord Buddha stayed and preached the immortal teaching to people. We have several references of Anguttarapa and Apana in Dhammapada attakatha, Majjhima Nikaya and Vinaya Pitaka. The area of Anguttarapa was the land on north Bihar just in the northern side of the Anga. According to Buddhist scripts a village is named as 'Apana' (A village surrounded by water). The indentification of Apana is however, obsure. In the area north of Munger and Bhagalpur, we have no big mounds except in the district of Begusarai, In this district at least half a dozen mounds are known such as Birpur, Gododih, Naulagarh Jogiadih, Masuriadih, Kaith and Jaimangala-garh etc. These areas are extended in about ten to fifteen miles of land. Some spots like Naulagarh and Jaimanglagarh bear some evidences of fortified establishemnts. River Balan, Kola, Kawar lake and Bainti used to provide water protection for the moats of forts of these sites. All these mounds yield NBP pot sherds in abundance including some fine pieces of Black & Red ware. Masuriadih is one of them. Among these mounds Jalmanglagarh and Masuriadih are in the midst of Kabar Jhil and Kola-Chowar, Both mounds are connected through a chanel of the Ganga and Gandak respectivaly. Between two mounds, the adjoining village of Jaimanglagarh has similarity with the Buddhist name such as Manjhawal.

A trial trench was dug by students of Archaeology of G.D. College at Masuriadih. The stratigraphical position indicates that above the virgin soil (Layer 6 yielded sherds of Black & Red ware along with the N.B.P. ware of early variety), it appears that the earliest site may have been at masuriadih. masuriadih in its beginning had been situated on the confluence of the Ganga and Gandaka in the Kola-Chawar. The site it situated north of Uren in the Munger district on the southern bank of the Ganga. From Anguttara-Nikaya, we come to know that Lord Buddha on way to Lumbani or Kapilvastu, crossed the Ganga from Uren to Anguttarap. So the village 'Apana' must have been located in the Begusarai district and most probably the mound of Masuriadih and Jaimanglagarh might have been its ancient sites. With this fact it appears that the area of Begusarai was known as Anguttarap at the time of Lord Buddha.

Here, it is an important question, who were the first inhabitants of the area, clearly depends upon the archaeological datas. From sattapath Brahman[2] we come to know that Aryan tribes came the Sarasavati river and settled on the western bank of Sadanira. Dr. Upendra Thakur identified Sadanira as the Gandaki which used to flow between Hajipur and Sonepur.

The excavation of Chirand reports a strata of black and red pottery widely found with the Aryan settlements of Rajasthan, M.P., U.P' In Bihar we have Black & Red pottery from Sonepur (Gaya) Oriup (Bhagalpur) and Chirand (Chapara). A fourth site we have is at Masuriadih (Begusarai) which is about 5 miles north of Jaimanglagarh. Thus, it is supposed that first inhabitant of the Begusarai land or the Anguttarapa were the Aryans or the later vedic folk.

Political History of the Region

The Anguttara Nikaya does not mention Anguttarapa as Janpada in the list of the sixteen Janapadas. It appears that the region was perhaps without any king and there is no detailed information about the nature of the political system prevailing at that time. Thus it appears that a few autonomous village units might have been like the clan system. Their economics were based on agriculture. The NBP culture existed upto 2nd century B.C. Dur-ing this period we have evidence of the existence of one dozen big and small villages. Amidst big villages we include sites like Jaimanglagarh, Naulagarh, Braipura and small village like Masuriadih, Mansurchaka, Jagiadih, Ranidih, Sanghawal and Bhagawanpur. The people of these villages had some connections among themselves and trade relations with the area of Vaisall, Magadh and Anga as well. As we know that rivers were the main route to enter in these areas, we have a legend prevalent in Naulagarh that in the time of Asoka, there had been a place for hanging the culprits at Naulagarh known as Fansiari. So it appears that Ashoka might have established some short of Administrative unit in the area. From Kautilya's Arthashastra we know that in the Mauryan period numerous agricultrual villages were established in the new basin and was called Sitagawan (raiyat Village), it is quite possible that few of the were established in this locality.

In this region before the advent of the Guptas we have no literary references. we have simply a red ware pot shered at Masuriadih. There is no cultural gap in between NBP ware and Red ware as it continued from the time of NBP upto the Gupta perrod. A Gupta seal has been found from Bhit mound near to Naula village. An inscription has been written on the seal as 'Gupta Adhikaran.' According to R.K. Choudhary during the time of Kumar Gupta-I, Govindagupta, the brother of Kumargupta-I was the governor of North Bihar.[3] In the Gupta period the population and number of habitational sites increased to a greater extent so that new basin area came into occupation. The sites at Naulagarh, Jaimanglagarh and others clearly prove this.

North Bihar was famous as the cradle of Brahmanism, as well as Buddhims in this region. The Pala remain scan be identified in Begusarai like Birpur, Jayamangalagarh, Naulagarh. Manjhawl, Maheshwara, Vikrampur; Sanghawl, Kaith Brait, Badi sankh, Sugharan Samho, Rajawara etc. and some parts of Mithila and Saharsa.

Viewed in the back ground, the Bangaon copper plate the Naulagarh inscripton and a silver coin of Vigrahpala- III (since lost) throw refreshing light on the history of palas in the North Bihar.[4]

The Palas are also credited with having started two other Viharas one at Phullahari near Munger and another at Naulagarh.[5]

Religion

The Pala rules were Buddhist. It is quite possible that a small Buddhist monastery was at Sanghawal few Buddhist stupa and monastries flourished in villages of Sanghawal, Maghawal, Majahawal of Begusarai district.

At th time of Hiuen-Tsiang there has been a few Buddhist monastary of Mahayana faith. After Hiuen Tsiang Saivism was getting its hold over Vaishali. That was the general development of religious faith in Tiribhukti. Mithila and its adjoining areas were in heavy impact of Saivism particularly the sakt cult. We have a lot of Icons of Buddha, Surya, siva, Chamunda, Durga, Reventa etc.

References :

1. Mahalase era. G.P. Dictionary of Pali Proper Names, Vol, I, Delhi. 1983, p. 22.
2. Satapath Brahaman, Vol. 1, Ch. iv.
3. Chaudhary, R.K. INC, Vol. VI, parts i.n. 1973, 99.
4. Chaudhary R.K, G. D. College Bulletin No. 1, JBRS, XXX VII. pp. 1-4.
5. G. D. College, Bulletin, 1952, NO.2, pp, 7-8 by R.K. Choudhary, Comprehensive History of Bihar p. 42

*Reader, Deptt of History
A.P.S.M. College, Barauni

Courtesy :
Jaimanglagadh
Journal of Historical Studies
Volume I, 2010.

N.B.P. Sites in the Close Vicinity of the Ganges in Begusarai District

Shailesh Kumar Sinha*

Amiya Krishna

The identification of a particular type of pottery with a particular cultural group of human race is a common practice with the archaeologists.[1] It is important not only in judging the cultural sequence at any excavated site[2] but at the same time it prima-facily indicates the importance of archaeological sites, during survey and exploration works. The Northern Black Polished ware has been taken as a pottery developed by the Aryans after their appearance on the land of Bihar.[3] Bihar is said to be the homeland of this so-called deluxe –ware of India.[4]

The Begusarai District of Bihar, situated between $25^{0}15'$N to $25^{0}45'$N and $85^{0}45'$E to $86^{0}\ 36'$E, has a glory to nourish many such archaeological sites popularly known as N.B.P. Sites among the history loving people. Few of them like Jaimangal Garh and Naulagarh have seen much talked about by the historians and regional archaeologist in the past and have successfully drawn the sight at National Level. But many of them are still awaiting the attention at higher level. Almost two dozen of such sites have been explored during the long survey and exploration work throughout the district.[5] Here, we are going to restrain ourselves in the close vicinity of the Ganga only.

The Holy Ganga marks the southern boundary of the district. The Burhi Gandak almost bisects it in the form of North and South Parts. The Western Part of the district between the Ganga and the Burhi Gandak is wider with respect to the Eastern part. In the west, the Bainti,the Balan and the Baya are active and divide the western part of the district in almost four sub parts:

1. Area falling between the Ganga and the Baya.
2. Area falling between the Baya and the Balan

3. Area falling between the Balan and the Bainti and
4. Area falling between the Bainti and the Burhi Gandak.

The Baya joins the Ganga in Teghra Sub-division and flows in the old bed of the Ganga itself. Therefore, here in the article we are going to cover the area south to the Balan in the west ; South to the Deoki, lost distributary of the Ganga in the central part and South to the Burhi Gandak in the Eastern Part of the District.

We have said earlier that much have been talked about the Northern part of the district. There are many N.B.P. Sites located in this region, and southern part of the district closer to the Ganga, is supposed to be a newer establishment. This is not true. There are several NBP sites in this part as well and they seem to be less important than none.

Sanghaul is a well known archaeological site in this region. Shograha Dih of Barauni is another familiar one to the regional archaeologists. Some recent findings and additional facts about the concerned topic are as follows:

SAVAI DIH

It is a remarkable archaeological site in the southern west end of the district in the close vicinity of the Ganga. Situated to the northern flank of the Baya, a distributaries of the Ganges joining the mainstream in the Barauni block, this site is at present in Bachwara block under Teghra Subdivision of the district. It is almost 40 Kms west to the district headquarter and and can be reached via Bachwara-Murli Tol. An old bunyan tree in the village Bhothari to the west of the embankment-popularly known as 'Badurwagachi, marks the destination of the approach motorable road leading to this site. The site is almost 1.5 Kms from the Bhothari Ram Janki Thakurwari close to the tree as well as the down way mark from the embankment.

This archaeological site is under agricultural practices at present. Through the top of the mound has been flattened for the purpose of agriculture, it is almost in tact as far as the remains beneath is concerned. The slope area of more than 100 m. in the peripheral form has been cut almost 1m. deep to flatten the mound. The mound area including the flattened slope is more than 500m x 500 m . According to the local residents of the nearby Bhothari village, the height of the mound would have been almost 3m. in its intact form. The Baya flows to the south. The famous Chamtha Diyara is just across the Baya in the south.

The potsherds found here are significant Apart from the NBP ware, some potsherds of BRW, Gray Ware (Plain) and a variety of red ware potsherds are found here. The BRW seems to be very specific as the red side is rough and some remains of polishing on the black side can be seen on it. This type of ware has been found over some other sites of the district as well, but the shining black polish over the deep penetrating black area is quite remarkable here. Potsherds of Red ware with painting in black are also noticeable due to its fine fabric and proper firing.

This almost intact mound is inviting the attention of the excavating agencies to reveal the hidden links of the regional history.

MASURIYA DIH

The landscape, the topology and the surface findings make this sight the most remarkable site in the district. It is situated in the Sadar block, almost 10 kms North East to the district headquarters. This almost intact mound is around 200m x 300m in size and almost 5m high at present. The topmost has been flattened for agricultural practices. We can reach here via Rajaura Sankh. The road upto Sankh is metalled and thereon motorable brick soled upto the western end of the mound. It is situated in the west-north of the famous Kola Chaur created by some distributaries of the Ganges like Deoki, Koyal (Kola) etc. Water confluence here even at present seizes our attention. All around the Kola Chaur, we can locate important archaeological sites. Manikpur, Chiriyadih and Kusmaut in the straight line to its East; Kaith, Baraith, Damdama, Shangokothi are slight northward to them. Suza and Majhanpur are to its south. The twin sites of Farida Dih is hardly 1 Km Eastward.

The site is remarkable as far as abundance of potsherds is concerned. Various types of BRW, Gray ware, NBP, black ware, black shipped, Red shipped and variety of Red ware potsherds can be seen on the surface. Potsherds of storage vessel, bowl, plate, basin, water jar, Cookware etc. are sufficient to prove it a rich archaeological site. The fabric is fine and the firing in proper in the majority of the potsherds. The potsherds are scattered in almost 5-6 acres of land.

Recent soil cutting in the eastern part of the mound during some infrastructure development work nearby is significant for archaeological study. It has opened the strata almost 5 m deep from the top. The 1.5 meter of soil cutting there has opened the N.B.P. layer. The upper strata contain the blackware and associated pottery whereas the lower has Grayware, BRW and associated potteries in the layer. Interestingly, Mashuriya Dih has evidence of fire in the NBP layer. The burnt soil deposit measures almost 1ft.thick throughout. This supports the hypothesis of the population shifting to the nearby twin mound of Farida Dih after the devastating disastrous fire here. It is interesting to know that Farida Dih, which is also intact at present, contains black ware and red ware potsherds in abundance. Masuriya Dih would have been inhibited once again but the fire in the NBP period there must have marked the beginning of inhabitation over twin mounds of Farida Dih. Moreover, Masuriya Dih must have been a remarkable site even in the NBP period. It would have been thickly populated at that time. The variety and abundance of NBP potsherds support this hypothesis. Not only this, the migration after the disastrous fire would have been towards Kaith and Manikpura as well where NBP is not frequent, and Chiriyadih and Damdama where NBP is found but not in abundance.

Apart from that, the remarkable finding of BRW in association with the NBP ware leads us to think that the original inhabitants may be the chalcolithic BRW people because

BRW potsherds are also in sufficient quantity here. S.N. Sahay has referred the iron acquainted NBP ware people who succeeded the BRW habitation at Champa.[6] The period representing the BRW using people who lived in association with the NBP ware people or NBP People who lived in association with BRW, people in 1A at Champa.[7] Therefore we cannot ignore the possibility of this site being a Neolithic Site in this region as the BRW potsherds are found in the section almost 1.5 M above the ground level.

Whatever be the truth, is buried under earth at present and awaits the attention of the authorities to come before the history loving mass of the region.

JOGIYA DIH

This is another NBP site situated in the Sadar Sub-division between Rajaura and Jhajh-Pul (Mohanpur) on the Begusarai-Manjhaul State Highway almost 12 Kms North to the district head quarters. In fact, the state Highway passes over the mound. This mound is almost intact in the centre and to the west but the top has been flattened due to agricultural practices. The Chanan streams being joint in the way, passes to its North and reaches the Kola Chaur. Though, the mound at preswnt seems to be a small one due to the soil cutting of eastward, it would have been 100m x 150 m x 5m in its intact form. NBP ware potsherds alongwith Black ware and various types of Redware potsherds are frequently found here. The famous site of Masuriya Dih is to its South-East and that of Chanan Dih to its west.

CHANAN DIH

This is another remarkable archaeological site situated 10 Kms northwest to the district headquarters in the Birpur Block under Sadar Sub-Division. We can reach here via Pachamha-Sahuri. This site is under Sahuri Panchayat, which is linked by metalled road with the district headquarters. A footpath through the agricultural field, leads to the mound, almost 2 Kms north to Sahuri. The mound is partially intact. The top has been flattened for the agricultural practices. The local people have tried to level the mound from three sides. The topology of this site is remarkable. The streams of Chanan seem to encircle the mound. This stream is a part of the distributaries Devki. The Birpur mound is northward from here.

The site is rich one as far as the potsherds and terracotta figurine is concerned. The 225m x 175 m x 4 m mound has variety of potsherds scattered over it. Potsherds of Black and Red ware, Gray ware, N.B.P. ware, Black ware and variety of Red ware can be seen here. The habitation of this Site is said to be shifted to Sahuri Deeh due to some epidemic according to local traditions. The fossil remains scattered here supports this tradition. The migration seems to happen during the Pala period towards Saraunza and Sahuri.

Apart from the above mentioned sites, there are few other NBP sites in this region. They are Bari Balia Mound, Maniappa, Kusmaut, Damdama and Sograha Dih (Barauni). These NBP Sites may indicate the route of migration in this region.

References:

1. Some observation on the NBP ware type- M.C.P. Strivastava, Page 58 The Journal of the Bihar Puravid Parishad Vol .III 1979

2. - ibid. -

3. The Northern Black Polished Ware in Bihar –Sita Ram Roy, Page 149 Patterns in Ancient India (edt. by B.P.Sinha)

4. Some observation on the NBP ware type- M.C.P. Srivastava, Page 59 The Journal of the Bihar Puravid Parishad Vol .III 1979

5. Website WWW. begusaraiheritage.com

6. The potteries of Champa, S.N.Sahay, Page No: 155. The Journal of the Bihar Puravid Parishad Vol. 1977

7. -ibid- Page 156

*Head, Deptt. of A.I.H., Culture & Archaeology,
G.D.College,Begusarai (Bihar)

Courtesy :
'Recent Archaeological Exploration and Excavation in Ganga Valley'
A National Seminar by A.S.I., Patna and Bihar Puravid Parishad
27-28 March, 2012, Patna

●●●

Clay Stupas of Begusarai

Shailesh Kr. Sinha*

Indian culture has enjoyed a remarkable dimension throughout the ages. Our diversified cultural profoundness is reflected by our unparalleled heritage. Stupas constitute a laudable part of this heritage.

'Mahaparinivvan sutta' has a references of Buddha preaching Ananda – "Chatu Mahapathe rajjo chakkavatissa thupang karoti'[1] (As Chakrabarti kings have 'Thupas' built on their tomb (Samadhi) his stupa also should be made on his Samadhi lying at a quadrivial). This shows the glory of Stupas.

Northern Bihar, like other part of our country has some remains of stupas. The region of Begusarai district is emerging as an important ancient Buddhist site on the basis of iconographical and other archaeological findings. The clay stupas, a rare type of architectural legacy of this region suggest it to be an important link of ancient Buddhist Circuit of this region. Herson (Hersain) and Dihi of Begusarai have caught the severe reflection of local historians and history loving people due to their stupas. It is remarkable that the stupas at both places belong to clay built category.

1.Herson (Hersain) Stupa

Situated under Manjhaul subdivision, almost 20 Km N.E. to the district headquarters, Harson (Harsain) is a village on the Eastern flank of the famous lake known as Kawar. It lies almost 86^0 10' 40" E and 25^0 36' 20" N with a remarkable landscape. The famous Jaimangal garh is situated to its S.W. and Kawar lake to its West & N.W. It is at present a group of four stupas lying to the west of Manjhaul Garhpura road. Almost 500 m. from the road, this set of stupa is a silent evidence of the glory of this region.As said earlier, it is a set of four stupas – all clay built, which segregates it from other stupas of the region. The central stupa is the largest one having 110 m Diameter and Height of 11m approx. Three smaller but similar and almost equidistant stupas lie to its north, south and west. It is popularly known as 'Pile made by monster' (Daitya Ka chhitta). An exploration team comprising students of G. D. College, Begusarai headed by one of the writers (Dr.S.K.Sinha) in the year 2003 reached the conclusion that it was a set of four stupas covered by thrashed pebbles. The central stupa seems to be three-tier and its outer surface seems to be 'Vajralepit.' The covering layer has deteriorated almost at the stage of disappearance due to negligence or lack of maintenance. The Singhali tradition. 'Mahavansha' has reference of covering the clay stupa with a layer of brick-dust and lime.[2] The Vishnu Dharmottar Purana also has references of such "Vajralepit" surface. This particular architectural tradition was using lime (kharsudha), brick dust (ittaka chunna), clay (mritika) seasam oil and many other things instead of bricks or stones to make the surface intact.[3]

At present, only the southern stupa is intact as it is covered by bushes. All the three other stupas including the central one have been cut almost to halves. Unauthorized expansion for agricultural purpose is posing a serious threat for their existence.

2.Dihi Stupa

Ekamba stupa is situated in Garhpura sub-division of the district almost 32km. N.E. from the district headquarters. Its locational destination is 86^0 09' 23" E and 25^0 39' 43' N. The Garhpura- Chaurahi road passes hardly 100 m South to the site.

It is remarkable to know that the same configuration plan seems to be adopted here at Dihi also as implemented at Herson. Unfortunately only the central and southern stupa measuring 75 m. x 75 m. x 10 m and 50 m. x 50 m. x 7 m respectively remained successful in saving its existence. The local people have flattened the two other smaller stupa for agricultural purpose due to their unawareness.

These two sets of stupas are remarkable as far as the religious traditions of the locality is concerned. We cannot ignore the possibilities of this region being a glittering part of 'Anguttarapa' of Maijhim Nikaya' used to lie North to Anga Janapada. The word 'Anguttarapa' itself sugest the region filled with water to the North of Anga. Pali literature points out that the region of 'Anguttarapa'was very dear to Mahatma Buddha and he had visited that region with his 1250 followers.[4] Undoubtedly this region would have been remarkable as far as Buddhism is concerned. The importance of these two sets of stupa, particularly of Herson increases many times due to its surroundings. The Jaimangalgarh and the mound of Garhkhouli are two important sites which should be seen with in context with the set of stupa. We can't ignore the possibility of Mahaviharas on these two sites. The name Garhkhouli can be treated as a garh or mound with Kholi or small chambers. This might be an indication of vihara near Herson stupa. Again the route from Herson to Dihi could be extended towards Mithila. We can even find a village named Vandwara (gateway of forest) near the Ganges almost 5 km south East to the district headquarter.

The remarkable NBP site of Masuriyadih falls between Vandwara and Herson. Does this suggest the possibility of some old route from the bank of the Ganga to Mithila?

Apart from that, Begusarai region seems much important as far as the Buddhist cult is concerned. A number of Buddhist icons have been found from different places of the district. Marichi placed at Rajwara railway crossing near Barauni, Tara of Birpur, Buddha from Sanghaul and Baliya along with many other icons and other Buddhist symbols displayed at District Museum, Begusarai as well as at K.P. Jaisawal Archaeological Museum, G.D.College, Begusarai are capable of establishing the fact that Begusarai used to be one of the few major Buddhist sites of North Bihar. Both stupas especially Herson stupas indicate the glorious religious past of the region which might be the second largest Buddhist site of North Bihar only after Vaishali.

It would be quite relevant here to remember the visit of four Chinese travelers coming to India after Hieun-tsang. Prof. R.K.Choudhary has mentioned those travelers.[5]

Hiemn-chiu (also known as Prakashmati)

Sin-chiu (also known as Charitvarma)

Chi-Hing (also known as Prajana deva)

Hui-lun (also known as Prajnaverma)

The above mentioned travelers had visited and stayed at Sin-Chu temple which was the most important Buddhist temple of Northern Bihar. The place is not determined yet. As Anguttarapa region lay between Videha one hand and Kusi country on the other , this Sin-chu temple must have been situated somewhere in Anguttarapa region.[6] Prof. Choudhary mentions that Sin-Chu had emerged as a vihara during the Palas. According to him there used to be a Phulhar or Pushpakar vihars on the northern bank of the Ganges Now, the questions arises whether the viharas made by the Palas at Jaimangal garh was that Phulhar? Certainly we don't have any written evidence to prove it but the location of Herson stupa and possibility of a vihara south East to it, supported by a number of Buddhist findings from sites nearby like Jaimangal Garh, Naula Garh etc. backs up the hypothesis of such vihara running around this place. The abundance of Buddhist sites in the district (like (Sanghaul, Kankaul, Meghaul, Manjhaul etc.). The Pala inscription from Naulagarh and number of Buddhist sculptures found every where in this region indicates its important. The four travelers staying or visiting the famous Sin-chu temple are supposed to return China via Nepal and Tibet crossing through almost heart of Mithila which is not very far from Herson – Dihi stupas. More over it could be connected by river Chanha flowing in this region. The configuration of the sets in the form of four stupa also invites sufficient attention. Does this indicate the homage paid to the four above – mentioned pilgrims of the cult?

The same configuration of the set of stupa can be seen at Dihi .Two Stupas- the central one (the largest) and a smaller one are intact there while two of them have been flattened by the local farmers, as claimed by the local residents. It is possible that the followers of that particular Buddhist cult would have been there and they also built the same set of stupa following the tradition from Herson,

There has been a bit confusion regarding the dating of the stupas. Few local historians have tried to establish their hypothesis saying it a construction of Mauryan era. There is almost nothing to prove this hypothesis. But during our exploration a sherd of N.B.P.W. was collected from the layer 6-7 feet above the present ground level, made open by the unauthorized soil-cutters at Herson. It has revealed the method and plan adopted for the construction of these stupas..It is almost clear that the whole stupa was constructed adding to the hammered layers upwards. In July 08 a team of A.S.I.Patna accompanied by the author along with the research scholars visited the Herson stupa. The senior representative of A.S.I. Patna, Mr.P.K.Mukherjee, Asst. Supt. Archaeologist found some potsherds representing the Gupta Age and concluded primafacily that these stupa represent the vajrayan cult of 11th-12th century A.D. Taking into account the Pala tradition and its prominence at Jaimanglagarh, we strongly feel that the Herson stupa came into existence as it is at present between post Gupta & Pala period. The pala findings from Jaimangla garh, which seems to be closely associated with Herson. It also indicates that the stupas of this region would have been constructed in accordance with the Pala support to the cult. Herson and Dihi are the indication of the glorious cultural development happening during the Pala-rule in this area. Buddhism was flourishing with the symbols of the cult found in this region. The concerned sets of stupas are glorious remnants of the Buddhist tradition flourishing in this region.

References :

1 Agrawala V.S.	Bhartiya Kala, page 136
Upadhaya Vasudeva	Prachin Bhartiya Stupa, Guha aivam Mandir, page 8
2 Mahavansha	ref. Bhartiya Kala, page 137
3 Vishnu Dharmottar Purana	3/40/1-3
4 Begusarai Abhigyangrantha	page 21
5 Choudhary, R.K.	History of Bihar, p. 82
Beal,	Life of Hieun Tsang, p. 17-36
6 Choudhary, R.K.	G.D. College , Bulletin-2

Head,
P.G. Dept. of A.I.H.C & Archaeology
G.D.College, Begusarai – 851101

Courtesy :
Mithila Prachya Prabha ,2012
Dept. of AIH Archaeology & Culture,
L.N.Mithila University, Darbhanga

●●●

Sculptures of Visnu and their influences on the people of Begusarai (Bihar)

Ram Shekhar Singh*

Begusarai is situnted on 85^0 45' East to 86^0 30' East nnd 25^0 15' to 25^{0}47' North. It is bounded by the district of Samastipur In the north, Lakhisarai and the river Ganga in the south and Samastipur as well as the Patna district in the west, The river Ganga, Burhi Gandak, Balan, Bainti, Baya and Chandrabhaga rivers flow through this dlstrict.

The entire district is full of hisitorical and archaeologlcal sites (begusarai heritage.com)

Jaimanglagarh and Naulagarh are very important among them. We find N.B.P. Ware, Black and Red Ware, Grey Ware, Black Ware sherds from these two mounds. Both the mounds are well fortified. We find moats around them, Thus we can place these forts as much back as (6th century B.C. We find antiquities from Mauryu period to late Medieval period from these mounds.

During Pala period we find so many stone sculptures from these forts as well as from mounds of Birpur, Baraipura, Sanghaul and other ancient sites, Brahmanical images like Sivalinga, Pahchmukhalinga, Uma-Maheswar, Sun images, Sakta images like Jaimangala, Durga and Vaisnava sculpture like Varaha, Visnu are scattered in this district. We have Buddhist images too. But overall stones seulplures of Vaisnava cult are dominant among them. Bihar is famous for promoting Vaisnavism since the Kusana period, We have stone image of Ekanamsa from Devangarh in the Nawadah district. Begusarai is not lagging behind. We also have an unfinished four handed sthanak stone image of Visnu in the Begusarai Museum, Begusaral.

We have two Varaha images in this district. One of them is samall stone image kept in a modern temple in the village of Rajaura, which is situated at N.H. 55. Another Varaha image had been reported by Prof. R.K. Choudhary, which was worshipped by, Iate Dr. Ganga Nath Jha of Manjhul, (Vide G.D. College Bulletin Series no. 2).

We also have stone image of Visnu from Jaimangalagarh. Late Dhiran Singh of the village Mohanpur lifted a life size stone sculpture from there and installed it in modern temple in front of his house, We also have a small size imnge of Visnu in a modern temple at Jaimangalagarh ltself. The State Museum, Begusarai, which ls called Begusarai Museum, Begusarai has another two Visnu lmage, We also have another stone image from Naulagarh which is preserved in Kashi Prasad Jayaswal Archaeologieal Museum, G.D, College, Begusarai,

Vaisnavism is one of the major branches of Hinduism along with Saivism and Saktism. It is focused on veneration of Visnu. The followers of Supreme lord Visnu lead a way of life promoting differential monotheism, It given importance to Lord Visnu and his ten incarnations.

The oldest religious text the Rigveda describes Lord Visnu as the Supreme diety in Visnu Sooktam. the Rigveda mentions supreme Lord 93 times.

The principal belief of Visnuu centered sects is the identification of Visnu or Narayana as the supreme god. The belief in the supermacy of visnu is based upon the many avataras of Visnu listed in Pauranik text.

The Philosophy of Vaisnavism is based on certain distinctive doctrines. it is one of the oldest living religions of India which upholds Lord Visnu as the ultimate reality. It believes that the exclusive and devoted worship of Visnu leads to the reliasation of the highest spiritual goal (Param Purusurtha) and for this purpose it has led down an ethical and religious discipline. The doctrines and belief of Vaisnavism are based on the philosophical theories that have been enunciated in the Upanisadas and the Vedanta Sütra. This provides the rational basis for Vasnava theology. The major part of the philosophical roots of Vaisnavism is found in the Vedanta theories. The philosophy of Vaisnavism is strongly centred around the concept of monotheism. It holds that Narayana is the highest personal God, The Supreme being. All the deities are said to have been created by him and all other deities, therefore parts of that one great being. All other countless being which are diferent from each other exist as his different aspects.

* Retd. Asst. Director,
Archaeology, Govt. of Bihar

Courtesy :
Indian Art History Congress
XXI Session - 2012 Guwahati
Printed - 2013, Kolkata

●●●

Begusarai:

A Stronghold of Buddhism

(With special reference to Archaeological remains)

Shailesh Kr. Sinha*
Amiya Krishna

Begusarai needs no introduction to people of Bihar. It has earned the reputation of being the biggest industrial hub of the state. But this materialistic introduction doesn't justify the glorious tradition this land bears. History has strengthened its roots deep here which is still visible in the form of almost 150 archaeological sites of the district. More than two dozen of these sites yield NBPW[1] which represents the golden era of Buddhism. A connected and coherent history of the area from the sixth century B.C. to the Mughal period can be presented on the basis of archeological findings of Naulagarh and numerous other sites of the district.

The region which Buddhist literature refer to as Anguttarapa had been an indispensable part of cultural history of India. 'Majjhimnikaya', 'Sanyuktanikaya' and 'Suttanipata Attakatha' mention that Lord Buddha had visited Apan Nigam of Anguttarapa.[2] Undoubtedly, locating the exact territory of Anguttarapa and Apan Nigam is a difficult task, but it is crystal clear that the region of Begusarai would have been an important part of that region.

The land of Begusarai is also a repository of black stone sculptures belonging to the early-medieval period. No doubt there are a large number of sculptures belonging to Hindu pantheon, but the Buddhist sculptures are specific and invite our special attention to be explained in this context. These sculptures have come before the history-loving people and the scholars in pieces or in introductory form. Few scholars have presented the iconographic or archaeological study related to the concerned subject but a little could be done to present them as a whole and explain them in the background of stronghold of the relevant cult in this region.

Important Buddhist Sculptures Of Begusarai

The sculptures found in this region reflect the archaeological potency of the district. Many Buddhist sculptures of the region are at present assets of the two museums of the district- the district museum Begusarai and Kashi Prasad Jaiswal Archaeological museum at G.D. College Begusarai. Many more are placed in the Garbhagriha of Hindu Temples and are being worshipped as Hindu deities. Few of them are placed under trees by the local devotees. Some specimens meeting the purpose of this article are:

Buddha Image from Balia

Three Black-stone sculptures of the Pala period were unearthed in 1996 during a civil construction work at block office, Balia and were put in the local P.S. premises to avoid any conflict. The district administration of Begusarai vide letter No. 1341 dated 4. 9. 1996 had requested the Dept. of A.I.H.& A. G.D. College, Begusari to assess the antique value of the sculptures. Dr. T.H. Dayal, the then Head of the concerned department observed the sculptures responding the request. Two of them were images of Buddha. Dr. Dayal has presented the description[3] as follows:-

a.) Buddha in Bhumisparsha mudra -

Height : 30.0 cm.

Width : 22.2 cm.

Two handed Buddha sitting in padmasana with his left hand resting in the lap and the fingers of the right hand touching the earth in *bhumisparsha mudra*.

The chakra is apparent over foot-sole. The upper half of the body exposed naked while the lower half covered with transparent dhoti having marks of lines. The crowned Buddha is adorned with a necklace. The *prabhamandala* is also decorated

The inscription in Pala-Brahmi seems to be – ***He Dhamma Hetu Prabhava.***

In our opinion,the deity should have been mentioned as Bodhisatva.

b.) Buddha in Bhumisparsha mudra -

Height : 29.5 cm.

Width : 20.0 cm.

Two handed Buddha sitting in *padmasana* over double petalled lotus with his left hand resting in the lap and the fingers of the right hand touching the earth in *bhumisparsha mudra*. The chakra is apparent over foot-sole and left palm. Urna in the middle of the two eyebrows. A lion depicted raising its paw on the both sides of the deity. A three line inscription in Pala-Brahmi not deciphered yet.

Buddhist sculptures from Sanghaul

Sanghaul Dih is the most important archaeological site in the close vicinity of the district headquarters. The legendry regional historian Prof. R.K.Choudhary and his colleagues from G.D.College,Begusarai explored this site in 1956.[4] This site has yielded many archaeological remains, sufficient enough to earn the reputation of a prominent Buddhist site in this region. Two black – stone broken sculptures of Buddha excavated (during private building construction work) from this site are at present exhibited at Kashi Prasad Jaisawal Archaeological Museum, G.D.College, Begusarai. Another sculpture of Asthanaka Buddha representing the same period excavated in the same manner in 2004 and was carried to the museum by one of the writers, Dr.S.K.Sinha. It is also displayed in the same museum. Some broken pieces of black stone sculptures can be seen at the Kali temple on this mound. It is remarkable to know that the two sculptures mentioned earlier are inscribed.

Description of these sculptures is:

a.) Buddha

9th-10th cen. A.D.

Black stone

Height : 16 cms.

Width : 19 cms

Buddha in Bhumisparsha mudra, seated over double-lotus. Central deity broken above the waist. Right hand broken above the elbow, fingers touching the earth. Left hand resting over left thigh, palm opened upward. To the left of the central deity a small figure of shalbhanjika carved out, a male figure to the left. Inscription to the left and right side of the pedestal. A lion and a female figure in worshipping posture to the right side whereas a lion and a triangular shape to the left in the pedestal.

b.) Buddha

9th-10th Cen.A.D.

Black Stone

Height : 48cms

Width : 33cms

Budha standing on double-petalled lotus in sthanak mudra, wearing sanghati, hands broken,decorated pillars near both hands, standing lion with its right leg over elephant's head and holding *mala* in its left leg. One deity in *tribhanga mudra* holding lotus in the hands on each side of the central deity.

c.) Buddha

9th -10th Cen.A.D.

Black stone

Height : 12cms

Width : 13cms

A broken piece of sculpture. The remains indicating it to be the sculpture of Padmaseen Buddha. Important due to the inscription.

Apart from the above mentioned sculptures of Buddha, some other findings related to the Buddhist identity of the site have been unearthed from here. They too have been preserved at the same museum. They are-

d.) Madhupatradharini

9th- 10th Cen. A.D.

Black stone

Height : 31cms

Width : 20cms

Only the central part of this female deity/figure is intact. The central figure right below the knee as well as the stele holding it is broken. The right hand of the figure is broken ahead elbow. The left hand holding a Madhupatra (a bowl carrying madhu).The motion and the swing of the broken right hand is indicating it to be bent towards the madhupatra. The central figure is displaying a remarkable twist of the upper part just above the waist. Ligaments and other parts of the body are heavy. Kundala, Armlet, Kankana, Necklace etc. apparent. Hair flock arranged. A horse in motion depicted to the right side of the central figure,a male figure holding the tree stretching his hand towards the central figure in *Yachakmudra* for Madhu. Impact of Buddhist Tantrayana can be seen over this sculpture.

e.) Votive Stupa

Few pieces of votive stupa of various sizes unearthed from here can be seen at the same museum mentioned above.

Buddhist sculptures from Birpur

Birpur is the block headquarters under sadar sub-division. It is almost 14 kms north to the dist headquarters. Baraipura lies almost 2 kms Northeast to Birpur. It caught the sight of historians even at national level in 1957 when many black stone sculptures of Pala period were unearthed during some reconstruction work in the twin pond here at Basaha Asthan. Very few sites even at state level have yielded such impressive black stone sculptures of Pala period as found at Birpur and Baraipura.

However, Birpur has yielded two Buddhist sculptures so far. They are-

a.) Tara at Bhairav Asthan

10th- 11th Cen. A.D.

Black stone

Height : 50cms

Width : 25cms

The two handed 'Tara' is placed at this newly built temple and is being worshiped as Brahma-Baba by the local Hindu devotees. It was earlier identified as 'Avalokiteshwara' by many regional historians. With its soft posture of ligaments and tender twist of the waist there should not be any confusion regarding its identification as female deity. The deity is in *Lalitasana* sitting on the double petalled lotus. Right leg is pendent over *'Mahambujapitha'* while the left is bent to rest on the Asana. The right palm of the deity is in front of the right knee and is exposed in the *'Varadmudra'* while the left hand is holding the stalk of a lotus flower. The palm is exposed in the *Abhaya mudra.*There is a smile on the deity's face. The crown is slight conical. Ornament like keyura, greevahar nupura,katimekhala and kundalas can be seen. Two full bloomed lotuses can be seen one each on the either side of the central figure above the shoulder line.

The decoration on the stele is sparse or say there is a little scope of doing so. It is slightly pointed on the top. Five Dhyani Buddhas are depicted on the top. All of them have been shown seated on double petalled lotus. The best possibility of specification advocates it being a superb piece of sculpture of Varad Tara.[5]

b.) Buddha (at present at Begusarai Museum)

10th cent. A D

Black stone

Buddha depicted in *Bhumisparsha Mudra*. Similar sculpture from Jaimangalgarha also displayed in the gallery.

Buddhist Sculpture from Barauni

Marichi at Rajwara railway-crossing

10th- 11th Cen. A.D.

Black stone

Height : 58.0cms

Width : 45.5cms

Four-handed Marichi in *pratyaleedha mudra* positioned over a chariot dragged by seven pigs. The sculpture is broken above neck. Hands also partially intact. Necklace, armlets, payal and katimekhala apparent. Posture of hands or *aayudha* carried by the deity can't be speculated as hands are broken. Though face is blunt, it seems to be Rahu as "Sadhanmala" suggests.

Seals and Sealing

Archaeological sites of Begusarai have yielded many seals and sealing of different historical periods. Many of them are preserved in Kashi Prasad Jaisawal Archaeological Museum, G.D. College, Begusarai. Dr.Prakash Chandra procured them for the college museum from the history-loving Tulsiyan family of Balia. Particularly, the seals having marks of Buddhism are specific. Few of them are as follows:-

a.) Seals having image of Buddha

More than half of the collection is inscribed and is having image of Buddha. The deity is shown seated on double-petlled lotus in Padmasana. Hands are folded in Vyakhyan mudra. The aabhamandala is plain. The carved sideline indicates that the image is placed in the niches. The inscription represents the Gupta-Brahmi.

b.) Seals having image of Avalokiteshwara

Few seals have image of Avalokiteshwara. A broken one is headless but other parts are intact. The deity is seated over a double petalled lotus in Lalitasana. Right leg resting on same *aasana* while the left pendent leg is placed over a similar but smaller lotus. Left hand supporting the weight of the body bent slightly backward while the right bent in Varad mudra. In another one,which has only upper half intact, the head is crowned and other features are similar.

c.) Seals having mark of votive stupa

A particular seal is black in colour and oval shaped. It is inscribed in Pala-Brahmi. It has a mark of votive stupa on the top. The other having mark of votive stupa on the bottom is almost circular and inscribed in Gupta-Brahmi.

Clay Stupa Of Begusarai

Begusarai district is emerging as an important ancient Buddhist site on the basis of other archaeological findings as well. The clay stupa, a rare type of this architectural legacy of this region suggests it to be an important link of ancient Buddhist Circuit of this region. Herson (Hersain) and Dihi of Begusarai must have been prominent Buddhist sites due to their stupa. It is remarkable that the stupa at both places belong to clay built category.

Herson (Hersain) Stupa

Situated under Manjhaul subdivision, almost 20 Km N.E. to the district headquarters, Harson (Harsain) is a village on the Eastern flank of the famous lake known as Kabar. It lies almost 86^0 10' 40" E and 25^0 36' 20" N with a remarkable landscape. The famous Jaimangal garh is situated to its S.W. and Kawar lake to its West & N.W. It is at present a group of four stupa lying to the west of Manjhaul Garhpura road. Almost 500 m. from the road, this set of stupa is a silent evidence of the glory of this region .As said earlier, it is a set of four stupa – all clay built, which segregates it from other stupa of the region. The central stupa is the largest one with the height of 11m and the diameter of 110m.Three smaller but similar and equidistant stupa are constructed to its north, south and west. It is popularly known as 'Pile made by monster' (Daitya Ka chhitta). The central stupa seems to be three-tier and its outer surface seem to be '*Vajralepit.*'

The covering layer has deteriorated almost at the stage of disappearance due to negligence or lack of maintenance. The Singhali tradition 'Mahavansha' has reference of covering clay stupa with a layer of brick-dust and lime.[6] The Vishnu Dharmottar Purana also has references of such 'Vajralepit' surface. This particular architectural tradition was using lime (kharsudha), brickdust (ittakachun), clay(mritika) sesame oil and many other things instead of bricks or stones to make the surface intact.[7]

At present, only the southern stupa is intact as it is covered by bushes. All the three other stupas including the central one have been cut almost to halves. Unauthorized expansion for agricultural purpose is posing a serious threat to their existence.

Dihi Stupa

Dihi (Ekamba) stupa is situated in Garhpura sub-division of the district almost 32km N.E. from the district headquarters. Its location is 86^0 09' 23" E and 25^0 39' 43' N. The Garhpura- Chhaurahi road passes hardly 100 m South to the site.

It is remarkable to know that the same configuration plan seems to be adopted here at Dihi also as implemented at Herson. Unfortunately, only the central and southern stupa having measurement of 70m diameter and 08m height and 50m diameter and 4m height respectively remained successful in saving their existence. Local people have flattened the two other smaller stupa(equal to the size of the smaller one mentioned above) for agricultural purpose due to their unawareness.

These two sets of stupa are remarkable as far as the religious traditions of the locality is concerned. We can't ignore the possibilities of this region being a glittering part of 'Anguttarapa' of 'Maijhim Nikaya.'

Pali literature points out that the region of 'Anguttarapa'was very dear to Mahatma Buddha and he had visited that region with his 1250 followers.[8] Undoubtedly this region would have been remarkable as far as Buddhism is concerned. The importance of these two set of stupa, particularly of Herson increases many times due to its surroundings. Jaimangalgarh and the mound of Garhkhouli are two important sites which should be seen in context with the set of stupa. We can't ignore the possibility of Mahaviharas on these two sites. The name Garhkhouli can be treated as a garh or mound with Kholi or small chambers. This might be an indication of vihara near Herson stupa. Again the route from Herson to Dihi could be extended towards Mithila. We can even find a village named Vandwara (gateway of forest) near the Ganges almost 5 km south East to the district headquarter.

The remarkable NBP site of Masuriyadih falls between Vandwara and Herson. Does this suggest the possibility of some old route from the bank of the Ganga to Mithila? Apart from that, Begusarai region seems much important as far as the Buddhist cult is concerned. A number of Buddhist icons have been found from different places of the district. Both of the stupa, especially Herson stupa, indicate the glorious religious past of the region which might be the second largest Buddhist site of North Bihar only after Vaishali.

It would be quite relevant here to remember the visit of four Chinese travelers coming to India after Hieun-tsang. Prof. R.K.Choudhary has mentioned those travelers.[9]

Hiemn-chiu (also known as Prakashmati)

Sin-chiu (also known as Charitvarma)

Chi-Hing (also known as Prajana deva)

Hui-lun (also known as Prajnaverma)

The above mentioned travelers had visited and stayed at Sin-Che temple which was the most important Buddhist temple of Northern Bihar. The place has not been determined yet. As Anguttarapa region lay between Videha on one hand and Kusi country on the other, this Sin-che temple must have been situated somewhere in Anguttarapa region.[10] We are going to discuss its location later in this article.

Some other indications

Apart from the above mentioned archaeological remains, there are some other indications supporting the profound Buddhist legacy of this district. Many of them are waiting to come before the world .We would like to start with the structural findings from Sanghaul. This western outskirts of Begusarai town has yielded many Black stone sculptures. Few Buddhist sculptures have been discussed earlier. In 1989, Prof. Phuleshwar Singh, Former Head, Dept. of A.I.H.& A., G.D. College, Begusarai managed to study the layers opened during some construction work following a report of some structure near the state tube-well.[11] Prof. Singh has reported four circular structures adjacent to each other, built on different platforms found in that trial trench in different subsequent times. He found the structures made of baked bricks of 5cm.x15cm.x30cm. The diameter of the structure was measured 194cm. to 205cm. The plinth of the structure was found 103cm. to 105cm. in height. Above the plinth the circular structure remained 50cm to 55cm. Prof. Singh has identified this circular structure as Votive stupa resembling with those found at Vikramshila.[12] So, it is clear that Sanghaul must have been a prominent Buddhist site at early-medieval period.

Birpur, which has found mention above in context with sculptures, also, would have been a Buddhist site. The excavation conducted by Dept. of A.I.H.& A., G.D.College, Begusarai at Birpur in 2004 (with the permission of A.S.I.) has added to the recognition of Begusarai as important Buddhist site .The Co-director of that excavation , Dr. Shailesh Kr. Sinha (one of the writers) found a curved structure in the section made of chiseled bricks bearing size of 26cm. x 16cm. x 6cm. which continues from Phase V to Phase IV (Muslim to Pala cultural phase).[13] The structure is embanked with large sized stones.The curve indicates that it must be a large structure. This type of structure usually uses to be granaries or Stupa. Now let us discuss the matter in the light of the findings of this excavation.

We must not forget that this excavation was conducted in a trench of 6 m x 4 m. So, we can easily conclude that the above mentioned structure was constructed in the Pala period over the dry river bed used to be active during and before the Mauryan period. The river must have been in the close vicinity. It is why the embankment of the structure was provisioned. It is relevant to mention that river Balan is still in action at a distance of 100-150m. Now, we must think whether a granary could have been constructed so close to the river? It doesn't sound logical. So there is a strong possibility of this structure being a stupa.

The above mentioned archaeological sources strongly suggest that Begusarai used to be a stronghold of Buddhism during the early-medieval period. Archaeological sites like Majhlapur (Sokha Baba sthan) and Maniappa bear the testimony of that glorious tradition. It would be remarkable to know that Dr. Nambar Singh has mentioned the name of Sarhapp, an 8th century poet in his thesis "Hindi Sahitya mein Apabhramsa Boli Ka Yogdan." It is said that Majhlapur was the birth place of that famous poet. Sarhappa was one of the 64 Siddhas of the Vajrayan sect of Buddhism. Maniappa is said to be named after Maniapp, who was a famous disciple of Sarhappa.[14]

Now let us try to connect the assonant clues discussed earlier. Prof. Choudhary mentions that Sin-Che had emerged as a vihara during the Palas. According to him there used to be a Phulhar or Pushpakar vihars on the northern bank of the Ganges. Now, the question arises whether the viharas made by the Palas at Jaimangalgarh was that Phulhar? Certainly we don't have any written evidence to prove it but the location of Herson stupa and possibility of a vihara south East to it, supported by a number of Buddhist findings from sites nearby like Jaimangal Garh, Naula Garh etc. backs up the hypothesis of such vihara running around this place. The abundance of Buddhist sites in the district (like Sanghaul Kankaul, Meghaul, Manjhaul etc.) the Pala inscription from Naulagarh, and number of Buddhist sculptures found everywhere in the region indicates its importance. The four travelers staying or visiting the famous Sin-Che temple are supposed to return China via Nepal and Tibet crossing through almost heart of Mithila which is not very far from Herson – Dihi stupa. More over it could be connected by river Chanha flowing in this region. The configuration of the set in the form of four stupa also invites sufficient attention. Does this indicate the homage paid to the four above – mentioned pilgrims of the cult?

The same configuration of the set of stupa can be seen at Dihi .Two Stupa- the central one (the largest) and a smaller one are intact there while two of them have been flattened by the local farmers, as claimed by the local residents. It is possible that the followers of that particular Buddhist cult would have been there and they also built the same set of stupa following the tradition from Herson.

There has been a bit confusion regarding the dating of the stupa. Few local historians have tried to establish their hypothesis saying it a construction of Mauryan era. There is almost nothing to prove this hypothesis. But during our exploration an N.B.P.W. potsherd was collected from the layer 6-7 feet above the present ground level, made open by the unauthorized soil- cutter at Harson. It revealed the method and plan adopted for the construction of these stupa .It is almost clear that the whole stupa was constructed adding to the hammered layers upwards. In July 08 a team of A.S.I. Patna accompanied by the authors along with research scholars visited the Herson stupa. The senior representative of A.S.I. Patna, Mr.P.K.Mukherjee, Asst. Supt. Archaeologist found some potsherds representing the Gupta Age and concluded primafacily that these stupa represent the vajrayan cult of 11th-12th century A.D. Taking into account the Pala tradition and its prominence at Jaimangalgarh, we strongly feel that Herson stupa came into existence, as it is at present, between post Gupta & Pala period. The Pala findings from Jaimanglgarh, which seems to be closely, associated with Herson shows the prominence of this dynastic rule here.

It is surprising that local historians have throughout ignored an important clue or so could it be that important feature of the old temple at Jaimanglagarh couldn't invite their sufficient attention. The *Lalat -bindu* of that temple used to bear the depiction of Buddha itself. So it is almost clear that the particular place would have been a Buddhist site known for the temple of that very cult. It is possible that it might have been a Hindu temple earlier or/and after the declination of Buddhism in this region. We don't have literary records supporting our hypothesis, but whatever the sites of Jaimanglagarh-Herson-Garhakhauli-Dihi speak, is all about the Buddhist prominence during the Palas.

The question arises whether Jaimangalgarh is the destination of that old Sin-Che temple where the four Buddhist travellers reffered earlier visited? The *Lalat-bindu* of the old temple at Jaimanglagarh and the set of four stupa at Herson and Dihi and their emergence during the Palas instigate us to respond positively. No doubt we need more research-oriented studies and further evidences to support our hypothesis, but we can't ignore these indications about the above mentioned Vihara and Temple. It also indicates that the stupa of this region would have been constructed in accordance with the Pala support to the cult. We strongly feel that Jaimangalgarh would have emerged as the famous Buddhist site much before the Pala dominance in this region. The famous 8th century-poet and Siddha of Majhlapur , Sarhappa, would have been associated with that Buddhist temple cum Siddhapeeth. Maniapp, his famous disciple would have just carried out the tradition. Both of them belonged to the close vicinity of Jaimangalgarh. The Pala dominance and their patronage to the cult just added to the glory of this worship place constructing the above-mentioned Vihara most probably at Garhkhauli or might be somewhere on the vast mound of Jaimangalgarh. Then came into existence the four famous stupa of Herson paying tribute to those four Chinese travelers mentioned earlier. Dihi just followed the tradition.

Jaimangalgarh would have emerged as the Hindu-Shaktipeeth only after the decline of the state patronage to Buddhism and favourable conditions for Shakt-cult of Hinduism with the emergence of Rajputa power here. Acceptance of Buddha in Hindu pantheon, especially in Vaishnavism, made it easier particularly in this region. The tradition of Baba Baudh Bali is still familiar in this region among the Hindu mass. This shows how Buddhism was accepted in Hinduism here and there would not have been much problem accepting the Buddhist worship place accordingly. So, there should not be any problem to accept the present shaktipeeth as the famous Buddhist temple just because of its present identity.

Stupas of Herson and Dihi ; the sculptures; the seals of Buddhist identity; the strong possibility of Sin-Che temple at Jaimangalgarh and the tradition of Sarhappa, Maniapp and Baba Baudh Bali- all are the indications of the glorious cultural development achieved during the Pala-rule in this area. Buddhism was flourishing with the symbols of the cult in this region. The concerned sets of stupas are glorious remnants of the Buddhist tradition flourishing in this region.

In the light of the above-mentioned references it is crystal clear that Begusarai used to be a stronghold of Buddhism during the early-medieval period.

References :

1. Sinha,S.K. & A.Krishna Archaeological Sites of Begusarai, Page 124-128
2. Majjhimnikaya (Hindi translation) Page 381
   Sanyuktanikaya(Hindi translation) II, Page 726
   Paramatthajotika (Suttanipata Attakata),II, Page 437
3. Dayal,T.H., Begusarai zile se prapt katipaya palakaleen pratimayen Paper presented in National seminar on 'The Art and Archaeology of Eastern India' org. by Govt. of Bihar, March 1997.
4. Choudhary, R.K. New Findings G.D.College, Bulletin- 4
5. same as ref. no. 1 Page 50
6. Mahavansha Agrawala V.S. Bhartiya Kala, Page 137

7. Vishnu Dharmottar Purana 3/40/1-3
8. Majjhimnikaya (Hindi translation) Page 381
9. Choudhary, R.K, History of Bihar Page 82
10. Choudhary, R.K. G.D.College, Bulletin- 2
11. Singh,Phuleshwar, Sanghaul ,the second largest Buddhist site of north Bihar Paper presented in National seminar on 'The Art and Archaeology of Eastern India' org. by Govt. of Bihar, March 1997.
12. ibid
13. same as ref. no. 1 Page 46-49.
14. same as ref. no. 1 Page 44 & 56

Head,
P.G. Dept. of A.I.H.C. & Archaeology
G.D. College, Begusarai - 851101

Courtesy :
DHAROHAR
(A Journal of Culture & Archaeology)
Vol.III , July 2013

●●●

Clues connecting the past

(With reference to Jaimangalgarh, Birpur and Nawalgarh)

Shailesh Kumar Sinha*
Amiya Krishna

History is deep – rooted in Begusarai. Various archaeological sites are its evidence. The potsherds explored over many of these sites indicate the continuity of habitation since BRW culture. There are around two dozens of NBPW sites in the district.[1] A connected and coherent history of the area from the sixth century B.C. to the Mughal period can be presented on the basis of archeological findings of many of these sites. Sculptures and local accounts in the form of manuscripts give us a clue that this region had established its identity during the Early Medieval times. Begusarai had been under the Palas in the early medieval period. The Naulagadh Inscription of Vigraha Pala and the black stone sculptures littered all over the region prove this. Much has been written about the Pala impact in this region.

After the Palas, Begusarai came under the influence of the Rajput rulers. A different style of black- stone sculptures, particularly belonging to the Shakt tradition can be seen in this region. The Rajput rulers established their kingdoms at three prominent places of historical importance. These were – Jaimangalgarh ,Birpur and Naulagarh or Nawalgarh. These three sites had come into existence much earlier but it is in this period of time that a common identity bound them with an intense regional political development .It was coming of a new political power in this region. Different Rajput clans established their political hold in this region. Here in this article we are going to highlight these three archaeological sites and connect the available clues to reconstruct the chapters of regional history.

Jaimangalgarh

Jaimangalgarh is the most famous and one of the earliest explored archaeological sites of Begusarai district having continuous cultural sequence. At present, this site is famous as a shaktipeeth and is popularly known for an old temple of a Goddess, Jaimangal Devi. It is under Cheriya Bariyarpur block of Manjhaul Sub-Division, almost 21 kms north to the district headquarters. It is about 5 Km north east to the sub-divisional headquarters. The Manjhaul-Garhpura road passes 1 Km west to this site. The famous Kabar Lake encircles this mound. The brief description of the site is -

Location	:	86^0 09' 20"E/ 25^0 35' 40" N'
Expansion	:	1000 m x 750 m
Height	:	5 m
Pottery found	:	Black slipped, NBPW, Red ware, Black ware

Jaimangalgarh is the second largest mound of the district only after Nawalgarh. It is a set of two mounds. The western part is separated by the main eastern part with the help of moat which encircles the eastern part of the mound. This part is fortified with bricks. The residential area on this mound inside the fort used to have extra-protection due to the moat. The western part outside the fortified area has frequent evidences of residential existence.

As mentioned earlier, it is one of the earliest explored site of the district. The mound came into light when late Prof. R. K. Choudhary thoroughly explored it and published an article on it in G. D. College Bulletin-2 as early as in 1952.[2] In 1955, a hoard of coins was unearthed from this site but only three silver coins could be procured by Late Prof Choudhary for examination. All of them belonged to the Tughlaq period[3] In 1958, during an excursion of the noted historians, three rows of wooden posts-five posts in each row and each at a distance of 7.5 feet were observed by Dr. R. S. Sharma in the middle of a tank, which was being dug out by the local authorities for public use. After a brief survey Dr. Sharma declared these posts as remains of ancient bridge[4] constructed during the Mauryan age probably to connect the settlement site with the set of stupa in the north-east. It might be a unique feature of this site.

In 1976-77, the tank east to the main temple yielded remains of a ring well.[5] The Directorate of State Archaeology took a trench on this mound and conducted vertical excavation but the report is still awaited. Another effort was made by the State Archaeology recently which does not seem justifying the prosperity of this mound.

The Majhaul- Garhpura road almost encircles the close vicinity of the site from south and east. The distance of the road is maintained up to Hersain. Here, almost 500 m from the road towards Jaimangalgarh mound, a set of stupa can be seen as a silent witness of the glory of this region. It is a set of four stupa – all are clay built. The central stupa is the largest one with the height of 11m and the diameter of 110m. Three similar and equidistant but smaller stupas are constructed to its north, south and west. It was popularly known as 'Pile made by monster' (Daitya Ka chhitta). The central stupa seems to be three-tier and its outer surface seem to be *Vajralepit*.The covering layer has deteriorated almost at the stage of disappearance due to negligence or lack of maintenance. The Singhali tradition **'Mahavansha'** has reference of covering clay stupa with a layer of brick-dust and lime.[6] The **Vishnu Dharmottar Purana** also has references of such *'Vajralepit'* surface. This particular architectural tradition was using lime (*kharsudha*), brick dust (*ittakachurna*), clay (*mritika*) sesame oil and many other things instead of bricks or stones to make the surface intact.[7]

At present, only the southern stupa is intact as it is covered by bushes. All the three other stupas including the central one have been cut almost to halves. Unauthorized expansion for agricultural purpose is posing a serious threat to their existence.

It is remarkable to know that the same configuration plan seems to be adopted here at Dihi also as implemented at Herson. Unfortunately, only the central and southern stupa having measurement of 70m diameter and 08m height and 50m diameter and 4m height respectively remained successful in saving their existence. Local people have flattened the two other smaller stupa (equal to the size of the smaller one mentioned above) for agricultural purpose due to their unawareness.

These two sets of stupa are remarkable as far as the religious tradition of the locality is concerned. We can't ignore the possibilities of this region being a glittering part of 'Anguttarapa' of **Maijhim Nikaya.'** Pali literature points out that the region of 'Anguttarapa'was very dear to Mahatma Buddha and he had visited that region with his 1250 followers.[8] Undoubtedly this region would have been remarkable as far as Buddhism is concerned. The importance of these two set of stupa, particularly of Herson increases many times due to its surroundings. Jaimangalgarh and the mound of Garhkhouli are two important sites which should be seen in context with the set of stupa. In our article 'Begusarai : A stronghold of Buddhism' published in 'Dharohar' vol III, we have raised strong possibility of the old Jaimangalgarh temple being Sin-che temple. At the same time we can't ignore the possibility of Mahaviharas on these two sites. The name Garhkhouli can be treated as a garh or mound with Kholi or small chambers. This might be an indication of vihara near Herson stupa. Again the route from Herson Dihi could be extended towards Mithila. We can even find a village named Vandwar (gateway of forest) near the Ganges almost 5 km south East to the district headquarter.

The remarkable NBPW site of Masuriyadih falls between Vandwar and Herson. Does this suggest the possibility of some old route from the bank of the Ganga to Mithila?

Apart from that, Begusarai region seems much important as far as the Buddhist cult is concerned. A number of Buddhist icons have been found from different places of the district. Both of the stupa, especially Herson stupa indicates the glorious religious past of the region which might be the second largest Buddhist site of North Bihar only after Vaishali.

In our opinion, the present religious identity of this site evolved during the later Pala rule in Bihar with the emergence of the Rajput power in this region. The set of stupa represents the early medieval period here whereas the black stone sculptures unearthed from here represent the late medieval. A four handed Vishnu in *Sambhanga mudra*, unearthed from this site, is placed in a newly built temple on the top of the mound near the old temple of Jaimangal Devi. A specific crown (different from Kirita), ajanulambi vanmala etc are apparent. The right lower hand of Vishnu is exposed in *Abhaymudra*. The deity is holding Sudarshan Chakra, Shankha, Shrifala and Gada (in the armpit). Garuda is also present there in worshipping posture.

Apart from this many sculptures unearthed from this site have been placed in different temples. One such is the following placed at Ram Janki Thakurwari, Garhpura.

Sun

Blackstone

Rajputa period

H – 50 cm

W – 30 cm

Standing sun holding lotus in two hands. Two female figures can be seen on each side. An identical (to Vishnu, Jaimangalgarh) sculpture of Chitragupta, unearthed from here or near about and representing the same period, is placed at present at Chitragupta temple, Bari Pokhar, Begusarai. The deity is adorned with the identical crown and has the same configuration of *Dasmasangula*.

Apart from the above Hindu deities, some Buddhist sculptures also have been unearthed from here. This supports the hypothesis of the religious transfusion here during the late medieval period. Some of the sculptures preserved in the district museum here are-

i) Buddha

Black stone

Height : 10cms

Width : 07cms

The Black stone sculpture is like other sculptures from Jaimangalgarh and belongs to the same school producing Vishnu at Jaimangalgarh and Chitragupta at chitragupta mandir, Bari Pokhar, Begusarai. The stretched eyes and crown of Buddha are identical to that of the above mentioned sculptures. Buddha is seated on a double- petalled lotus in *bhumisparsha mudra*

ii) Buddha

Black stone

Height : 07 cms(approx)

Width : 04 cms (approx)

Two identical small-sized sculptures of Buddha in *bhumisparsha mudra* are also displayed.

The above mentioned religious feature of Jaimangalgarh is remarkable and to our opinion is the result of the acceptance of Buddha in the mainstream religious cult. At the same time we can't ignore the fact that Buddhism in this region would not have resisted for its identity due to lack of any political patronage.

The history of the region falling between the golden days of the Palas and the expansion of the Karnats from Simraon Garh seems to be influenced by the Rajput. Even at the time of the Karnats rule in this region, it seems that Rajputa used to exercise dominating influence over this area. After the downfall of the Pala rule over this area, it came under Karnata rule.

The Maheshwara Inscription of Feroz Etigin (1290-91 A.D.) edited by Prof. Choudhary in 1956 proves the shifting control over this region. Feroz Etigin was the regional administrator appointed by Ruknuddin Kaikas (1291-1302) A.D. Later on the Oinwaras came in the light to replace the Karnata power somewhere in the half way mark of the 14th century. On the basisof the descriptions of Mulla Taquia, Prof. R.K.Choudhary indicates that Haji Illiyas subjugated Tirhut and divided the kingdomin two parts. River Burhi Gandak was fixed as the boundary line and Oinwara Kameshwara was forced by him north to it.[9] Thus Jaimangalgarh came under the Oinwaras. Later the region came under the Mugals and then the British colonial rule. the vestiges of the British rule still exist in Manjhaul.

Birpur / Baraipura

Birpur is the block headquarters under sadar sub-division. It is almost 14kms northward to the district headquarters. Baraipura is almost 2 kms northeast to Birpur. It caught the sight of historians at even national level when many black stone sculptures of Pala period were unearthed during some reconstruction work in the twin pond here at Basaha Asthan in 1957.[10] Very few sites even at state level have yielded such impressive black stone sculptures of Pala period as found at Birpur and Baraipura.

Location : 86^{0}04'15"E- 86^{0}05'15"E/
25^{0}31'15"N25^{0}31'45"N

Birpur excavation – 2004 : Outcomes[11] There are not less than four mounds- One at Birpur Market and others at Baraipura Basaha Asthan, Chamunda Asthan and Nonefar mound. The mound at Birpur Market is the largest and highest of all. An excavation was conducted by P.G. Department. of A.I.H &Archaeology, G.D. College Begusarai with an objective to discover the cultural sequence of the region. The mound near the market and close to the river Balan was selected for the purpose. The market area itself is a part of a huge mound and is thickly populated but the western concerned part has no habitation at present.

In course of our several explorations, potsherds of BRW and NBPW were observed scattered everywhere on the mound. But in the excavation Phase I, hardly yielded few pieces of NBPW potsherds. The muddy layer stopped any further excavation. It might be due to the site selection closer to the river. Phase II here is significant due to the remains of a structure as well as the frequent findings of Black Ware potsherds. The Remains of a brick built structure of a courtyard soled with burnt bricks was observed in this phase. Bricks used in the main construction as well as in the floor of the courtyard measure equal i.e. 35cm x 23cm x 6cm. This construction at the depth of 697cm.indicate the evidence of a well-established habitation over this place. An inscribed sealing was also collected from this cultural layer. The findings from this layer clearly suggest this site being as important economic center in the region during 1st and 2nd century B.C. They resemble with that of Pandgarh found in the same cultural phase.

Another remains of a structure was observed in the phase III slight above the end mark of the second cultural phase. Potsherds of various designs of red slipped ware were also found in this layer indicating the habitation of Gupta- settlements in this region.

Few medicinal leaves were found in the same layer near the oven. This is clear indication that the oven found in this layer was not one serving domestic purpose. It must be serving the purpose of medicine-preparation here in this cultural phase for which this particular site earned a reputation throughout the years. Mahendri, a village 12 kms southeast from Birpur, is still famous for the same tradition.

The remains of structure continued in the phase IV. The remarkable finding in this layer was the remains of a circular wall in the southern section. The upper portion of the wall was found ruined/dismantled but the lower part was intact to some extent. The curve was forced using chiseled bricks. It could be the remains of a stupa or a granary. Never the less a further south ward excavation is needed to identify the structure and reveal the importance of the site in this phase. The bricks used in the wall measured 26 cm x 16 cm x 6 cm. This layer yielded variety of potsherds in handful number. Tradition of Gupta-layer found continued in pottery making with bright red polishing on few of them. Some yellowish red ware potsherds were also found.

The phase V at this site is characterized by many structures made of bricks during Muslim rule. Remains of white powder, iron ores and few pieces of burnt iron were also collected near by the oven. It could be the indication of industrial activity at Birpur because three ovens were found in this phase. The lower layer of this phase yielded potshard of red ware prominently where as the upper layer which has got flattened at the top due to agricultural practices, also produced few green ware potsherds of Muslim culture.

Overall, we can say that the brief excavation proved the uninterrupted cultural continuity of Birpur at least from Black Ware cultural layer to till date. The surface finding of the potsherds of BRW and NBPW suggest that history must be stretched to earlier times with respect to what was revealed during the excavation.

As mentioned earlier Birpur/Baraipura has yielded a variety of black stone sculptures. Mr Johnston noticed a Sun sculpture as early as in 1918 and reported it.[12] Many of these sculptures are placed in the garbhagriha of newly built temples here. Few earlier reported sculptures are traceless. Few broken pieces are lying unprotected under trees and in the temple premises. Some are protected in local museums. Hence, the sculptures procured from here can be put under the following categories:-

1. Sculptures placed in the local temples

i) Birpur Bhairav Asthan (Tara)

The two handed 25cm x 50cm black stone 'Tara' is placed at this newly built temple which is being worshiped as Brahma-Baba by the local Hindu devotees. The black stone deity was earlier identified as 'Avalokiteshwara' by many regional historians. With its exposed breasts, soft posture of ligaments and tender twist of the waist there should not be any confusion regarding its identification as a female deity. The deity is in Lalitasana sitting on the double petalled lotus. Right leg is pendent on 'Mahambujapitha' while the left is bent to rest on the Asana. The right hand of the deity is close to the right knee and is exposed in the 'Varadmudra' while the left hand is holding the stalk of a lotus flower in the middle fingers and the palm is exposed in the Abhaya mudra. There is a smile on the deity's face. The crown is slight conical. Ornaments like keyura, greevahar, Nupura, Katimekhala and Kundalas can be seen. Two full bloomed lotus can be seen one each on the either side of the central figure above the shoulder line.

The decoration on the stele is sparse or say there is a little scope of doing so. It is slightly pointed on the top. Five Dhyani Buddhas are carved on the top. All of them have been shown seated on double petalled lotus. It is a specimen sculpture of Varad Tara.

ii) Birpur Sun Temple (Surya)

A standing sun of black stone representing the early pala period, unearthed from the field nearly, has been placed in this small temple-like structure. The two handed 77cm x 143cm sun is standing on a big lotus throne bearing the relief of seven horses of the divine chariot. His two hands are holding two stalk of full bloomed lotus.The deity is flanked by several divine attendants like Usha, Pratyusha, Dandi, Pingala, Samjana and Mahasveta.

The pointed stele is sparsely decorated having three figures- two of flying gandharvas on both sides on the top and the face of a tiger in the middle of those celestial being. The flank of the stele is carved with some twisted line symbolizing the emergence of sun flames.

iii) Basaha Asthan, Baraipura (Basaha, Surya)

This is one of the mounds of Baraipura having the twin-ponds which yielded many broken and intact black stone sculptures. A new temple has been made in 1990, 5m ahead of the old one which according to local residents, was built almost 125-150 years ago. At the time of laying foundation of the present temple, people reported the evidence of brick-wall deep in the layer. We can't ignore the possibility of some old worship place here as the twin ponds just in front of and in the right side of the new temple yielded nearly half a dozen sculptures. At present, a superb piece of Pala sculpture art in the form of Basaha is placed in the temple. A beautiful sculpture of sun is also placed in the temple behind the Basaha. But the sculpture of Basaha is so remarkable that the place is known as Basaha Asthan.

The Basaha is shown in sitting posture folding all his four legs. The front two legs seem to provide the essential attention and mobility. It measures 107cm(L) x 42cm(W) x 70cm(H).The sun is highly decorated. The deity is accompanied by Usha and Pratyusha. The two handed deity is holding two full-bloomed lotus, one each in both hands. The sculpture measures 107cm (H) x 52cm (W). Both of the sculptures represent the matured pala period.

iv) Chamunda Asthan, Baraipura (Chamunda)

A black stone sculpture of the Pala period is placed in this old temple, said to be built almost 125-150 years ago. The eight handed deity is holding Damru, vessel, dagger, danda and munda. One left hand is touching the lips while the rest two upper hands are holding an elephant. The work of a scorpion is apparent on the stomach. The sculpture measures 52cm x 100cm.

v) Vishhar Asthan, Baraipura (Revant)

A black stone sculpture of Revant representing the Rajputa period is placed in the Vishhar Asthan, very close to the Balan river. Riding over a highly caparisoned horse, the two handed deity is probably holding a cup in his right hand. The deity is booted. A dog is running besides the horse. The rhythm of the caparisoned horse is remarkable. Though the craftsmanship isn't up to the level as displayed in some other sculptures in the region, the movement of the horse is touching the perfection.

2. Sculptures at Museums

i) Harihar (K.P.J.A.Museum)

10th Cen.A.D.

Black stone

Birpur, Begusarai (Bihar)

Height : 16 cms

Width : 13 cms

Intact to some extent above the waist. Form of Vishnu in the left side while that of Shiva in the right. Accordingly the Kirita mukuta in the left and Jatamukuta in the right over head. Only the right upper hand of the four handed deity intact which is holding Parashu.

ii) Vishnu (Begusarai Museum)

9th Cen.A.D.

Black stone

Birpur, Begusarai (Bihar)

Only the upper half of the two handed Vishnu is intact to some extent. Both hands broken from elbow, a short Kirita over head, adorned with kundal, keyur and necklace. A plain round *Aabhamandala* behind the head.

iii) Nandi (Begusarai Museum

9th Cen.A.D.

Black stone

Birpur, Begusarai (Bihar)

The highly decorated sculpture is showing some sign of decay.

iv) Buddha (Begusarai Museum)

10th Cen.A.D.

Black stone

Birpur, Begusarai (Bihar)

Height : 16 cms

Width : 13 cms

Buddha depicted in Bhumisparshamudra. Similar sculpture from Jaimangalgarh also displayed in the gallery.

V) Vishnu (Begusarai Museum)

9th Cen.A.D.

Black stone

Birpur, Begusarai (Bihar)

Only the upper half of the two handed Vishnu is intact to some extent. Both hands broken right below the arm. Greevahar, keyur, kundala, upnavit and the kirit mukut is apparenti.

3. Sculptures at present traceless[13]*

As mentioned earlier, some sculptures finding space in the photographs as Birpur sculptures, are traceless at present. It is suspected that they might have fallen in the hands of some illegal traders of antiquities. A brief description of these are :-

i) Vishnu (1)

A marvelous Black stone four handed Sthanak Vishnu . Holding Chakra and Shankha in the two left hands. Right lower hand exposed in Varad mudra while holding Gada in the upper hand. Kiritmukut, Ajanulambi vanmala, upnaveet, kundala, greevahar, keyur, katimekhala etc are apparent. Bhudevi and Saraswati in the two sides. Two Flying Gandhrvas on the top of the stele.

ii) Vishnu (2 A)

Almost identical Vishnu but stele sparsely decorated. Seems to be earlier respectively.

iii) Vishnu (2B)

Features are identical but larger than the previous one. Most decorative of the three Vishnu sculptures. Crown identical to that of Jaimangalgarh Vishnu or Chitragupta at Bari Pokhar, Begusarai.

iv) Dancing Ganesha

A superb piece of Black stone eight handed Dancing Ganesha holding Pash, Anguliya, Parshu, Modak, Swadant and Ankush in his six hands. One left hand is raised in dancing posture while the right one is in *Abhaymudra.* Two lady attendants perhaps Riddhi and Buddhi on the both sides of the Mahambujapeeth. The mouse is in front of the Mahambujapeeth.

iii) Narsinh

A rare form of Vishnu sculpture. Four handed pratyaleedh Narsinh holding Hiranyakashyap on his thigh and pulling out his intestinal parts. Adorned with regular features of Vishnu except a crown. The deity is not holding any *aayudh* or *prateek.* Two upper hands are raised while the rest two are engaged with the demon king.

Naulagarh/Nawalgarh It is one of the most famous archaeological sites of the district. It is situated on the northern flank of the Bainti, almost 20km. north-northwest to the district headquarters of Begusarai and almost 3.5 kms. in the same direction to the block headquarters of Birpur. The huge mound is almost intact and is under agriculture practices. The Birpur-Sanjat road intersects this mound. The remains of fortification over this mound has been explored several times by dept. of A.I.HC &.Archaeology, G.D. College, Begusarai

Location	:	86^0 04' 00" E / 25^0 33'15" N
Expansion	:	1500 m x 1000 m
Height	:	3m
Pottery found	:	BRW, Grey ware, Black slipped ware N.B.P.W, Red ware

Naulagarh is a huge mound. It is expanded right from Bhith(Bhit) in the east to Fansiare Tola in Makhwa Panchayat in the west, The Balan in the east and the Bainti in the south create a remarkable topology for the mound. Both of them join in the east almost 1km. from here. In fact, this huge mound seems to be divided in three parts:

(i) The central fortification area covered by a 3m wide fortification wall made of baked bricks.

(ii) Sodhni mound measuring 400m x 100m to the north of the fort.

(iii) The mound of Dih and Bhit to the east of the fortified area.

Naulagarh is one of the earliest explored sites of the district. The Dept. of History and A I H & C, G.D.College, Begusarai: under supervision of Prof. R.K.Choudhary explored and surveyed this site in 1950-52. A local resident Shri Ram Nath Singh had gifted the antique collection from this site to the Meseum of G.D.College, Begusarai.[14] A black stone sculpture bearing the inscription of Vigraha Pala III is protected and displayed in the Museum (Dept. of A.I.H.C & Archaeology). The concerned inscription is narrated in **On Bihar, Buletin-2** of G.D.College, Begusarai.

Naulagarh is remarkable for its multicultural background and continuous cultural sequence. A number of coins- from punch marked coins to muslim coins- have been reported to be explored by local people during agricultural practices. The southern part of the mound nearing the Bainti, the Balan, and the Burhi Gandak connect this site to the heart of Mithila as well as to the outer world.

There is a strong possibility of a dockyard in the southern end of the mound. The 200m x 100m old tank which is connected by river Bainti with a 50m wide deep Channel, seems to be made for the purpose of transportation. It is possible that the .southern side of the tank would have been a platform for loading-unloading of goods. The Bainti connects it to Birpur which could be a medicinal trade centre in ancient times and religious centre during the Palas and the Rajputa period.

According to the local tradition, this particular tank used to be a secret path of the royal family to go outside but the topology and the finding till now doesn't support this traditional story.

The expansion and the evidence of dockyard as well as the expanded NBPW influenced area strongly suggest this site to be the Apan Nigam mentioned in the Buddhist literature.

Naulagarh has yielded few black stone sculptures. Some of them are reported missing by local residents. Nevertheless, there are few preserved in K.P.J.A.Museum at G.D.College, Begusarai.

Goddess

10th Cen. A.D.

Inscribed, Black stone, broken

Naulagarh, Begusarai

Height : 54 cms.

Width : 53 cms.

Upper left of this high relief sculpture is completely broken, deity seated on double petalled lotus in Lalitasana. Left leg bent while the right hanging in the front of the Asana placed over another double petalled lotus, smaller in size. Right hand intact below the elbow and placed over the thigh. The right palm opened upward carrying 'Shri Phala' pressed with the middle finger, Kankana in the right wrist. Left hand completely broken but remains indicating it to be placed over left thigh. The lower part of a vanmala between right thigh and left leg indicating the Ajanulambini pushpamala deity would be having Mani Mekhala in the waist with its pendents hanging. The left foot sole showing some holy symbol.

One female attendant holding Chamar on the both sides of the main deity. Decorated pedestal Ganapati seated over a double-petelled lotus to the extreme left. Brahma and Brahmani with folding hands to its next, decorated flower in the middle, two female figures seated over lotus offering prayers and a decorated Kalash to the extreme right.

The flexibility of the waist, the tenderness of the ligaments and the twist suggesting it to be a female deity and the pedestal showing indication of the sculpture of Lakshmi.

Vishnu

10th Cen. A.D.

Black stone

Naulagarh, Begusarai (Bihar)

Height : 49 cms (broken)

Width : 86 cms.

Only the platform of this large sculpture exists. The two legs just above the ankle can be seen. Indication of one deity each on the two sides of the central deity standing over two double-petalled lotus. Pedastal decorated with many figures. To the extreme left a female figure worshipping, next to it a male figure indicating to be Brahma due to its beard and 'mala' (Akshamala) in the hand. Two half blossomed flowers in the centre of the pedestal. Garuda with folding hands next to it towards left and a couple offering prayer to the extreme left. Figures on the pedestal are bent over knee. Remains indicating the central deity to be Vishnu.

Door Panel

9th-10th cen. A.D.

Black stone

Naulagarh, Begusarai (Bihar)

Height : 90 cms

Width : 20 cms.

The rectangular door panel decorated with four lineal carvings. An attendant wearing sacred thread holding Parashu in the left hand and the right hand in *Abhayamudra*. Kundala and neclace apparent.

The above description shows that all the three sites described here have continuous legacy of more than two thousand years. There are archaeological evidences supporting the identity of this region during the early medieval times though history had taken shapes much earlier here. After the Pala dominance was over in this region, like other parts of the northern Bihar, it witnessed the advent of the Rajput power. Chandela, Parmara, Solanki and Chauhan clans entered this region. As far as the local traditions of the Rajput legacy is concerned, we come to know about three local rulers- Nawal Sinh, Jaimangal Sinh and Bir Sinh who are supposed to be the rulers of Naulagarh, Jaimangalgarh and Birpur respectively. Chandela particularly seems to rule this region. According to Dr R.K.Choudhary they were originally Bhar (Bharshiva) and belonged to ruling class.[15] Chamunda is said to be their ***adidevi.*** Prof Chaudhary has tried to connect[16] the two sites – Nawalgarh and Jaimanglgarh consenting that the later was the religious center of the rulers from Nawalgarh. The administrative – cum-commercial aspect of Nawalgargh is also reflected by the geographical and archaeological evidences. We would like to add to this hypothesis connecting Birpur also. Jaimangalgarh might be the royal religious center in this referred period but Birpur has elements of a mass religious center. These Rajput rulers brought with them a particular type of art – reflected in iconography as well as in architecture. Birpur has vestiges of this political changeover. We strongly feel that the emergence of the Shakt cult, sculptures of Chamunda, Mahishasurmardini, Bhairav etc and iconographical features like tribal crown of the deities are the reflections of this political changeover. Jaimangalgarh, Nawalgarh and Birpur are three major sites connecting the history of this region particularly of the period which has remained sidelined unfortunately. We talk about Anguttarapa, about the Palas, about the Chakwaras, about the Mugal or British rule in Begusarai but ignore the history between the Palas and the Muslim rule in Begusarai. A complete and comprehensive History must come before the history lovers for the sake of mere History.

References :

1. Archaeological sites of Begusarai , Dr S.K.Sinha & Dr A. Krishna Appendix
2. G.D.College Bulletin Series No.-2 Page 13- 17
3. On Bihar, G.D.College Bulletin Series-4 Appendix III Page-3
4. New finds from Jaimangalgarh R.C.Prasad Singh ,On Bihar, G.D.College Bulletin Series-4
5. Archaeological sites of Begusarai, Dr.S.K.Sinha & Dr. A. Krishna, page-67
6. Bhartiya Kala, Vasudeosharan Agrawal page-137
7. Vishnudharmottar puran, 3/40/1-3

8. Majjhim Nikay, Potliya Sutta (2.1.4)
9. Archaeological sites of Begusarai , Dr S.K.Sinha & Dr A. Krishna page-46
10. Bihar District Gazetteers Munger 1960, page 463.
11. A brief report on Birpur Excavation submitted to A.S.I.
12. Bihar District Gazetteers Munger 1960 page 463.
13. Bihar District Gazetteers Munger 1960 Appendix
14. G.D.College Bulletin Series-1
15. Begusarai Abhijnan Granth page 16
16. G.D.College Bulletin Series-2 page 16

*P G Dept.of AIH Archaeology & Culture
G.D. College, Begusarai -851101

Courtesy :
Dharohar
(A Journal of Culture & Archaeology)
vol.IV & V ,July 2016

●●●

हिन्दी आलेख

बेगूसराय जिले से प्राप्त कतिपय पालकालीन बौद्ध प्रतिमाएँ

ठाकुर हरेन्द्र दयाल*

बिहार प्रदेश में स्थित बेगूसराय जिले का अपना प्राचीन इतिहास है। कब से यहाँ आबादी बसने लगी, इसके विषय में अभी ठीक से पता नहीं लगाया जा सका है। लेकिन बौद्धकाल में यहाँ आबादी का अस्तित्व मिलता है। बेगूसराय जिले के विभिन्न भागों से उत्तरी कृष्णमार्जित मृदभाण्ड[1] प्राप्त हुए हैं। इन बर्त्तनों की तिथि बौद्धकालीन आंकी गयी है। यहाँ मौर्यकालीन लकड़ी के पुल जयमंगलागढ़ से प्राप्त हुए हैं। जयमंगलागढ़[2] से मौर्येत्तर तथा कुषाणकालीन मूर्त्तियाँ[3] प्राप्त हुई हैं। बाद में गुप्तकालीन ब्राह्मी लिपि की एक मुहर[4] भी प्राप्त हुई है।

गुप्तकाल के बाद भी यहाँ आबादी रही। पालकालीन अनेक अवशेषों का पता चला है। बेगूसराय जिले के विभिन्न स्थानों से पालकालीन विष्णु,[5] गणेश,[6] अप्सरा,[7] शिव अर्घा,[8] सूर्य[9] तथा कुछ बौद्ध प्रतिमायें प्राप्त हुई हैं। यहाँ बेगूसराय से प्राप्त कतिपय पालकालीन बौद्ध प्रतिमाओं का वर्णन प्रस्तुत किया जायेगा। ये प्रतिमाएँ राजवाड़ा ग्राम (बरौनी प्रखण्ड), सिंघौल (बेगूसराय प्रखंड), बलिया (बलिया प्रखण्ड) से प्राप्त हुई हैं।

इन बौद्ध प्रतिमाओं पर प्रकाश डालने से पूर्व यह बताना आवश्यक है कि पालकालीन अनेक प्रतिमाएँ चाहे ब्राह्मण या बौद्ध धर्म की हों, काले पत्थर की बनी हैं। यहाँ यह उल्लेखनीय है कि काले पत्थर, कसौटी के पत्थर या स्लेट पत्थर की मूर्त्तियाँ[10] पालयुग में निर्मित की जाती थीं। ऐसे पत्थरों की बनी मूर्त्तियाँ जी0 डी0 कॉलेज, बेगूसराय के काशी प्रसाद जायसवाल संग्रहालय तथा बेगूसराय जिला संग्रहालय में सुरक्षित हैं। बिहार तथा बंगाल पर पाल राजवंश का आधिपत्य था। इसके फलस्वरूप इन प्रदेशों में ऐसे प्रस्तर की प्रतिमाएँ उपलब्ध हुई हैं। बिहार प्रदेश के नालन्दा, राजगृह तथा अन्य स्थानों[11] के अलावे बेगूसराय[12] जिले के विभिन्न स्थलों से ऐसे पत्थरों की प्रतिमाएँ मिली हैं। बिहार प्रदेश में स्थित राजमहल और मुंगेर के खड़गपुर की पहाड़ियों[13]

में ऐसा पत्थर अधिक मिलता है। मुंगेर जिले में सीता कोहबर से प्राचीन स्लेट पत्थर निकालने की खान का पता चला है जिससे बहुत बड़े पैमाने पर (शायद पालयुग में ही) पत्थर निकाला गया, यह स्पष्ट है[14]। अब यह प्रश्न उठता है कि गंगा के दक्षिणी तट पर स्थित पहाड़ियों से बेगूसराय जिले के स्थानों तक किस प्रकार ऐसे पत्थर लाये गये होंगे। इस प्रश्न का उत्तर देना कठिन नहीं है। यह अनुमान लगाना सही है कि गंगा नदी के द्वारा नावों पर लादकर पत्थर उत्तरी तट तक लाये गये होंगे। गंडक नदी तथा अन्य छोटी नदियों के मार्ग से जयमंगलागढ़, नौलागढ़ आदि स्थानों तक ये पत्थर पहुँचाये गये हों। जहाँ नदी मार्ग संभव नहीं होगा वहाँ स्थल मार्ग से पाषाण–खण्डों को लोग ले गये होंगे। इसके साथ यह भी प्रश्न उठता है कि क्या कलाकारों या मूर्त्तिकारों ने पत्थर के खदान में ही इन मूत्तियों का निर्माण किया या प्राप्ति भी स्थान में पत्थरों को लाकर? इस प्रश्न का उत्तर भी दिया जा सकता है कि खदान में पत्थरों को तराशकर मूर्तियों को लाने में इनपर खरोंच पड़ने तथा इनके क्षतिग्रस्त होने का डर था। अतः यह संभव प्रतीत होता है कि पत्थर खण्डों को खदान से लाकर प्राप्ति–स्थानों में मूर्त्तिकारों ने मूर्त्तियों का निर्माण किया होगा।

सर्वप्रथम बलिया प्रखण्ड से प्राप्त दो बुद्ध प्रतिमाओं का विवरण प्रस्तुत किया जायेगा। बेगूसराय जिला मुख्यालय से पूर्व की ओर 20 कि0 मी0 की दूरी पर राजमार्ग संख्या 31 तथा पूर्वोत्तर रेलवे के लखमिनिया स्टेशन के दक्षिणी ओर बलिया प्रखण्ड का कार्यालय स्थित है। इस प्रखण्ड कार्यालय परिसर में एक नवीन भवन की नींव काटते समय काले पत्थर की तीन मूर्त्तियाँ प्राप्त हुई। इन मूर्त्तियों को लेकर स्थानीय लोगों में बड़ा विवाद उठ खड़ा हुआ। अतः वहाँ के लोगों में शान्ति बनाये रखने के उद्देश्य से वहाँ के पदाधिकारियों ने इन मूर्त्तियों को बलिया थाना में पुलिस विभाग के अधिकारियों की देखरेख में सुरक्षित रख दिया। बेगूसराय जिला पदाधिकारी ने पत्रांक 1341 दिनांक 04.09.1996 में इन मूर्त्तियों के अध्ययन करने का आग्रह किया। दि0 07. 09.1996 को लेखक ने बलिया प्रखण्ड में जाकर पुलिस पदाधिकारियों से बातचीत की और इन मूर्त्तियों का अध्ययन किया। दो बुद्ध प्रतिमाएँ भूमिस्पर्श मुद्रा में तथा एक विष्णु प्रतिमा है। यहाँ केवल दो बौद्ध प्रतिमाओं का अध्ययन प्रस्तुत किया जायेगा।

भूमिस्पर्श मुद्रा में बुद्ध :

यह मूर्त्ति काले कसौटी पत्थर की बनी है और इसपर कहीं–कहीं पर धूमिल लाल रंग का अवशेष है। यह प्रतिमा 30 से0 मी0 लम्बी तथा 22.2 से0 मी0 चौड़ी हैं। इस प्रतिमा का चौड़ा वक्षस्थल, क्षीण कटि तथा कोमल बाहें अत्यन्त मनोहर हैं। इसके मुख पर नारी–सुलभ कोमलता व्याप्त दिखाई गयी है। पालकालीन प्रस्तर मूर्त्तियों की यह विशिष्टता है। इस युग की अन्य प्रतिमाओं में भी यह विद्विष्ट गुण प्रदर्शित होता है।[15] इस युग की प्रतिमाओं के मुखमण्डल पर

नारी सुलभ कोमलता प्रदर्षन करने का कारण क्या था? पालयुग में तंत्रयान का प्रभाव अधिक था। अतः इसके फलस्वरूप ''शान्ति'' का महत्त्व इतना बढ़ गया था कि पुरुष–देवताओं की मूर्तियों में भी नारी सुलभ कोमलता चेहरे पर व्याप्त दिखाई गयी। कलाकारों ने मूर्तियों के अंग की रचना में मानवीय भावना तथा आध्यात्मिक भावना का समावेश किया है।

यह स्वतंत्र तथा त्रि–आयामी मूर्त्ति है। इसकी पीठ चौरस है। पालयुग की अनेक प्रतिमाओं की पीठ चौरस बनायी जाती थी। लगता है कलाकार ने इस काल की मूर्त्तियों की पीठ गढ़ने में अधिक तत्परता और लगन नहीं दिखाई, जितनी की त्रि–आयामी मूर्त्ति बनाने में चाहिए थी। इस कारण सामने और बगल में मूर्त्ति पूरी और चौकोर कटी मालूम पड़ती है, पर पीछे से चिपटी भी है। इस कारण दर्शक की दृष्टि मूर्त्ति की पीठ पर वस्तुतः आसानी से पड़ती है। लगता है कि यह प्रतिमा किसी वृक्ष या दीवार के सहारे खड़ी की गयी होगी, इसलिए मूर्त्तिकार ने इस प्रतिमा की पीठ को चौरस कर दिया लेकिन अलंकृत नहीं। यह विशेषता पालयुगीन अन्य मूर्त्तियों में भी पाई जाती है।[16]

विचाराधीन प्रतिमा में कमल पुष्प की मृदुल पंखुड़ियों की अच्छी तरह से प्रदर्शित करने का प्रयास किया गया है। बुद्ध पद्मासन में हैं और उनके दोनों पैरों के तलवे ऊपर की ओर तथा इनके बायें हाथ की हथेली गोद में और दाहिने हाथ की अंगुलियाँ भूमिस्पर्श मुद्रा में हैं। इनके तलवे पर चक्र का चिह्न है। आँखें आधी खुली हैं। बौद्ध साहित्य[17] से ज्ञात होता है कि बुद्ध ने शरीर के परिमार्जन के लिए कठोर तप किया, परन्तु काया–क्लेष उन्हें उनके निश्चित लक्ष्य तक पहुँचा नहीं सका। इसकी निष्फलता अनुभव करने के बाद अन्ततोगत्वा बुद्ध बोधगया में एक अश्वत्थ वृक्ष की छाया में ध्यानमुद्रा में रत हो गये। प्रस्तुत मूर्ति से बुद्ध के द्वारा ध्यान लगानेवाली घटना का परिचय प्राप्त होता है।

इस प्रतिमा की कटि से ऊपर का भाग नग्न है लेकिन कटि के नीचे के भाग में पारदर्शी धोती का अंकन है जिसपर पतली रेखाओं का अंकन है। पालयुग की अनेक प्रतिमाओं पर ऐसे अधोवस्त्र का अंकन मिलता है।[18] इसके अतिरिक्त इस प्रतिमा पर विभिन्न आभूषणों का अंकन है। इसके मस्तक पर मुकुट व गले में हार है। यहाँ यह उल्लेखनीय है कि पालयुग में हिन्दू देवी–देवताओं की प्रतिमाओं को आभूषणों से आभूषित दिखाने की परम्परा थी। बौद्ध मूर्त्तिकारों पर भी इसका प्रभाव पड़ा। पालयुग के बुद्ध तथा बोधिसत्व की मूर्त्तियों के मस्तक पर मुकुट और शरीर पर अनेक प्रकार के आभूषणों का अंकन कर मूर्त्तिकारों ने भारतीय अलंकारप्रियता की परम्परा प्रतिष्ठित करने का बहाना ढूँढ लिया। आभूषणों का चाव इतना अधिक बढ़ा कि विरागी बुद्ध को भी सिर पर मुकुट और गले में हार लिये प्रदर्शित किया जाने लगा। ऐसी मुकुटधारी बुद्ध प्रतिमाएँ राजगृह और नालन्दा में भी मिली है।[19]

आलोच्य प्रतिमा की प्रभावली अलंकृत बनायी गयी है और बुद्ध के सम्पूर्ण शरीर से जुड़ी है। इस प्रतिमा की बाँई तथा दाहिनी ओर एक–एक सिंह को अपने पंजों को उठाये खड़ा प्रदर्शित किया गया है इससे मूर्त्ति में गति का आभास मिलता है।

प्रस्तुत प्रतिमा की दाहिनी ओर पालकालीन ब्राह्मी लिपि में एक अभिलेख उत्कीर्ण है। इसके अनेक अक्षरों को पढ़ा नहीं जा सकता है। लगता है यह बौद्ध धर्म की प्रसिद्ध उक्ति है–

"हे धम्मा हेतु प्रभवा"।

पद्मासन में बुद्ध की प्रतिमा :

बलिया प्रखण्ड कार्यालय से ही बुद्ध की एक अन्य प्रतिमा प्राप्त हुई है। यह भी काले पत्थर की प्रतिमा है। बुद्ध मुकुट, हार आदि आभूषणों से आभूषित हैं। इनकी दोनों पतली भौहों के मध्य ऊर्णा अंकित है। यह मूर्ति भी पद्मासन में है। इसका बाँया हाथ गोद में तथा दाहिना हाथ भूमिस्पर्श मुद्रा में है। इनके बायें हाथ की तलहथी तथा दोनों पैरों के तलवों में चक्र के चिह्न का अंकन है।

यह मूर्त्ति दोहरे कमलासन पर आसीन है। मूर्त्ति के दोनों ओर एक–एक सिंह को पंजा उठाये प्रदर्शित किया गया है। यह मूर्त्ति 29.5 से0 मी0 लम्बी तथा 20 से0 मी0 चौड़ी है। ऊपर का भाग खण्डित है। इसका पृष्ठ भाग समतल तथा चौरस है। लगता है किसी देवस्थान की दीवार या किसी वृक्ष के सहारे खड़ी की जाने के लिए इसका भी निर्माण किया गया होगा। इसके पृष्ठभाग पर तीन पंक्तियों में पालकालीन ब्राह्मी लिपि में एक अभिलेख अंकित है, जिसे तत्काल पढ़ा नहीं जा सका है।

संघौल से प्राप्त बुद्ध :

बेगूसराय नगर से 2 कि0 मी0 पश्चिम संघौल ग्राम स्थित है। इस ग्राम से पालकालीन मूर्त्तियाँ मिली थी। यहाँ एक खण्डित बुद्ध की प्रतिमा मिली है। यह भूमिस्पर्श मुद्रा में है। इसका दाहिना हाथ भूमिस्पर्श मुद्रा में तथा बायाँ हाथ गोद में है। यह पद्मासन में है और दोनों पैरों के तलवे ऊपर की ओर है। बायीं ओर तथा दाहिनी ओर एक–एक नारी प्रतिमा है। जिनकी पहचान करना कठिन है। कमलासन के नीचे दो सिंह तथा एक भक्त की आकृतियाँ उत्कीर्ण हैं।[20] यहाँ एक अभिलेख अंकित है लेकिन अस्पष्ट है। प्रो0 राधाकृष्ण चौधरी ने इसे पढ़ने का प्रयास किया था। लगता है अभिलेख का उत्कीर्णक लेखन–कला में सिद्धहस्त नहीं था। प्रो0 चौधरी का विचार है कि बाद में इस प्रतिमा पर अभिलेख को उत्कीर्ण किया गया[21] और लगभग 800 ई0 से 1000 ई0 के बीच इस अभिलेख की तिथि निर्धारित की जा सकती है। प्रो0 चौधरी ने "विरूपा" पढ़ा है।[22] इस व्यक्ति के पहचान के विषय में बताना कठिन है। बिहार में इस नाम से एक सिद्ध लेखक की जानकारी है। राहुल सांकृत्यायन[23] ने बताया है कि पाल सम्राट देवपाल

का समकालीन 'विरूप' था जिसने 18 ग्रंथों की रचना की थी। इससे अधिक इस व्यक्ति तथा विचाराधीन मूर्त्ति के विषय में कुछ नहीं कहा जा सकता है।

राजवाड़ा से प्राप्त मारीची की खण्डित प्रतिमा :

राजवाड़ा ग्राम (बरौनी प्रखंड) बरौनी रेलवे जंक्शन के पूर्व गुमटी संख्या 61 के पास भूमि को खोदते समय प्राप्त हुई थी। यह मूर्त्ति गुमटी के पास एक वृक्ष के नीचे रखी हुई है। वहाँ के स्थानीय लोगों का विश्वास है कि इस प्रतिमा के कारण यहाँ पर बस दुर्घटनाएँ नहीं होती, अगर होती हैं तो यात्रियों की मृत्यु नहीं होती। इसे लोग मुड़कटवा बाबा कहते हैं। लगता है कि लोग इस प्रतिमा को नहीं पहचान सके। यह देवता की नहीं बल्कि देवी की प्रतिमा है। यह ब्राह्मण धर्म की नहीं बल्कि बौद्ध धर्म की देवी है। यह भी काले कसौटी पत्थर की बनी प्रतिमा है। इसका पृष्ठभाग चौरस है और पृष्ठ की ओर से मापने पर 54 से0 मी0 लम्बा है लेकिन खड़ा करने के लिये नीचे की ओर 4 से0 मी0 नुकीला भाग है। अतः कुल मिलाकर 58 से0 मी0 लम्बा है। यह प्रतिमा चौड़ाई में 45.5 से0 मी0 है।

यहाँ पत्थर खण्ड के बीच भाग में प्रमुख देवी का अंकन है जिसका मस्तक खण्डित है लेकिन इसके गले में हार, कमर में कमरधनी, पैर में पायल तथा बाहों में बाजूबन्द है। कमर के नीचे पारर्दशक वस्त्र पर कई वक्र रेखाएँ अंकित हैं। इसका दाहिना पैर जंघा से टूटा हुआ है लेकिन घुटना से नीचे पूरी तरह सुरक्षित है और वस्त्र से दोनों पैरों को ढका दिखाया गया है। प्रतिमा के बायें पैर की अगुलियाँ बायीं ओर मुड़ी हैं। यह प्रतिमा चतुर्भुजी है। इसके सामने का बायाँ हाथ केहुनी से टूटी है और बाँह पर बाजूबन्द है। इस हाथ की अंगुलियाँ हृदय के पास है। पीछे का बायाँ हाथ भी टूटा हुआ है। अतः हाथों में आयुधों तथा मुद्राओं के विषय में कुछ पता नहीं चलता है। यह प्रतिमा प्रत्यालीढ़ आसन में हैं और सात सुअरों से जुटे रथ पर सवार है। इस रथ में दाहिनी ओर तीन, बायीं ओर तीन और बीच में एक सुअर है। इन सुअरों का मुख का अग्र भाग लम्बा है और दाँत वक्र दिखाये गये हैं। दाहिनी ओर के तीन सुअर दाहिनी ओर और बायीं ओर के सुअर बायीं ओर देख रहे हैं। इन सभी पशुओं के गले में हार है। लगता है गले में घंटी है ओर इनके कान लम्बे हैं। इनके आगे का पैर मुड़ा है जिससे ''गति'' का आभास होता है। लेकिन पीछे के शरीर का भाग और पैरों को नहीं दिखाया गया। इन सुअरों के अंकन से इस प्रतिमा की पहचान करना संभव है। यह मारीची देवी की प्रतिमा है जिसका सम्बन्ध प्रकाश तथा सूर्य से है। तिब्बत के लामा इसकी आराधना सूर्योदय के समय करते हैं।[24] हिन्दुओं के सूर्य देवता के समान यह रथ पर आरूढ़ रहती है। लेकिन दोनों में अन्तर है कि सूर्य के रथ को सात अश्व खींचते हैं, जबकि मारीची के रथ में सात सुअर लगे रहते हैं। विचाराधीन प्रतिमा में एक चालक का अंकन है लेकिन वह अस्पष्ट है। अतः इसकी पहचान करना कठिन है। लेकिन अन्य मूर्त्तियों तथा साधनों में (शुकरारूढ़ाम्) मारीची देवी शूकर पर सवार बतायी गयी है। उसका रथ

चालक या तो बिना पैर की एक देवी या राहू है जिसके मस्तक दिखाये जाते हैं। यहाँ पर यह उल्लेखनीय है कि मारीची तथा वज्रवाराही बौद्ध देवियों को कुछ लोग एक मानते हैं। लेकिन यह विचार मान्य नहीं है क्योंकि दोनों में अन्तर है। व्रजवाराही को उनके पति हेरूक के साथ यव–युम मुद्रा में बताया गया है। लेकिन मारीची का अंकन अकेले किया जाता है और वैरोचन इनके परिवार के प्रमुख हैं। दूसरा अन्तर यह है कि हेरूक पड़े हुए शव पर सवार प्रदर्शित किये जाते हैं। अतः वज्रवाराही का भी वाहन शव है। लेकिन मारीची को भी शव पर सवार नहीं प्रदर्शित किया जाता है। हेरूक तथा वज्रवाराही के सम्मिलित रूप में वज्रवाराही तंत्र है लेकिन मारीची के साथ वैसा कोई तंत्र नहीं है। वज्रवाराही शव पर नृत्य–मुद्रा में प्रदर्शित की जाती है, लेकिन मारीची हमेशा आलीढ़ मुद्रा में खड़ी तथा रथ पर सवार रहती है और नृत्य मुद्रा में नहीं रहती है।[25] व्रजवाराही को डाकिनी कहा गया है लेकिन मारीची को देवी।[26]

साधनमाला से मारीची के छः प्रकार के रूपों का पता चलता है। लेकिन विचाराधीन प्रतिमा का मस्तक खण्डित है। अतः यह पता नहीं चल पाता है कि इसका तीन या पांच या छः मुख है। प्रस्तुत प्रतिमा में देवी के सहचारियों का अंकन है। प्रमुख देवी प्रतिमा की दाहिनी ओर चतुर्भुजी देवी का अंकन है जिसके दोनों दाहिने हाथ टूटे हैं लेकिन दोनों बायाँ हाथ सुरक्षित है। पीछे बायाँ हाथ उठा है जिसमें कुछ आयुध हैं जिसकी पहचान करना कठिन है। सामने का बायाँ हाथ ह्रदय के पास स्थित है। इस देवी के गले में हार है और इसका दाहिना पैर ऊपर उठा है बायाँ पैर सीधा जमीन पर स्थित है। इस प्रतिमा में देवी को पारदर्शक वस्त्र में दिखलाया गया है। उसके पैर के पास बैठा हुआ एक भक्त है जिसके हाथों में माला है। मारीची देवी की प्रतिमा के बायीं ओर चतुर्भुजी एक अन्य देवी की प्रतिमा का अंकन है जिसके पीछे का दाहिना हाथ ऊपर उठा हुआ है जिसमें कोई वस्तु है। सामने का बायाँ हाथ ह्रदय के पास अवस्थित है। यह प्रतिमा भी विभिन्न आभूषणों से आभूषित है। इसका मुख भग्न है लेकिन दाहिना पैर सीधा और बायाँ मुड़ा हुआ है। देवी मारीची की इन दोनों सहचारियों की पहचान करना कठिन है। लेकिन साधनमाला[27] में मारीची देवी के चार सहचारियों वर्त्ताली, वाडाली, वराली तथा वराहमुखी का वर्णन है। विचाराधीन प्रतिमा में दो सहचारियों की प्रतिमाएँ खंण्डित है। अतः पहचान करना कठिन है। रथ चालक की प्रतिमा के नीचे तथा सुअरों के ऊपर वाले भाग में पालकालीन ब्राह्मी लिपि में एक लेख अंकित है जो अस्पष्ट है। अतः इसे पढ़ना संभव नहीं हो पाया है।

निष्कर्ष :

उपर्युक्त तथ्यों से यह स्पष्ट हो जाता है कि अन्य स्थानों के अतिरिक्त बेगूसराय जिले पर पाल राजाओं का आधिपत्य था। उस युग में पाल–कला की काफी विकास हुआ। बेगूसराय जिले में पालयुगीन ब्राह्मण तथा बौद्ध प्रतिमाएँ मिली हैं। पाल युग में मूर्त्तियों की विशेषताएँ निर्धारित

हो चुकी थीं। तिब्बती इतिहासकार तारानाथ ने ''धीमान'' और उसके पुत्र ''वित्तपाल'' को पूर्वी भारत की मूर्त्तिकला का जन्मदाता कहा है। इनका समय नौवीं सदी था, जिस समय धर्मपाल और देवपाल सम्राट थे। नालन्दा के उत्खनन से यह प्रमाणित हो गया है कि नालन्दा विश्वविद्यालय पाल–कला का प्रमुख केन्द्र था। पाल राजाओं के संरक्षण में ही मध्यकालीन पूर्वी शैली का मगध में ही अभ्युदय हुआ। नालन्दा योगाचार तथा वज्रयान का प्रधान केन्द्र था और इसलिए संभवतः यहीं इनसे संबंधित मूर्त्तियों का निर्माण होने लगा और रूप निश्चित किये गये। तान्त्रिक बौद्ध धर्म का प्रधान सिद्धान्त था–शक्ति की आराधना। इसलिए स्त्री–प्रतिमाएँ विभिन्न मुद्राओं और आसनों में शक्ति के विभिन्न रूपों और गुणों को अभिव्यक्त करती हुई बनने लगी। यह बराबर ध्यान में रखा गया कि सभी मूर्त्तियाँ अत्यन्त आकर्षक और श्रृंगार रस से ओत–प्रोत हों। इसलिए इस युग की पुरुष–मूर्त्तियाँ तथा बुद्ध, बोधिसत्व तथा अन्य देवताओं की मूर्त्तियों में नारी सौन्दर्य और शक्ति का प्रदर्शन किया गया। गोलाकार चेहरा, कोमल मूर्त्तियाँ सुन्दर और आकर्षक हैं जिससे पालकालीन कलाकारों की दक्षता का परिचय मिलता है। इन सभी मूर्त्तियों में पालकालीन मूर्त्तिकला की विशेषताएँ मिली हैं। ये सभी प्रतिमाएँ कसौटी पत्थर की हैं, प्रभामंडल प्रतिमा के सम्पूर्ण शरीर से सम्बन्धित हैं। प्रभा मंडल अलंकृत है, ऊपर में नुकीला है और पृष्ठ भाग चौरस है। ये सभी मूर्त्तियाँ आभूषणों से आभूषित प्रदर्षित किया गया है। यहाँ तक कि विरागी बुद्ध को भी आभूषणों से आभूषित प्रदर्शित किया गया है। इन मूर्त्तियों पर अंकित अभिलेखों को अभी तक ठीक से पढ़ा नहीं जा सका है।

सन्दर्भ सूची :

1. रामशरण शर्मा : प्राचीन भारत में भौतिक प्रगति एवं सामाजिक संरचनायें, पृ0 154;

   प्रो0 राधाकृष्ण चौधरी ने भी बेगूसराय जिले में स्थित नौलागढ़ तथा जयमंगलागढ़ आदि स्थानों से कृष्णमार्जित मृदमाण्डों के टुकड़ों को प्राप्त किया जो जी0 डी0 कॉलेज के प्राचीन भारतीय इतिहास एवं पुरातत्व विभाग से सम्बद्ध काशी प्रसाद जायसवाल संग्रहालय में सुरक्षित है।
2. जी0 डी0 कॉलेज बुलेटिन संख्या 4 में न्यू फाइन्डस फ्रॉम जयमंगलागढ़ प्लेट सं0 2; तुलनीय राधाकृष्ण चौधरी, *इकोनोमिक हिस्ट्री ऑफ एन्सियन्ट इण्डिया,* पृ0 1271 ।
3. जयमंगलागढ़ में रेस्ट हाउस के निकट एक तालाब की खुदाई करते समय बहुत–सी पशु मृण्मूर्त्तियाँ मिली हैं जिनके पीठ पर वृतों का अंकन है। ऐसी प्रतिमायें पटना संग्रहालय में सुरक्षित हैं जिन्हें मौर्येत्तरकालीन माना गया है। अतः समता के आधार पर जयमंगलागढ़ से प्राप्त मृण्मूर्त्तियों को कुषाण मान सकते हैं। जयमंगलागढ़ से प्राप्त मृण्मूर्त्तियाँ बेगूसराय जिला संग्रहालय में सुरक्षित हैं। पटना संग्रहालय में वैसी मूर्त्तियों के विवरण के लिए देखें *टेराकोटा फिगराइन्स इन पटना म्यूजियम,* आर्क0 4275, अश्वमूर्ति।
4. राधाकृष्ण चौधरी : *''द इंडियन न्यूमिसमैटीक क्रोनिकल''* खण्ड 2, भाग 1–2, 1973 पृ0 99–101 प्लेट –2 (बी), नौलागढ़ के लिए विस्तार से देखें **जी0 डी0 कॉलेज बुलेटिन संख्या–4** राधाकृष्ण चौधरी (सं0) **बेगूसराय अभिज्ञान ग्रन्थ** (1973); **जे0 ब0 डी0 आर0 एस0 1952; डी0 आर0 पाटिल कृत एन्टिक्वेरियन**

रिमेन्स ऑफ बेगूसराय; पी0 सी0 राय चौधरी 8 (सं0) **मुंगेर डिस्ट्रीक्ट गजेटीयर।**

5. बेगूसराय प्रखंड कार्यालय के उत्तर एक मंदिर में एक विष्णु प्रतिमा तथा वीरपुर ग्राम में मईया–धिया तालाब के किनारे बने एक खपड़ैल मंदिर में एक अन्य विष्णु प्रतिमा सुरक्षित है।

6. बेगूसराय नगर से पश्चिम स्थित संघौल ग्राम में।

7. राधाकृष्ण चौधरी : जी0 डी0 कॉलेज बेगुसराय बुलेटिन संख्या–4 एपेन्डिक्स 3 प्लेट संख्या 2 ।

8. वीरपुर के एक तालाब से शिव अर्घा प्राप्त जो बेगूसराय संग्रहालय में सुरक्षित है।

9. बेगूसराय के विभिन्न स्थानों से सूर्य प्रतिमाएँ मिली हैं। बरौनी की सूर्य प्रतिमा जी0 डी0 कॉलेज बुलेटिन सं0 4 एपेन्डिक्स 3 प्लेट–1; प्रोसिडिंग ऑफ हिस्टोरिकल कॉग्रेस, आगरा अधिवेशन 1956; जर्नल ऑफ बिहार यूनिवर्सिटी 1959 (जी0 डी0 कॉलेज के काशी प्र0 जायसवाल संग्रहालय में सूर्य की दो प्रतिमायें सुरक्षित हैं तथा एक कईथ बराइत ग्राम में है। अतः बेगूसराय जिले में पाँच सूर्य प्रतिमायें पालकालीन हैं।)

10. बी0 पी0 सिन्हा : ''भारतीय कला को बिहार की देन'' पृ0 126, चित्र संख्या 87, 89, 90, 91, 921 तुलनीय राधाकृष्ण चौधरी, जी0 डी0 कॉलेज, बुलेटिन संख्या–1, नौलागढ़ प्लेट 1, 4, बुलेटिन संख्या–4, 5 ए0 5 बी, 5 सी।

11. बी0 पी0 सिन्हाः ऊपर उल्लिखित, पृ0 126 और आगे।

12. सन्दर्भ के लिए देखे पाद टिप्पणियाँ 5, 6, 7, 8

13. बी0 पी0 सिन्हा : ऊपर उल्लिखित, पृ0 126

14. आर्कियोलौजिकल सर्वे ऑफ इण्डिया, ऐनुअल रिपोर्ट 1926, पृ0 152 .

15. बी0 पी0 सिन्हा : ऊपर उल्लिखित पृ0 126 और आगे

16. वही

17. महानिद्देश, पृ0 476, विनय–पिटक का महावग्ग 1, 1, 7।

18. बी0 पी0 सिन्हा : ऊपर उल्लिखित, चित्र संख्या 90, 91, 92, 93, 96, 95, 99।

19. वही, पृ0 126।

20. राधाकृष्ण चौधरी : जी0 डी0 कॉलेज बुलेटिन संख्या–4, प्लेट सं0 4, ऐपेन्डिक्स 3 पृ0 2

21. वही

22. वही

23. राहुल सांकृत्यायन : पुरातत्व निबन्धावली पृ0 148 तथा 176

24. विनयतोष भट्टाचार्य : दी इण्डियन बुद्धिस्ट आइकोनोग्राफी, पृ0 207।

25. वही पृ0 217 और आगे।

26. वही पृ0 207 और आगे।

27. वही पृ0 208।

* पूर्व विभागाध्यक्ष,
प्रा. भा. इतिहास एवं पुरातत्त्व विभाग,
जी. डी. कॉलेज, बेगूसराय

सौजन्य :
आर्ट एण्ड आर्कयोकाँजी ऑफ इर्स्टनइण्डिया
सं0–नसीम अख्तर
पुरातत्व निदेशालय, कला, संस्कृति एवं युवा
विभाग, बिहार, पटना 2006

●●●

वीरपुर (जिला बेगूसराय) से प्राप्त कतिपय पालकालीन मूर्तियाँ

ठाकुर हरेन्द्र दयाल*

मिथिला क्षेत्र की परिधि उत्तर में हिमालय, दक्षिण में गंगा नदी, पूर्व में कोशी तथा पश्चिम में गण्डक है। इस क्षेत्र के अन्तर्गत दरभंगा, मधुबनी, समस्तीपुर, बेगूसराय, खगड़िया, सहरसा, मधेपुरा, पूर्णियाँ जिले आते हैं। निःसंदेह बेगूसराय जिला इस क्षेत्र के अन्तर्गत आता है। बेगूसराय जिला के विभिन्न भागों, जैसे बरौनी, राजवारा, संघौल, बेगूसराय, कंकौल, राजौरा, जयमंगलागढ़, नौलागढ़, वीरपुर एवं बलिया से पालकालीन प्रस्तर मूर्तियाँ प्राप्त हुई हैं। यहाँ पर केवल वीरपुर से प्राप्त पालकालीन मूर्तियों का विवरण प्रस्तुत किया जायेगा।

बेगूसराय मुख्यालय से 10 कि0 मी0 की दूरी पर वीरपुर ग्राम स्थित है। इसे वीरपुर संघाराम भी कहा गया है। यह स्थान बेगूसराय से पक्की सड़क से जुड़ा है। वैसे तो इस ग्राम में अनेक प्रतिमाएँ हैं, परन्तु यहाँ मात्र काले पत्थर की प्रतिमाओं का विवरण प्रस्तुत किया जा रहा है। ऐसे काले पत्थर की प्रतिमाएँ पाल युग में निर्मित की जाती थीं। बेगूसराय क्षेत्र पर पालों का आधिपत्य था।[1] आठवीं सदी के पूर्वार्द्ध में अराजकता से तंग आकर जनता और नेताओं ने बंगाल के गोपाल नामक व्यक्ति को राजा चुना, जिसने पाल राजवंश की स्थापना की। गोपाल द्वारा बिहार प्रदेश पर विजय प्राप्त कर लेने पर उसके पुत्र धर्मपाल ने सम्भवतः पाटलिपुत्र को फिर से बसाया और अपनी राजधानी बनायी। देवपाल ने मुद्गगिरि या मुंगेर में अपनी राजधानी रखी। मगध की ऐतिहासिक गरिमा से प्रभावित होकर ही बंगाली पालवंशियों ने इसे अपना केन्द्र बनाया और यहीं से पाल साम्राज्यवादी नीति तथा पाल कला और संस्कृति की किरणे उत्तर–भारत में चमकीं। पाल साम्राज्य धर्मपाल और देवपाल के समय में पूर्व में आसाम और पश्चिम में कन्नौज तक फैल चुका। पर पाल राजाओं को बराबर त्रिपक्षीय संघर्ष में उलझा रहना पड़ा। भारतीय सार्वभौम सत्ता के प्राप्ति हेतु राष्ट्रकूटों, गुर्जर–प्रतिहारों और पालों में कई पीढ़ियों तक संघर्ष होते रहे। कुछ

समय के लिए तो गुर्जर–प्रतिहारों ने बिहार और उत्तर–बंगाल पर भी आक्रमण किया। पाल–युग में राजनीतिक उथल–पुथल के बावजूद पाल राजाओं के तीन सौ वर्ष तक के शासन में बिहार–बंगाल में कला का महत्वपूर्ण विकास होता रहा। राजनीतिक उतार–चढ़ाव के बावजूद इस युग में धर्म और कला के विकास में लोग संलग्न रहे। बेगूसराय जिले पर भी शासन था। यही कारण है कि यहाँ से अनेक पालकालीन प्रतिमाएँ उपलब्ध हुई हैं।[2]

वीरपुर से प्राप्त अधिकांश प्रतिमाएँ काले पत्थर की हैं। राजमहल और मुंगेर के खड़गपुर पहाड़ी में ऐसे काले पत्थर बहुतायत में मिलता है। मुंगेर जिले में सीता कोहवर में प्राचीन स्लेट पत्थर निकालने की खान का पता चला है, जिससे बहुत बड़े पैमाने पर (शायद पालयुग में ही) पत्थर निकाला गया था।[3]

वीरपुर ग्राम से प्राप्त निम्नलिखित प्रतिमाएँ हैं–

सूर्य प्रतिमा (भगवान स्थान)

वीरपुर ग्राम के हरिहरटोला मे भगवान स्थान पर काले पत्थर की सूर्य प्रतिमा है। यह खड़ी प्रतिमा है। इसकी लम्बाई नीचे से ऊपर (प्रभामंडल तक) *4′11 1/2* है बीच में सूर्य की प्रतिमा है। इसका स्टेला (प्रभावली) अधिक अलंकृत नहीं है और इसके ऊपर का भाग नुकीला है। इसका स्टेला प्रतिमा के समस्त शरीर से जुड़ा दिखाया गया है। प्रभावली से मूर्ति को पीठ की तरफ से जोड़ दी गयी है। इस कारण दर्शक की नजर मूर्ति की पीठ पर आसानी से नहीं पड़ती है। लगता है कलाकार ने मूर्ति की पीठ गढ़ने में सामने और बगल से मूर्ति पूरी और चौकोर कटी मालूम पड़ती है। ऐसे प्रभावली पालकालीन अन्य प्रतिमाओं[4] में दृष्टिगत होते हैं। विचाराधीन प्रतिमा के प्रभावली के ऊपरी भाग पर विद्याधर माला धारण किये हुए उड़ते दिखाये गये हैं।

यह बहुत ही आकर्षक मूर्ति है। यह विभिन्न आभूषणों से आभूषित है। इसके मस्तक पर लम्बा मुकुट, गले में हार, कमर में कमरधनी और हाथों में आभूषण दिखाए गये हैं। पाल कालीन प्रतिमाओं में आभूषण दिखाने के प्रमाण मिलते हैं। इस युग के कलाकारों ने बड़े चाव से प्रतिमाओं पर आभूषणों के अंकन किये है।[5]

सूर्य–प्रतिमा का गोलाकार चेहरा, कोमल और चिकने अंग और वक्षः स्थल चौड़ा दिखाया गया है। इसमें नारी–सुलभ कोमलता झलकती हैं इस युग में हिन्दू धर्म तथा बौद्ध धर्म पर तंत्रयान का प्रभाव था जिसमें शक्ति की प्रधानता थी। इस कारण बराबर ध्यान इस बात का रखा गया कि सभी मूर्तियाँ अत्यन्त आकर्षक और श्रृंगार–रस से पूर्ण हों। यही कारण है कि पालकालीन कला में पुरुष–मूर्तियों में भी नारी सुलभ कोमलता का अंकन किया गया था।

सूर्य–प्रतिमा का गोल चेहरा, लम्बे कान, नुकीला नाक तथा दोनों भौहों के बीच मे टीका दर्शनीय है। इस प्रतिमा के दोनों पैरों में लम्बे जूते दिखाये गये हैं। यह उल्लेखनीय है कि

प्रतिमाओं में उनके पैरों की अंगुलियों को दिखाने की परम्परा नहीं थी। उनके दो पैर या तो रथ में छिपे हैं या लम्बे जूते पहने प्रदर्शित किए गये हैं। उत्तर भारत की अधिकांश सूर्य मूर्तियों के पैर में घुटनों तक फीतेदार बूट हैं और कमर में अव्यड्.य पड़े हैं। यही वाराहमिहिर द्वारा उल्लखित 'उदीच्यवेश' है। ***भविष्यपुराण*** से ज्ञात होता है कि शक स्थान में विश्वकर्मा ने सूर्य की मूर्ति बनाई। सारा विश्व सूर्य के तेज को सहन करने में असमर्थ हो गया। अतः सूर्य के कहने पर विश्वकर्म्मा ने उनके शरीर के तीक्ष्ण तेज को कम करने के लिए खगद पर चढ़ाया, पर घुटने के नीचे का भाग छूट गया। उस भाग के तेज को मनुष्य की आँखें सहन नहीं कर सकती थीं, अतः लम्बा बूट पहनना पड़ा।[6] इस प्रकार सूर्य–मूर्ति की पूजा शक–स्थान से भारत आई, और संभवतः सर्वप्रथम यहाँ मेशी पुरोहितों ने ही इसकी पूजा–अर्चना आरम्भ की होगी। इसके संबंध में कुछ ठीक से नहीं कहा जा सकता है। यह भी कहा जाता है कि सूर्य उपासक ईरान से भारत आये। वे ही शाकदीपीय ब्राह्मण कहलाए।

भविष्यपुराण में भी इसी बात का उल्लेख है कि शक–स्थान से मेशी पुरोहित भारत बुलाये गये और उन्होंने सूर्य की पूजा के द्वारा कृष्ण के पुत्र 'साम्ब' को श्वेत कुष्ट से मुक्त किया। यह प्रतिमा सात अश्वों से युक्त रथ पर सवार प्रदर्शित की गई है। घोड़ों की उठती टापों और मुद्रा से अतिशय गति, स्फूर्ति और शक्ति की अभिव्यक्ति होती है। घोड़ों के लगाम थामे अरूण को दिखाया गया है। यह पैर से हीन है इसलिए इसके पैरों का अंकन नहीं किया गया है। सूर्य –प्रतिमा की दाहिनी ओर पिंगल की आकृति है जिसकी लम्वाई 1'3'' है। इसके एक हाथ में लेखनी तथा दूसरे में स्याही का पात्र है। यह आकृति भी आभूषणों से युक्त है जिसके चेहरे पर दाढ़ी प्रदर्शित की गई है। इसके बगल में सूर्य की पत्नी छाया का अंकन है, जिसकी लम्बाई एक फुट है। यह भी आभूषणों से आभूषित है और इसके एक हाथ में चँवर है। वहीं पर दूसरी ओर, हाथों में धनुष लिए उषा का अंकन है।

सूर्य के दोनों पैरों के पास महाश्वेता और बाई ओर दंडी का अंकन है। यह आकृति *1' 3 1/2''* लम्बी है। इसके बाएँ हाथ में दण्ड है और दाहिनी हाथ अभय मुद्रा में है। इसके पास ही संज्ञा देवी का भी अंकन है। इन सभी तथ्यों से यह प्रतीत होता है कि यह प्रतिमा उदीच्चवेश में है।

सूर्य प्रतिमा (बसहा स्थान)

वीरपुर के एक भाग में मईया–धीया पोखर के किनारे बसहास्थान में एक खपड़ैल मकान (वर्तमान में मंदिर– सं.) में सूर्य के काले पत्थर की प्रतिमा स्थापित है। इस प्रतिमा की प्राप्ति इसी पोखर से की गई थी। इस प्रतिमा की प्रभावली ऊपर से नुकीली है। इस प्रतिमा की कुल लम्बाई 3'6'' तथा चौड़ाई 2' फीट है। इसकी प्रभावली काफी अलंकृत है। इसके ऊपरी भाग में कीर्तिमुख

का अंकन है। सिंह के मुख से पुष्प माला निकलती प्रदर्शित की गई है। दोनों ओर एक –एक विद्याधर अपने हाथों में माला धारण कर उड़ते दिखाये गये हैं। प्रभावली पर मकर और घोड़े की आकृतियाँ उत्कीर्ण हैं। इन सभी के अंकन प्रभामंडल को सुसज्जित करने के लिए किये गये हैं।

सूर्य का गोल चेहरा तथा बिलासमय मुस्कान दर्शनीय है। इसके मस्तक पर मुकुट, ललाट पर टीका, गले में हार, वनमाला और कमर में कमरधनी का अंकन है। यह सूर्य–प्रतिमा दो भुजाओं वाली है। इसके दाहिने तथा बाएँ हाथों में एक–एक लम्बे नालवाले कमलपुष्प हैं। इसके कमर में लटकते कटार और पैरों में लम्बे जूते हैं। सूर्य – प्रतिमा के पैरों के पास विभिन्न आभूषणों से युक्त महाश्वेता है। सूर्य कमलपुष्प पर खड़े है। वहीं पर उनका सारथी अरूण बैठा है तथा कमल के नीचे सात घोड़े की आकृतियाँ अंकित है। इनमें तीन दाहिनी ओर और तीन बायीं ओर और एक घोड़ा बीच में बने वृत्त से निकलता हुआ दिखाया गया। इस प्रतिमा की दाहिनी ओर मस्तक पर मुकुट, गले में हार पहने, दाढ़ी– युक्त पिंगल की आकृति है। इनेक हाथों में लेखनी तथा दावात का अंकन है। पिंगल की बाई ओर विभिन्न आभूषणों से आभूषित एक नारी–प्रतिमा है जो अपने दाहिने हाथ में चंवर धारण की हुई है। पिंगल के पास दाहिनी ओर मुख किये दौड़ती हुई उषा की आकृति है, जिसके हाथों में धनुष–वाण है। मुख्य प्रतिमा की बाई ओर एक देवी का अंकन है जो संज्ञा हो सकती है। इसी देवी की ओर एक पुरूष की आकृति है जो दंडी है। इसके हाथों में दण्ड है। इसके पास ही प्रत्युषा धनुष धारण किये प्रदर्शित की गई है।

विष्णु प्रतिमा (वसहा स्थान)

वीरपुर के बसहा स्थान में ही एक विष्णु प्रतिमा स्थापित है। यह सूर्य प्रतिमा के बगल में ही है। कहा जाता है कि इसके निकट वाले पोखर से ही प्रतिमा की प्राप्ति हुई थी। इसकी प्राप्ति का सही समय ज्ञात नहीं है। यह प्रतिमा भी काले पत्थर की है और नीचे से ऊपर तक स्टेला 3′ लम्बी तथा 16″ चौड़ी है। लेकिन बीच में अंकित विष्णु प्रतिमा 23″ लम्बी है। यह स्थानक चतुर्भुजी प्रतिमा है। इसके पीछे के दाहिने हाथ में गदा, सामने का दाहिना हाथ अभयमुद्रा में, पीछे के बाएँ हाथ में चक्र तथा सामने के बाएँ हाथ में शंख है। इस प्रतिमा के मस्तक पर मुकुट, ललाट पर टीका, गले में हार, कमर में कमरघनी तथा पैरों में पाजेब हैं। प्रतिमा के कमर के नीचे रेखाओं से युक्त धोती है, लेकिन कमर के ऊपर के भाग में कोई परिधान नहीं है।

बसहा (बसहा स्थान)

बसहा स्थान से ही बसहा की प्रतिमा प्राप्त हुई है। जिसे सूर्य तथा विष्णु की प्रतिमाओं के पास ही स्थापित किया गया है। शिव के वाहन वृषभ की यह आकृति काले पत्थर की है। इसकी कुल लम्बाई 3′6″ तथा चौड़ाई 2′ है। यह उकडू बैठे वृषभ की प्रतिमा है। इसकी दो सीगें अच्छी

तरह से प्रदर्शित किये गये हैं तथा गले में लटकती घंटी भी भली प्रकार दिखायी गयी है। यह प्रतिमा अनेक आभूषणों से अलंकृत है। इसके कूबड़ को अच्छी तरह दिखाया गया है।

महिषासुरमर्दिनी (काली स्थान)

वीरपुर के काली स्थान से महिषासुरमर्दिनी की प्रतिमा प्राप्त हुई है। इसे एक वृक्ष के नीचे स्थापित किया गया है। यह भी काले पत्थर की प्रतिमा है। यह प्रतिमा उलटे कमल पुष्प पर प्रदर्शित की गई है। यह खंडित बहुभुजी प्रतिमा है। भैंसे के रूप में महिषासुर की आकृति भी अंकित है। इसका मस्तक धड़ से अलग दिखाया गया है।

अवलोकितेश्वर (भैरव स्थान)

वीरपुर के काली स्थान से महिषासुरमर्दिनी की प्रतिमा प्राप्त हुई है। इसे एक वृक्ष के नीचे स्थापित किया गया है। यह भी काले पत्थर की प्रतिमा है। यह प्रतिमा उलटे कमल पुष्प पर बैठी प्रदर्शित की गई है। इसका दाहिना पैर लटका हुआ है और बायाँ पैर कमलासन पर स्थित है। अवलोकितेश्वर के मस्तक पर मुकुट, कान में कर्णफूल, गले में हार, हाथ में भुजबंध और कंगन और कमर में कमरघनी है। इसका दाहिना हाथ वरद मुद्रा में तथा बायाँ हाथ कमल पुष्प से युक्त है। इस प्रतिमा की दाहिनी ओर एक बैठे हुए भक्त की आकृति का भी अंकन है।

चामुण्डा (भैरव स्थान)

इस स्थान के पास एक वृक्ष के नीचे काले पत्थर की चामुण्डा की प्रतिमा है। (वर्त्तमान में मंदिर में सथापित– सं) इसका मस्तक खंडित है। यह अष्टभुजी प्रतिमा है, जिसके चार दाहिने हाथ खंडित हैं, लेकिन चार बायें हाथों में तीन विद्यमान है और एक खंडित है। इसके सामने वाले बायें हाथ की अंगुलियाँ विस्मय मुद्रा में, दूसरे हाथ में खट्वांग तथा तीसरे हाथ में एक खंडित मस्तक का लम्बा केश है। यह प्रतिमा विभिन्न आभूषणों से आभूषित है। इसकी वक्षस्थल की पसलियाँ दिखाई पड़ रही हैं और पेट धँसा है। इसके वक्षस्थल पर एक वृश्चिक का अंकन है। यह देवी मुण्डमाल पहनी है। **मार्कण्डेय पुराण**[7] से ज्ञात होता है कि चण्ड और मुण्ड राक्षसों की हत्या करने से इन्हें चामुण्डा कहा गया है। वीरपुर के बगल के एक गाँव से चामुण्डा की तथा बरैपुर से रेवन्त की मूर्ति भी पाई गई हैं।

वीरपुर से पालकालीन काले पत्थर की अनेक प्रतिमाएँ मिली है। इससे इस स्थान पर पालों के आधिपत्य की पुष्टि होती है। दूसरी बात यह है कि यहाँ से सूर्य, विष्णु, बसहा, महिषासुरमर्दिनी, अर्धा, चामुण्डा, अवलोकितेश्वर की प्रतिमाएँ प्राप्त हुई हैं। अतः ये प्रतीत होता है कि यहाँ पाल काल में विभिन्न धार्मिक सम्प्रदायों के अनुयायी मिल–जुल कर रहते थे। हिन्दू तथा बौद्ध प्रतिमाओं की प्राप्तियाँ यह संकेत करती हैं कि इन दोनों सम्प्रदायों के बीच मनमुटाव नहीं था। इस क्षेत्र में बौद्ध प्रतिमाओं की प्राप्ति एक महत्वपूर्ण बात है। बेगूसराय जिले के राजवारा से

मारीचि और बलिया से बुद्ध प्रतिमाएँ मिली थी। संघौल के उत्खनन से तो अनेक पूजक स्तूप के अवशेष भी मिले हैं। इन प्राप्तियों से बेगूसराय जिले में पाल युग के दौरान बौद्ध धर्म क अस्तित्व का पता चलता है। लेकिन वीरपुर में हिन्दू तथा बौद्ध सम्प्रदायों की प्रतिमाओं की प्राप्ति बहुत महत्वपूर्ण है। यहाँ इस ओर संकेत करना आवश्यक है कि इस युग में कलाकारों ने प्रतिमा लक्षणों के आधार पर मूर्तियों का निर्माण किया। उन्हें कल्पना के आकाश में उड़ने की स्वतंत्रता नहीं थी, बल्कि वे प्रतिमाशास्त्र के नियमों से बंधे थे। जो भी प्रतिमाएँ इस युग में बनाई गई उनमें नारी सुलभ कोमलता का प्रदर्शन किया गया। सबसे महत्वपूर्ण तथ्य यह है कि कलाकारों ने प्रतिमाओं के शरीर पर अनेक प्रकार के आभूषणों को चित्रित करने का प्रयास किया है। कलाकारों में आभूषणों के प्रति इतना आग्रह था कि विरागी बुद्ध और बौद्ध प्रतिमाओं पर भी आभूषण प्रचूरता से दिखाये गये हैं।

संदर्भ सूची :

1. बी0 पी0 सिन्हा, भारतीय कला को बिहार की देन, पटना, 1958, पृ0 126.
2. राधा कृष्ण चौधरी, दी जायसवाल आकिर्योलोजिकल ऐण्ड हिस्टोरिकल सोसाइटी बुलेटिन संख्या 1, पृ0 11.
3. आर्क्योलाजिकल सर्वे ऑफ इण्डिया, ऐनुअल रिर्पोट, 1925–26, पृ0 152–153.
4. तुलनीय, बी0 पी0 सिन्हा, पूर्वोक्त, चित्र संख्या 89, 90, 91, 92, 93, 95, 96.
5. वही।
6. वृहत्संहिता, 59.
7. मार्कण्डेय पुराण, अध्याय 87, 25.

*पूर्व विभागाध्यक्ष,
प्रा0 भा0 इति0 एवं पुरातत्व विभाग
जी0 डी0 कॉलेज बेगूसराय

सौजन्य :
आर्ट एण्ड आर्कयोकॉंजी ऑफ मिथिला
मु. सं0–एस. के. सिन्हा, सं. अतुल कु. वर्मा एवं अन्य
पुरातत्व निदेशालय,
कला, संस्कृति एवं युवा विभाग, बिहार, पटना 2006

●●●

बेगूसराय के प्रमुख धरोहर–1

शैलेश कुमार सिन्हा*

श्री श्याम मंदिर, उलाव

श्री राधेश्याम मंदिर बेगूसराय जिले का एक अनूठा एवं विशिष्ट धरोहर है। यह मंदिर बेगूसराय जिला मुख्यालय से पश्चिम लगभग 3 कि.मी. की दूरी पर अवस्थित है। राष्ट्रीय उच्च पथ 31 से दक्षिण उलाव ग्राम में सड़क से सटे उत्तर दिशा में निर्मित भव्य प्रवेश द्वार से इस मंदिर को पहचाना जा सकता है।

श्रीमति श्यामकुमारी ने सन् 1857 ई0 में इस मंदिर का निर्माण करवाया था। मंदिर के पुजारी के अनुसार यह मंदिर लगभग तीन वर्षों में बनकर पूरा हुआ तथा इसमें लगभग नौ लाख रूपये व्यय किये गए। पूर्व में संभवतः इस मंदिर का नाम श्याम मंदिर था लेकिन बाद में यह राधेश्याम मंदिर के नाम से अभिज्ञात हुआ।

यह मंदिर परिकोटे के अंदर आयताकार आकृति में निर्मित है। इसका स्थापत्थ इंडो–रोमन कला से प्रभावित प्रतीत होता है।

इसकी अनुपम चित्रकारियाँ इसका महत्वपूर्ण सौन्दर्य पक्ष है। मंदिर के अंदर की दीवारें विभिन्न कथानक एवं सौन्दर्यपरक चित्रों से अलंकृत है। दीवारों पर निर्मित ये चित्र विभिन्न रंगों से बने हैं। इसकी चित्रकारी अत्यंत सूक्ष्म एवं संतुलित है, किन्तु सुरक्षा एवं संरक्षण के अभाव में इन महत्वपूर्ण चित्रों के आकर्षण में धीरे–धीरे कमी आती जा रही है तथा कुछ चित्र विनिष्ट होने की कगार पर है।

चित्रकारियाँ – श्याम मंदिर की चित्रकारियाँ तत्कालीन कला की अद्भुत मिसाल हैं। सुर्खी चूने से किये गए प्लास्टर के ऊपर सफेद पतला लेप लगा हुआ है जिस पर मंदिर के अंदर चतुर्दिक चित्रकारियाँ हैं। ये समस्त चित्रकारियाँ मंदिर के आंतरिक भागों में ही किये गए हैं। मंदिर की सभी दीवारें चित्रों से भरी पड़ी हैं। यह चित्रण दरवाजे के मेहराव तथा उसके ऊपर

के समस्त दीवारों पर बने हुए हैं। रामायण, महाभारत, स्वर्ग–नरक की घटनाएँ, ऋषि–मुनियों तत्कालीन परिस्थितियों का चित्रण, बेलबूटे फूल–पत्तियाँ तथा फलों के साथ–साथ ज्यामितिक आकृतियों के चित्रण भी अत्यंत बारीकी से उकेरे गए हैं। चित्रकारियों के साथ मिथिलाक्षर (उत्तरी शैली) का प्रयोग ऐतिहासिक तथ्यों को और भी स्पष्ट करता है।

इस मंदिर के पूर्वी दीवार के ऊपर रामकथा से संबंधित घटनाओं का चित्रण किया गया है जबकि पश्चिमी दीवारों पर कृष्ण–लीलाओं की सुन्दर अभिव्यक्ति है। पूर्वी दीवार के प्रमुख चित्रण में शंकर, ब्रह्मा, इन्द्र व नारद, विश्वामित्र के साथ राम–लक्ष्मण का प्रस्थान, यज्ञ करते विश्वामित्र, श्री राम द्वारा तारकासुर बध, अहिल्या उद्धार, विभिन्न आकृतियों की छोटी–बड़ी नौकाएँ/विमान, राम–लक्ष्मण तथा सहेली के साथ जानकी फुलवाड़ी मे,ं जनकपुर के विभिन्न विमानों का प्रदर्शन, जनकनंदिनी द्वारा वरमाला प्रदान किया जाना, परशुराम विवाद, विवाह विधान में भाग लेने वाले विभिन्न कर्मचारी एवं कर्मी तथा राजतिलक का चित्रण अत्यंत आकर्षित करने वाला है।

पश्चिमी दिशा में कृष्ण की विभिन्न लीलाओं को अत्यंत रोचक ढ़ंग से प्रस्तुत किया गया है। मंडप में भी विभिन्न प्रकार की आकृतियाँ चित्रित हैं। इनमें समुद्र मंथन जिसमें राक्षस के लिए "**राछत**" शब्द की उपयोग किया गया है। राजा के विवरण के रूप में अंकित अभिलेख '**रो कु राजा जनक पुरनेवासी**' तथा '**अलख राजा तपकना**' अंकित है। इसके अतिरिक्त कमला नदी, भागीरथ–प्रयास, विभिन्न लोकों–इन्द्रलोक, कैलाश तथा दुर्वाशा ऋषि का अत्यंत प्रभावकारी चित्रण किया गया है। स्तम्भों के मेहराब में अनेक फूल–पत्तियाँ एवं फलों का चित्रण है। फलों को अत्यंत जीवंत एवं आकर्षक रूपों में प्रदर्शित किया गया है। फलों में अंगूर, पपीता, खीरा, अमरूद, नारंगी आम, तरबूज, अनानास आदि उल्लेखनीय है।

मंडप के प्रवेशद्वार के ऊपर बाईं ओर कमला माता एवं दाहिनी ओर महिषासुर मर्दिनी का ओजपूर्ण चित्रांकन है।

मुख्य मंदिर के प्रवेश द्वार के अन्दर विष्णु के विभिन्न अवतारों का अत्यंत आकर्षक विवरण है। इनमें मत्स्य, कच्छप, बराह, नरसिंह, वावन, परशुराम उल्लेखनीय है। प्रवेशद्वार के दाहिनी दरवाजे के ऊपर गंगा–यमुना की आकृतियाँ 'आर्य मंदिर शैली' के अनुरूप चित्रित है।

इस तरह श्री राधेश्याम मंदिर स्थापत्य की भिन्न शैली तथा अनुपम चित्रकारियों की दृष्टि से इस क्षेत्र के साथ–साथ बिहार प्रांत की अमूल्य निधि है। इसकी सुरक्षा एवं संरक्षण हम सबों की जिम्मेदारी है।

राधेश्याम मंदिर की वास्तु संरचना :– मंदिर का तोरण द्वार उत्तरी दिशा में (वर्तमान) उलाव के मुख्य सड़क से सटा हुआ है। तोरणद्वार काष्ठ निर्मित विशाल किवाड़युक्त है। इसकी चौड़ाई 11 फीट तथा ऊँचाई लगभग 12 फीट है। तोरणद्वार के ऊपर गुम्बदयुक्त छत निर्मित है जो पूरब एवं पश्चिम में सलग्नित कमरों से जुड़ा हुआ है। इसकी चौड़ाई लगभग 25 फीट है।

तोरणद्वार में प्रवेश करने के बाद द्वार के दोनों ओर दो मूर्तियाँ स्थापित हैं, जिनकी मुखाकृति अंदर की ओर मंदिर की दिशा में है। बाईं ओर गरूड़ की आकृति है तथा दाहिनी ओर हनुमान की आकृति बनी हुई है। प्रवेशद्वार के बाद एक विस्तृत एवं खुला प्रांगन है। लगभग 90 फीट लम्बे एवं 90 फीट चौड़े प्रांगन के बाद मुख्य मंदिर निर्मित है।

राधेश्याम मंदिर की आधार पीठिका 90 फीट **X** 55 फीट है जिस पर संपूर्ण मंदिर की संरचना है। इसमें 20 फीट **X** 28 फीट का एक गर्भगृह तथा 28 फीट **X** 28 फीट का एक बारह स्तंभों पर आधारित आकर्षक मंडप निर्मित है। इनके स्तम्भ बारह पहले हैं। ये छोटे–छोटे कई स्तम्भों के समूह प्रतीत होते हैं। गर्भगृह तथा मंडप तीन दिशाओं पूरब, पश्चिम तथा उत्तर में 11 फीट 6 ईंच चौड़े बरामदे से घिरा है। गर्भगृह एवं मंडप के मध्य बारह फीट चौड़ा स्थान है जो संभवतः पूजा आराधना अथवा प्रदक्षिणापथ के रूप में प्रयुक्त होता होगा। गर्भगृह के पीछे दक्षिण दिशा में 3 फीट का एक गलियारा या प्रदक्षिणापथ है। गलियारे के दक्षिण सटे हुए तीन कोठरियाँ निर्मित हैं।

मंदिर के पूर्वी एवं पश्चिम दिशाओं में 10–10 दरबाजे बने हैं। जबकि मुख्य प्रवेश द्वार जो उत्तर दिशा में है तीन दरवाजे एवं दो झरोखे से युक्त है। मंदिर की तीन दिशाओं में अलग–अलग सीढ़ियाँ बनी हुई हैं।

यह मंदिर दो मंजिला है। चारों दिशाओं में मध्य को छोड़कर दो तल्ले भवन निर्मित हैं ऊपर की भवन नीचे की ही अनुकृति प्रतीत होती है।

समग्रता से यह मंदिर प्रासाद एवं मंदिर का सम्मिश्रण है।

अंकुरीनाथ महादेव पंचमंदिर, उलाव

यह मंदिर बेगूसराय जिला मुख्यालय से पश्चिम लगभग 3 कि0 मी0 की दूरी पर राष्ट्रीय उच्च पथ 31 से दक्षिण में उलाव ग्राम में अवस्थित है। यह श्याम मंदिर के पश्चिम में कुछ ही दूरी पर है।

यह मंदिर अंकुरीनाथ महादेव पंचमंदिर के नाम से भी स्थानीय लोगों में ज्ञात है। स्थानीय लोगों की ऐसी मान्यता है कि यहाँ के शिवलिंग भूमि से स्वयं प्रकट हुए हैं इसलिए इन्हें अंकुरीनाथ के नाम से पुकारा जाता है। इसके निर्माता के संबंध में स्थानीय लोग एकमत नहीं हैं।

वर्तमान में यह पंचायतन मंदिर का स्वरूप लिए हुए है। यह मंदिर चारो ओर घिरा हुआ है। इसका मुख्यद्वार पश्चिम दिशा में है। इसको दक्षिणी और उत्तरी दीवार 26 मी0 लम्बा तथा पूर्वी और पश्चिमी दीवार लगभग 30 मी0 लम्बा है। इसके चारो दिशाओं में बरामदा है तथा प्रत्येक कोने में मंदिर स्थापित है। गर्भगृह (मुख्य मंदिर) प्रांगण के मध्य में निर्मित है। मुख्य मंदिर पाषाण निर्मित है जबकि शेष चारो मंदिर मिट्टी के ईंटों से बने हुए हैं। मंदिर स्थापत्य की दृष्टि से ये दोनों भिन्न–भिन्न कालों में निर्मित प्रतीत होते हैं। मुख्य मंदिर उत्तर मध्यकालीन है, जबकि शेष मंदिर बाद के कालों में बने हुए दृष्टिगोचर होते हैं।

गर्भगृह या मुख्य मंदिर स्थापत्य की दृष्टि से अत्यंत आकर्षक हैं। इसके शिखर अलंकरण से परिपूर्ण हैं। पाषाण खंडों पर उकेरी गई आकृतियाँ परिपक्व शिल्पियों की देन है। मुख्य मंदिर का आधार आयताकार है। यह 5 मीटर X 2मी0 60से0मी0 की है। गर्भगृह वर्गाकार है। इसकी बाहरी दीवार 2 मी0 60 से0मी0 X 2 मी0 60 से0मी0 की है। गर्भगृह की आंतरिक माप 1 मी0 90 सेमी है। इसके मध्य में खण्डित शिवलिंग स्थापित है। गर्भगृह के सामने खुला हुआ मण्डप है जो 2 मी0 50 से0मी0 X 2 मी0 50 से0मी0 की है। गर्भगृह का प्रवेशद्वार पश्चिम दिशा में है। मुख्यमंदिर का चबूतरा वर्तमान स्थल से 65 से0मी0 ऊँचा है। अनुमानतः यह मंदिर आधार से शिखर तक 10 मीटर के लगभग ऊँचा है। मंदिर के सामने निर्मित मंडप के छत चार पाषाण खंडों पर आधारित है। स्तम्भ के ऊपरी सिरे पर कमल की आकृति उत्कीर्ण की गई है। स्तम्भ के ऊपर छत से सटे हुए प्रत्येक स्तम्भ से बर्हिमुखी मनुष्याकृति है। यह आकृति अपने मुख पर ऊँगली रखे हुए है जो किसी संकेत का प्रतीक है। दो स्तम्भों के मध्य मेहराब बने हुए हैं जिस पर विभिन्न प्रकार की फूल–पत्तियाँ उत्कीर्ण है। मंडप के छत के ऊपर चार पहलों में कार्निस बने हुए हैं तथा इसके ऊपर जालीनुमा रेलिंग बनाई गई है। इसके शिखर आर्य शैली के हैं तथा मुख्य शिखर की चारों दिशाओं में दो–दो उरूश्रृंग बने हुए हैं।

गर्भगृह के मुख्य द्वार के ऊपर ललाट बिन्दु पर गणेश की आकृति उत्कीर्ण है। ऐसा प्रतीत होता है कि इस मंदिर के गर्भगृह में स्थापित शिवलिंग तथा अन्य मंदिरों में स्थापित काले रंग की मूर्तियों को, जो पालकालीन हैं एवं इस क्षेत्र में प्रायः मिलती हैं, स्थानीय लोगों ने लाकर यहाँ स्थापित किया है। यह तथ्य इस बात से भी स्पष्ट होता है कि इस पंचमंदिर के दक्षिण–पूर्वी कोण के मंदिर में स्थापित सूर्य सफेद पत्थर के हैं जबकि पश्चिमी कोण की प्रतिमा काले पत्थर की है। उत्तर–पूर्वी कोण पर स्थापित शिव पार्वती सफेद तथा उसके निकट स्थापित बसहा काले पत्थर की है। इसके निकट काले पत्थर की कई भग्न प्रतिमाएँ भी है। उत्तर पूर्वी कोण में सफेद पत्थर के गणेश स्थापित हैं। मंदिर की चारो दिशाओं में निर्मित बरामदे की चौड़ाई 3 मी0 20 से0मी0 है तथा प्रत्येक कोण पर निर्मित मंदिर के अंदर का माप 3 मी0 10 से0मी0 X 3 मी0 10 से0मी0 वर्गाकार है। इस तरह उत्तर मध्यकालीन यह मुख्य मंदिर कलात्मक दृष्टि से अत्यन्त उत्कृष्ट धरोहर है।

हरसाई स्तूप

हरसाई स्तूप समूह बेगूसराय मुख्यालय से लगभग 20 कि0मी0 दूर मंझौल अनुमंडल के अंतर्गत विश्व प्रसिद्ध पक्षी बिहार एवं ऐतिहासिक जयमंगलागढ़ के उत्तर पूर्व में हरसाई गाँव में अवस्थित है। यह मंझौल गढ़पुरा रोड से लगभग 1/2 कि0मी0 पश्चिम में है।

यहाँ चार स्तूपों का एक समूह है जो स्थापत्य की दृष्टि से बिहार में प्राप्त अन्य स्तूपों से पूर्णतः पृथक है। इनमें एक मुख्य स्तूप है जो तीन स्तूपों के मध्य अवस्थित है एवं सबसे बड़ा है।

एक स्तूप पश्चिम में दूसरा दक्षिण में तथा तीसरा उत्तर में निर्मित है। ये स्तूप लगभग समानदूरी पर निर्मित हैं। 2003 में मेरे सर्वेक्षण (दल) के क्रम में इसे उद्‌घाटित किया जा सका। पूर्व में इसके दो स्तूप ''दैत्य का छीट्टा''' नाम से अभिज्ञात था। यह स्तूप समूह मिट्टी से निर्मित है तथा स्तरीकृत है। अवशेष को देखने से ऐसा लगता है कि यह स्तूप त्रिस्तरीय है तथा इसका बाहरी आवरण वज्रलेपित है। सिंहली अनुश्रुति 'महावंश' जो ईसा पूर्व प्रथम और द्वितीय शताब्दी की रचना मानी जाती है, में भी स्तूपों पर सुरखी चूना के लेप का विवरण आया है। इस दृष्टि से यह स्तूप केसरिया स्तूप से प्राचीन तथा अधिक महत्वपूर्ण प्रतीत होता है।

इसके मुख्य स्तूप की ऊँचाई 65 फीट तथा चौड़ाई 360 फीट है। यह हीनयानी स्तूप इस क्षेत्र की एक महत्वपूर्ण ऐतिहासिक उपलब्धि है। पाली साहित्य में भगवान बुद्ध के अंगुत्तराप भ्रमण का उल्लेख मिलता है। भगवान बुद्ध का यह प्रिय चारिका स्थल रहा है। 'मज्झिम निकाय' की अठ्‌कथा में इसे अंगजनपद के सटे गंगा नदी के उत्तर आप अर्थात पानी वाला भाग को अंगुत्तराप कहा गया है। (मज्झिम निकाय – अठ्‌कथा 2, 1, 4) इस दृष्टि से इस स्तूप की महत्ता और भी बढ़ जाती है। बौद्ध काल में जयमंगलगढ़ में महाविहार होने के संकेत मिलते हैं। जयमंगलगढ़ के निकट होने के कारण इस पूजन स्थल का सीधा संबंध महाविहार से स्थापित होता है। ध्यातव्य है कि हरसाई गांव के पूर्वी भाग में सड़क से सटे भू–भाग से खेती के क्रम में भवनों के भग्नावशेष मिलते रहे हैं। अतः यहाँ भी बौद्ध विहार होने की संभावना से इन्कार नहीं किया जा सकता। इस तरह जयमंगलागढ़ के पूर्वोत्तर दिशा में अवस्थित हरसाईं ग्राम अथवा गढ़ में यदि बौद्ध विहार के अवशेष प्राप्त होते हैं तो प्राचीन बौद्ध, पाली साहित्य मज्झिम निकाय, महावग्ग और सूतनिपात अठ्‌कथा में वर्णित अंगुत्तराप जनपद और उसमें गौतम बुद्ध का 1250 अनुयायिओं के साथ धर्म–प्रचार के लिए आने की कथ से संबद्ध होकर इन स्तूपों की महत्ता उजागर होती है।

अतः बौद्धकालीन इस स्मारक की महत्ता को दृष्टिगत कर इसके संरक्षण की तत्क्षण आवश्यकता है। यह इस क्षेत्र के साथ–साथ बिहार एवं भारत की अमूल्य धरोहर है, जिसे कुछ स्वार्थी तत्वों के द्वारा ध्वस्त किया जा रहा है। इसे अविलम्ब सुरक्षित एवं संरक्षित कर ही हम अपनी संस्कृति की इस अमूल्य विरासत को बचा पायेंगे और आनेवाली पीढ़ी को उसकी सांस्कृतिक सम्पदा सौंपकर अपने दायित्व का निर्वहन कर सकेंगे।

* विभागाध्यक्ष,
स्नातकोत्तर प्रा. भा. इतिहास संस्कृति एवं पुरातत्त्व
जी. डी. कॉलेज, बेगूसराय

सौजन्य :
धरोहर
(संस्कृति एवं पुरातत्त्व को समर्पित शोध पत्रिका)
प्रथम अक, 2007
बेगूसराय

बेगूसराय संग्रहालय

जितेन्द्र कारजी*

बेगूसराय जिला की प्राचीन महत्ता, पुरातात्विक एवं ऐतिहासिक सामग्री की बहुलता, कलाकृतियाँ तथा सांस्कृतिक सम्पदाओं की सुरक्षा, सवंर्द्धन एवं जनहित में उनके प्रदर्शन के उद्देश्य से वर्ष 1981 में बिहार सरकार ने जिला मुख्यालय में 'बेगूसराय संग्रहालय' नाम से संग्रहालय की स्थापना की।

संग्रहालय की स्थापना में तत्कालीन जिला पदाधिकारी श्री ए0 के0 रथ, डा0 पी0 गुप्ता, डा0 अखिलेश्वर कुमार, श्री शिवदानी सिंह आदि व्यक्तियों की महत्वपूर्ण भूमिका रही है।

संग्रहालय बेगूसराय बस स्टैण्ड तथा रेलवे स्टेशन से 1 कि0मी0 की दूरी पर पूर्वोत्तर रेलवे गुमटी के सामने स्थित है। इस संग्रहालय में बेगूसराय के विभिन्न प्राचीन ऐतिहासिक स्थलों से प्राप्त पुरातात्विक महत्व की सामग्री, कलाकृतियाँ, प्राचीन एवं अर्वाचीन सिक्के, प्रस्तर मूर्तियाँ, हस्तलिखित ग्रन्थ आदि भिन्न–भिन्न प्रकार की वस्तुएँ जनहित में संग्रहित और प्रदर्शित हैं।

मृणमूर्तियाँ :– मौर्यकाल से लेकर पालकाल तक पकी मिट्टी के बर्तनों के ढ़िकरे, भवन की ईंट, मानव, पशु–पक्षी की आकृति के खिलौने, चूड़ियाँ, मनके, मुहरें, गुलेल की गोलियाँ, गेन्दाकार गोले आदि इस संग्रहालय में विद्यमान हैं।

मुद्राएँ :– प्राचीन काल से आधुनिक काल तक के सिक्कों का एक बड़ा संग्रह इस संग्रहालय में है। पाँचवीं सदी ई0 पूर्व के भिन्न–भिन्न आकार एवं वजन के ताम्बे एवं चाँदी के आहत् (पंचमार्क) सिक्के, जिनके अग्रभाग पर सूर्य, शंख, स्वास्तिक, पशु, मानव, अर्द्धचन्द्र आदि तथा पृष्ठभाग पर कमल, नदी, मछली के चिह्न अंकित मिलते हैं, काफी मात्रा में संग्रहित हैं। इसके अतिरिक्त ताम्बे के ढ़ालुए सिक्के भी हैं जिनके अग्रभाग पर रेलिंग के अन्दर वृक्ष तथा पृष्ठ भाग पर हाथी के उपर महावत का अंकन है। इन चिन्हों का वास्तविक अर्थ या उद्देश्य क्या था यह कहना बड़ा कठिन है। संभवतः स्वर्णकारों की कोई संस्था रही होगी और संस्था के सभी

सदस्य सिक्कों पर अपना–अपना चिन्ह अंकित कर दिया करते थे। सिक्कों पर किसी राजा का नाम नहीं मिलता है।

पालकालीन चाँदी के छोटे–छोटे गोल सिक्के भी हैं जिनके अग्रभाग पर देवनागरी लिपि में **'श्री विग्रह'** अंकित है तथा पृष्ठ भाग पर यज्ञ वेदी। कर्णाट वंशीय राजा गोविन्द चन्द्र देव की स्वर्ण मुद्रा, 13 वीं, 14 वीं शताब्दी के मुसलमान राजाओं के फारसी लेख युक्त ताम्बे एवं चाँदी के गोल सिक्के, मुगल राजाओं के ताम्र एवं रजत सिक्के, देशी रियासतों, इस्ट इंडिया कम्पनी, ब्रिटिश इंडिया तथा स्वतंत्र भारत की विभिन्न मुद्राएँ इस संग्रहालय की बहुमूल्य निधियाँ है।

प्रस्तर मूर्तियाँ :– संग्रहालय में काले पत्थर से निर्मित पालकालीन बौद्ध, हिन्दू देवी–देवताओं की मूर्तियाँ संग्रहित हैं। हिन्दू मूर्तियों में मुख्य रूप से गणेश, दुर्गा, नन्दी, विष्णु, शिव, पिडडाल, सूर्य आदि की प्रधानता है।

वर्ष 1984 में जयमंगलागढ़ से प्राप्त तथा काला पत्थर से निर्मित एक नवग्रह पट्ट भी है। यह पालकालीन शिल्प का सुन्दर उदाहरण है। नवग्रह पट्ट की लम्बाई 1 मी0 4 से0मी0, चौड़ाई 43.5 से0मी0 तथा मोटाई 9 से0मी0 है। साधारणतया नवग्रह पट्ट पर ग्रहों की संख्या 9 होती है। परन्तु इस पट्ट की विशेषता है कि इस पर नवग्रह के अलावे प्रारम्भ में विध्ननाशक गणेश की मूर्ति बनी है। कुल दस मूर्तियां हैं। पट्ट के ऊपरी हिस्से पर फूल पत्तियों की सुन्दर नक्काशी है। सभी आकृतियाँ प्रभामंडल युक्त कमलासन पर खड़ी हैं। कमलासन के अग्रभाग पर ग्रहों के वाहनों की छोटी–छोटी सुन्दर आकृतियाँ बनी हैं जिनसे ग्रहों को पहचानना आसान है। सभी ग्रहों के प्रतीक चिन्ह उनके हाथों में है। यह पट्ट पूर्वी भारतीय कला शैली का अद्‌भुत उदाहरण है। मध्य भारतीय शैली में गणेश की मूर्ति अंत में पायी जाती है। ग्रह पट्ट बनाने की कला वास्तव में मथुरा शैली में गुप्त काल में प्रारम्भ हुई। पालकला शैली में यह पूर्ण विकसित रूप में दिखती है।

हस्तलिखित ग्रन्थ :– तालपत्र, भोजपत्र एवं वसहापत्रों पर मिथिलाक्षर तथा प्राचीन देवनागरी लिपि में हस्तलिखित विभिन्न प्रकार के धर्मग्रन्थों का सुन्दर संग्रह इस संग्रहालय में उपलब्ध है जो विद्वान एवं शोधकर्त्ताओं के लिए महत्वपूर्ण तथा उपयोगी सिद्ध हो सकता है।

संग्रहालय में प्रवेश निःशुल्क है।

संग्रहालय सोमवार (साप्ताहिक अवकाश) के अतिरिक्त प्रत्येक दिन 10 बजे प्रातः से 5 बजे संध्या तक खुला रहता है।

संग्रहालय की ओर लोगों को आकर्षित करने हेतु विभिन्न तरह के शैक्षणिक एवं सांस्कृतिक कार्यक्रम भी आयोजित किए जाते हैं।

संग्रहालय की ओर लोगों को आकर्षित करने हेतु विभिन्न तरह के शैक्षणिक एवं सांस्कृतिक कार्यक्रम भी आयोजित किए जाते हैं।

संग्रहालय बिहार सरकार के कला, संस्कृति एवं युवा विभाग के अन्तर्गत संग्रहालय निदेशालय के प्रशासनाधीन है।

*बेगूसराय संग्रहालय,
बेगूसराय

सौजन्य :
धरोहर प्रथम अंक – 2007
बेगूसराय

●●●

काशी प्रसाद जायसवाल पुरातात्विक संग्रहालय जी0डी0कॉलेज, बेगूसराय

अनिल कुमार*
कुंदन कुमार*

काशी प्रसाद जायसवाल पुरातात्विक संग्रहालय बिहार राज्य के बेगूसराय शहर में स्थित गणेशदत्त महाविद्यालय के प्राचीन भारतीय इतिहास एवं पुरातत्व विभाग का विभागीय संग्रहालय है। इस संग्रहालय की स्थापना बिहार के सपूत एवं प्रसिद्ध भारत विद् डा0 काशी प्रसाद जायसवाल के नाम पर की गई। इसकी स्थापना का मूल उद्वेश्य बेगूसराय तथा इसके आस–पास बिखरे सांस्कृतिक धरोहरों को संग्रहित और संरक्षित कर क्षेत्रीय इतिहास समृद्ध कर इतिहास को समग्रता प्रदान करना है।

के0 पी0 जायसवाल पुरातात्विक संग्रहालय का उद्‌घाटन तत्कालीन जिलाधिकारी मुंगेर, **श्री टी0 पी0 सिंह, आई0 सी0 एस0** के कर कमलों द्वारा **सितम्बर 1947 ई0** को सम्पन्न हुआ। संग्रहालय की स्थापना में **प्रो0 राधाकृष्ण चौधरी**, **श्री जी0 डी0 चक्रवर्ती**, तात्कालीन प्रधानाचार्य एवं **प्रो0 सच्चिदानंद सिंह** ने महत्वपूर्ण भूमिका निभाई।

इस संग्रहालय के पुरावशेष स्थानाभाव के कारण लम्बी अवधि तक प्रदर्शन का मोहताज रहे।, परिणामस्वरूप छात्र एवं आम दर्शक संग्रहालय से अपरिचित रहे। **सन 1999 ई0** का वर्ष इस संग्रहालय के लिए सौभाग्यशाली रहा जब प्राचीन भारतीय इतिहास के गवेषक **प्रो0 शैलेश कुमार सिन्हा** की नजर संग्रहालय के बिखरे पुरावशेषों पर पड़ी। प्रो0 सिन्हा के अथक प्रयास एवं परिकल्पना, **प्रो0 फुलेश्वर सिंह**, तत्कालीन विभागाध्यक्ष के नेतृत्व एवं **डा0 एन0 एन0 सिन्हा**, तत्कालीन प्रधानाचार्य के सहयोग ने महान इतिहासकार प्रो0 राधाकृष्ण चौधरी के अभूतपूर्व योगदान एवं त्याग को नमन् करते हुए उनकी स्मृति में प्रो0 राधाकृष्ण चौधरी मेमोरियल

हाल (पूर्व प्रधानाचार्य कक्ष) में दिनांक 27 मार्च 2000 को संग्रहालय को पुर्नस्थापित किया। इसका उद्घाटन तत्कालीन कुलपति ल0 ना0 मि0 वि0 दरभंगा, **डा0 हरिहर भक्त** के कर कमलों द्वारा सम्पन्न हुआ। फलतः के0 पी0 जायसवाल पुरातात्विक संग्रहालय को स्वतंत्र अस्तित्व, नाम एवं दर्शनीय स्वरूप प्राप्त हुआ। इस संग्रहालय को शैक्षणिक एवं पर्यटन की दृष्टि से बिहार राज्य के एकमात्र महाविद्यालय स्तरीय संग्रहालय होने का गौरव प्राप्त है। आज यह शोधकर्त्ताओं, विद्वानों एवं छात्रों के आकर्षण का केन्द्र है।

इस संग्रहालय में संग्रहित पुरावशेष नौलागढ़, जयमंगलागढ़, वीरपुर, बरैपुरा, मसुरियाडीह, सिंघौल, बरौनी के अतिरिक्त अंतिचक (भागलपुर) एवं कुछ निकटवर्त्ती स्थानों के हैं।

अंगुत्तराप' नाम से प्राचीन भारत में ज्ञात बेगूसराय जिला बुद्धकाल से आज तक के क्रमिक इतिहास का साक्षी है। इस संग्रहालय में संरक्षित एवं प्रदर्शित विभिन्न कालों (मौर्य, कुषाण, गुप्त, पाल एवं मुसलमान) की मूर्तियाँ, अभिलेख युक्त मुहरें, सिक्के, मनके आदि इसके प्रमाण हैं। इस संग्रहालय में संग्रहित अधिकांश कलाकृतियाँ '**तुलस्यायन**' परिवार की ओर से प्रो0 (स्व0) राधाकृष्ण चौधरी को प्रदान की गई थी। इस संग्रहालय को गौरवशाली एवं समृद्ध बनाने में '**डा0 पीयूष गुप्ता**, **डा0 ए0 कुमार** एवं अन्य विद्वतजनों की महत्वपूर्ण भूमिका रही है। दानकर्त्ताओं, छात्रों के साथ–साथ जनसहयोग ने भी इस संग्रहालय को समृद्ध एवं दर्शनीय बनाने में महत्वपूर्ण भूमिका अदा की है। संग्रहालय के माध्यम से समय–समय पर बुलेटिन एवं पत्रिकाएँ प्रकाशित होती रहती हैं जो इसकी जीवंतता एवं शैक्षणिक स्तर को उजागर करती है।

संग्रहालय के संग्रह एवं कलाकृतियाँ बेगूसराय आने वाले विद्वानों एवं कलाप्रेमियों को आकर्षित करती रही है। यहाँ पाषाण की छोटी–बड़ी लगभग 40 मूर्तियाँ, लगभग 85 मृण्मूर्तियाँ, लगभग 30 मिट्टी की मुहरें, मनके, सिक्के, बटखरे, पाषाण उपकरण, जीवाश्म, बहुमूल्य मोतियाँ, मृदभांड, अभिलेख एवं अन्य सामग्रियाँ प्रदर्शित हैं।

संग्रहालय के प्रमुख पाषाण मूर्तियों में सूर्य, बुद्ध, शिव, विष्णु (पद), कार्तिकेय, बौद्धदेवी, पूजक स्तूप, द्वारपाल, नर एवं नारी प्रतिमाएँ प्रमुख हैं। इनमें नौलागढ़, वीरपुर, बरैपुरा, सिंघौल, रजौड़ा और जयमंगलागढ़ से प्राप्त काले पत्थर की पालकालीन मूर्तियाँ उल्लेखनीय हैं। पूर्वी भारतीय मध्यकालीन स्थापत्य कला के चरमोत्कर्ष का परिचायक पालकालीन सूर्य प्रतिमा संग्रहालय की अमूल्य निधि है। संग्रहालय के नवीनतम् संग्रहों में सिंघौल से प्राप्त बुद्ध की काले पत्थर की पालकालीन प्रतिमा महत्वपूर्ण संग्रह है।

मौर्य एवं शुंगकालीन (ई0 पू0 320 से 180 ई0 पू0) मृण्मूर्तियाँ भारतीय कला के सौन्दर्य का अनुपम उदाहरण है। साँचे में ढ़ालकर मृण्मूर्त्तियों का निर्माण कुषाणों से लेकर गुप्तों तक व्यापक रूप से प्रचलित रहा। ये आग पर पकाकर बनाई गई हैं। ये मूर्तियां अपने–अपने कालों के

विभिन्न शैलियों को प्रदर्शित करती हैं। मृदभाड़ों में रक्तकृष्ण, उत्तरी कृष्णमार्जित, धूसर मृदभांड, काले मृदभांड, मुस्लिम पात्र आदि प्रदर्शित है। संग्रहित मिट्टी की मुहरों पर कई चित्र एवं लेख उत्कीर्ण हैं। ये अधिकांश पालकालीन हैं।

संग्रहालय में पंचमार्क एवं मुसलमान काल के बहुमूल्य सिक्के भी प्रदर्शित हैं। काष्ठशिल्प एवं धातुओं की विभिन्न सामग्रियाँ भी मौजूद हैं। धातु की सामग्रियों में वज्र, अष्टधातु से निर्मित चकिये आदि प्रमुख हैं। ये पत्थर, मिट्टी एवं बहुमूल्य रत्नों से निर्मित मनके, लकड़ी एवं अनाजों के जीवाश्म तथा हड्डी के औजार भी संग्रहित हैं।

बेगूसराय पुरातात्विक एवं सांस्कृतिक दृष्टिकोण से सम्पन्न है। लगातार हो रहे सर्वेक्षण एवं अन्वेषण से प्राप्त पुरावशेषों के संग्रहण के लिए के0 पी0 जायसवाल पुरातात्विक संग्रहालय के विस्तार की प्रबल संभावनाएँ हैं।

धरोहरों को सुरक्षित एवं संरक्षित रखने का यह एक महत्वपूर्ण केन्द्र है।

*शोधार्थी,
ल. ना. मि. विश्वविद्यालय
दरभंगा

सौजन्य :
धरोहर
प्रथम अंक, 2007

बेगूसराय के प्रमुख धरोहर–2

शैलेश कुमार सिन्हा *

बेगूसराय की धरती अपने गर्भ में हजारों वर्षों से विभिन्न सांस्कृतिक स्तरों को समेटे हुए है। यह हमारे गौरवपूर्ण ऐतिहासिक पृष्ठभूमि का प्रतिफलन है–इस क्षेत्र की सामाजिक एवं सांस्कृतिक समरसता का सुदृढ़ आधार। किन्तु विरासत के प्रति हमारी अनभिज्ञता तथा सांस्कृतिक मूल्यों में ह्रास ने हमारे गौरवशाली अतीत को विस्मृत कर दिया है। इतिहास भविष्य का आईना है। इसे सहेजकर आने वाले कल को थाती के रूप में प्रदान कर ही हम अपने बिखरे हुए अस्तित्व को बचा सकते हैं तथा कल के स्वर्णिम भविष्य की कल्पना कर सकते हैं।

हमारे विशाल देश में क्षेत्र विशेष की अपनी भौगोलिक संस्कृति है। सत्ता के विकेन्द्रीकरण के साथ सल्तनत काल में अनेक क्षेत्रीय राज्यों की स्थापना हुई। क्षेत्र विशेष की अपनी भौगोलिक संस्कृति तथा क्षेत्रीय शासकों के प्रोत्साहन से स्थापत्य की क्षेत्रीय शैलियों का प्रादुर्भाव एवं विकास हुआ। मध्यकालीन सांस्कृतिक संरचना का ललित रूप उसका सर्वाधिक महत्वपूर्ण अंग है। इस काल में ललित कला विविध रूपों में प्रकट हुई। इनमें वास्तुकला प्रमुख है।

हमारी वास्तुकला परम्परा अति श्रेष्ठ थी पर इस्लाम की आवश्यकताओं के अनुरूप न थी। इस्लाम के अनुयायी जब भारत आये, अपने साथ मिश्रित कला परम्परा भी साथ लाये। इस क्षेत्र में मुसलमान किसी एक स्थान से नहीं अपितु भिन्न–भिन्न क्षेत्रों से आये। विविध विदेशी शैलियाँ इनके साथ इस देश में आई। ये शैलियाँ उनकी परम्परा एवं आवश्यकता के अनुरूप थीं। उन्हें मस्जिद, मीनार, मकबरा, गुम्बद, दुर्ग, महल और विशाल द्वारों की आवश्यकता थी। इस्लामी वास्तु परम्परा को मेहराबी परम्परा कहा जा सकता है। यह मेहराबी परम्परा समस्त इस्लामी वास्तु में देखी जा सकती है। इस्लाम की सादगी सर्वविज्ञ है। इस्लामी वास्तु तकनीकी परम्परा परिस्थितियों से प्रभावित थी।

भारत में तुर्को के आगमन पर जहाँ विध्वंस पर वास्तु निर्माण हुआ, वहीं धीरे–धीरे नवनिर्माण भी हुआ। इस समन्वित वास्तु शैली के प्रादुर्भाव में पर्याप्त समय लगा।

मध्यकाल में विविध प्रकार के स्थापत्यों का निर्माण हुआ। सामान्यतः यह निर्माण शासकीय प्रश्रय एवं पोषण में हुआ। अफगान और मुगल शासकों के समय में पूर्ण समन्वयपरक स्थापत्यों का निर्माण हुआ। ऐसे मुस्लिम स्थापत्य में बिहार के सासाराम में स्थित शेरशाह का मकबरा उल्लेखनीय है। मुस्लिम सत्ता के विकेन्द्रीकरण के साथ क्षेत्रीय मुस्लिम सत्ता का प्रादुर्भाव हुआ। इसी के साथ जौनपुर, मालवा, गुजरात, कश्मीर, मुल्तान, बंगाल, बिहार, आसाम व दक्षिण आदि स्थलों में क्षेत्रीय मुस्लिम स्थापत्यों का निर्माण हुआ। इनमें क्षेत्रीय रंग उभरकर सामने आया।

मध्यकालीन बिहार के सांस्कृतिक विकास में सूफियों का योगदान अत्यंत महत्वपूर्ण है। तेरहवीं शताब्दी तक सूफीवाद के अंतर्गत चौदह शाखाएँ स्थापित हो गए। प्रत्येक सिलसिले के सूफियों ने अपनी परम्पराओं को सुरक्षित रखने का प्रयास किया। इन शाखाओं में नक्सबंदिया की स्थापना चौदहवीं शताब्दी में ख्वाजा बहाउद्दीन नक्सबंद ने की थी। इस शाखा के शिष्यों में शेख अहमद फारूख सरहिंदी प्रमुख हैं जो मुज्जद्दिद अर्थात इस्लाम धर्म के सुधारक के नाम से भी प्रख्यात हैं। इनका का जन्म सरहिन्द में 1563 ई0 में हुआ था। ये बहुत प्रतिभाशाली व्यक्तित्व के थे। उन्होंने अपने 'मक्तूबातों' (पत्रों) के द्वारा यह उपदेश दिया है कि संसार की सृष्टि ईश्वर ने की है इसकी तुलना उसके प्राणियों से नहीं की जा सकती। मुज्जदिद ने वजुदिया एवं सुहूदिया विचारधाराओं का समन्वय किया। शेख अहमद सरहिंदी का 63 वर्ष की आयु में (1625 ई0) स्वर्गवास हो गया। उन्होंने इस्लाम के उद्देश्यों को व्यावहारिक रूप प्रदान किया तथा एक क्रमबद्ध धर्मप्रचार का कार्य प्रारंभ किया। शेख अहमद सरहिंदी ने ख्वाजा मासूम को अपना उत्तराधिकारी घोषित किया। बादशाह औरंगजेब इनके मुरीद थे। इस शाखा के प्रमुख सूफियों में शाह वलीउल्लाह भी एक थे। इनका जन्म औरंगजेब के शासनकाल में 1703 ई0 (1176 हिजरी) में हुई। इसी कड़ी के शेख सुल्तान लखमिनियाँ में आकर बस गये, ऐसी मान्यता है।

इन सूफियों का प्रभाव बेगूसराय के क्षेत्रीय इतिहास पर भी दृष्टिगोचर होता है। लखमिनियां क्षेत्र इसका ज्वलंत उदाहरण है।

बेगूसराय के सांस्कृतिक एवं धार्मिक इतिहास को प्रामाणिक एवं तथ्यपरक बनाने में यहाँ के स्मारकों का महत्वपूर्ण योगदान है। मस्जिद एवं मकबरा इस क्षेत्र के इस्लामिक संस्कृति को अभिज्ञात करने का एक महत्वपूर्ण स्त्रोत हैं। बेगूसराय क्षेत्र में लम्बी अवधि तक मुसलमानों का शासन रहने के कारण अनेक ऐतिहासिक मस्जिदों का निर्माण हुआ जो अपने काल के साक्ष्य हैं। ये उत्तर मुगलकालीन स्थापत्य का प्रतिनिधित्व करते हैं। इन मस्जिदों में बड़ी बलिया मस्जिद (ध्वंसावशेष), मस्जिदे सुल्तानियाँ, लखमिनियाँ, नूरपुर मस्जिद एवं सरायनूरनगर (मंसूरचक) उल्लेखनीय हैं।

बेगूसराय के प्रमुख मस्जिद

बड़ी बलिया मस्जिद एवं दरगाह

इस मस्जिद के ध्वंसावशेष एक विशाल टीले के उत्तर–पश्चिम दिशा में अवस्थित हैं। बेगूसराय जिला मुख्यालय से यह 16 कि0मी0 पूरब में अवस्थित है। वर्तमान टीला 1200 कट्ठा के परिक्षेत्र में विस्तृत है। प्राप्त पुरावशेषों से ज्ञात होता है कि यह स्थल मुसलमान काल से पूर्व भी आवासित था। 690 हिजरी में अलाउद्दीन खिलजी की सैनिक छावनी इस आवासित टीले के 5 कि0मी0 पूरब में लगी थी। शाह अलाउद्दीन बुखारी (900 हिजरी) के काल में यह टीला आवासित था।

बड़ी बलिया मस्जिद के आज से लगभग 500 वर्ष पूर्व निर्मित होने के प्रमाण मिलते हैं। यह मस्जिद लाल पत्थर तथा ईटों से निर्मित है। वर्तमान में इस मस्जिद के ध्वंसावशेष ही मिलते हैं। खण्डहर के रूप में मस्जिद की मुख्य कक्ष के अवशेष अपने स्थापत्य की खूबियों को आज भी प्रदर्शित कर रहे हैं। दुर्भाग्यवश इस मस्जिद को स्थानीय लोगों की अज्ञानता का शिकार होना पड़ा है। इस ऐतिहासिक स्मारक की उपेक्षा संस्कृति के प्रति जनमानस की उदासीनता का द्योतक है। (जबकि इसके बगल में एक नवीन विशाल मस्जिद का निर्माण किया गया है।) यहाँ पर कई महान हस्तियों के मजार भी निर्मित हैं। यह मस्जिद इस क्षेत्र का सर्वाधिक प्राचीन मस्जिद स्थापत्य का नमूना है। शाह अलाउद्दीन बुखारी (1451–1526 ई0), जो सूफी परम्परा के महान संत रहे हैं, यहाँ 1493 ई0 में पधारे, ऐसी मान्यता है। यहाँ प्रत्येक वर्ष उर्स का भी आयोजन किया जाता है। कहा जाता है कि गांधी जी यहाँ के दरगाह को देखने सन् 1915–16 ई0 में आये।

बड़ी बलिया मस्जिद के ध्वंसावशेष से उसकी प्राचीनता एवं कलात्मक अभिव्यक्ति के प्रमाण मिलते हैं। ईटों पर फूल–पत्तियों के उकेरे गए डिजाईन, जो छेनियों से काटकर बनाये गये प्रतीत होते हैं, तत्कालीन कला की उत्कृष्टता के द्योतक हैं। मस्जिद के प्रमुख भाग ईटों से की गई कारीगरी से आच्छादित है। ऐसा विश्वास है कि यह मस्जिद प्रसिद्ध निजामुद्दीन औलिया दरगाह मस्जिद की प्रतिकृति है।

कहा जाता है कि शाह अलाउद्दीन बुखारी जिनका जन्म 1451 में बुखारा में हुआ, का यहाँ 1493 में बड़ी वलिया में आगमन हुआ। इनके साथ पंडित उदत पांडे भी कन्नौज से यहाँ आए। इन दोनों के वंशज आज भी मस्जिद के निकट निवास कर रहे हैं। यह तत्कालीन सामाजिक समरसता का एक अनुकरणीय उदाहरण है। इनके वंशजों में सैयद शाह इफ्तेखारूल हक (जिनका जन्म लगभग 1920 में हुआ) तथा इनके छोटे भाई सैयद शाह फिरोजउल हक हैं। 'शो राफा की नगरी', जो क्यामुद्दीन कुरैशी के द्वारा लिखित तथा निजामी एकेडमी कराँची, पाकिस्तान से प्रकाशित है, में इस क्षेत्र के क्षेत्रीय इतिहास एवं वंशावलियों का विवरण मिलता है। (डा0 ज़फ़र

हबीब साहब एवं सैयद शाह फिरोजउल हक साहब के प्रति हम अपनी कृतज्ञता व्यक्त करते हैं जिन्होंने हमें महत्वपूर्ण जानकारियाँ दी।)

मस्जिदे–सुल्तानियाँ

यह मस्जिद बेगूसराय जिला मुख्यालय से 18 कि0मी0 पूर्व में अवस्थित है। यह $86^0 19'45''$ एवं $25^0 24'45''$पर अवस्थित है। यह मुगल शासक औरंगजेब का समकालीन है। कहा जाता है कि यह आज से लगभग 300 वर्ष पूर्व निर्मित हुआ। इस मस्जिद की स्थिति अच्छी है किन्तु इसका रखरखाव अपेक्षित है। मस्जिद का मीनार अष्टपहल है। यह फिरोज (गौड़) स्थापत्य की अभिव्यक्ति प्रतीत होती है। मीनार का शीर्ष चौपहल बीदर शैली का है। इस मस्जिद में प्रयुक्त ईंट (20 x 8 x 8) cm की है। Sanctury के सामने अवस्थित हॉल 20 मी0 X 5 मी0 है। इसका मेहराब 2 मी0 चौड़ा एवं 3 मी0 ऊँचा है। इसका Astle 3.6 मी0 चौड़ा है। इसका Nave 2.6 मीटर है। इसके मुख्य हाल में कुरान की आयत लिखी हुई थी जो दुर्भाग्यवश रंग रोगन से छुप गयी है। मस्जिद की दीवार 5 मीटर ऊँची है।

यह मस्जिद तीन गुम्बदों से युक्त है। इसके मध्य एवं मुख्य गुम्बद की परिधि 18.90 मीटर है जबकि मध्य के दोनों ओर की गुम्बदें 17.70 मीटर की परिधि के हैं।

इस मस्जिद की नींव के चारों ओर नदी से बचाव का प्रबंधन दिखाई पड़ता है। कहा जाता है कि गंगा इसके समीप बहती थी। वर्तमान में गंगा की धारा यहाँ से 8 कि0मी0 दूर चली गयी है।

इस मस्जिद के निर्माण के संबंध में स्थानीय लोगों में एक सौदागर की कहानी अत्यधिक प्रचलित है। इसके अनुसार घनश्याम नामक एक सौदागर ने इस मस्जिद का निर्माण करवाया। कहा जाता है कि घनश्याम व्यापार के सिलसिले में बलिया के निकट से गंगा से गुजर रहा था तो उसका जहाज गंगा की धार में फँस गया। अत्यधिक परिश्रम के बाद भी जब जहाज को संकट से नहीं उबारा जा सका तो अंततः यह सौदागर उत्तरी दिशा में अवस्थित एक टीले पर पहुँचा, जहाँ सूफी संत शेख सुल्तान से इसकी मुलाकात हुई। उनके आशीर्वाद एवं शुभकामना के फलस्वरूप वह अविलंब संकट से मुक्त हो गया। बाद में इस सौदागर ने अपनी कमाई का हिस्सा सूफी संत को भेंट करना चाहा लेकिन उन्होंने इसे लेने से इंकार किया और कहा कि उन्हें इसकी कोई आवश्यकता नहीं है। अंत में घनश्याम के अत्यधिक अनुरोध पर मस्जिद के निर्माण हेतु उसके धन को स्वीकार किया गया। फलतः घनश्याम के द्वारा उस धन से मस्जिद का निर्माण हुआ। परम्परा के अनुसार सूफी संत ने अपनी पुत्री का विवाह सौदागर से किया। घनश्याम ने इस्लाम धर्म स्वीकार कर लिया और वह घनश्याम अब्दुल्ला के नाम से जाना जाने लगा। मस्जिदें–सुल्तानियाँ इसी परम्परा का प्रतिफलन है।

नूरपुर मस्जिद

नूरपुर मस्जिद बेगूसराय जिला मुख्यालय से लगभग 12 कि0मी0 पश्चिम में अवस्थित है। यह अत्यंत आकर्षक, अनुपातिक एवं राजशाही है।

गंगा इस मस्जिद के निकट से बहती थी। ध्यातव्य है कि इस क्षेत्र का अधिकांश मस्जिद किसी–न–किसी नदी के किनारे अवस्थित है। यह तत्कालीन सामरिक, व्यापारिक एवं सांस्कृतिक परिस्थितियों के संकेतक है। गंगा नदी इस मस्जिद के निकट बहती थी तथा इसके निकटस्थ अवस्थित टीले पर मुगल सैन्य टुकड़ी निवास करती थी। इस टीले को मुगलिया डीह के नाम से भी जाना जाता है।

इस मस्जिद में 1213 हिजरी का एक लेख काले पत्थर पर उत्कीर्ण है, उसके अनुसार मीरन अली की आत्मा की शांति के लिए उनके मुलाजिम अजीजुल्लाह ने एक मजार एवं उसके निकट एक मस्जिद का निर्माण करवाया।

चूँकि मीरन अली अज़ीं आलम
रख़्त बर बस्त सूए दारि करार
बहरे ऊ खाक़सार अजीजुल्लाह
मसजिदी साखतई करीब मज़ार
साल तारीख ब शनो अज राज़ी
इ मुसल्ली ब्या नमाज़ गुज़ार (1213 हिजरी)

(पत्थर पर अंकित फारसी लेख के अनुवाद के लिए मो0 मरगुब तथा मो0 कसीमुल हक के प्रति हम अपनी कृतज्ञता अभिव्यक्त करते हैं।)

वहाँ के निवासी के पूर्वज मुल्तान से आकर बसे हैं। मुल्तान से आने वालों में शाह अबुल रहमान मुल्तानी के पुत्रों का नाम सिजरा (वंशावली) में अंकित है। ये चौदह पुश्त से यहाँ निवास कर रहे हैं। मुल्तान से आये शाह अबुल रहमान मुल्तानी के पुत्र निकट के अलग–अलग क्षेत्रों में बस गये। इनमें शाह आसिफ आसिफपुर गढ़हरा, शाहनुर–नुरपुर एवं शाह सलीम – सलीमपुर में बस गये। स्थानीय लोगों से इस क्षेत्र में बसे अलग–अलग नामों की चर्चा आती है – इस्लाम और सलीम। इसके बाद शाह बली का नाम भी उल्लखित हैं।इस मस्जिद का प्रवेश द्वार अतिविशिष्ट है। इस क्षेत्र के अन्य मस्जिदों की तुलना में इसके द्वार का निर्माण सुरक्षा को दृष्टिगत कर बनाया गया है। द्वार के दोनों ओर प्रहरी कक्ष की व्यवस्था है। अन्दर से बाहर के दृश्यों को देखा जा सकता है किन्तु बाहर से किसी भी आक्रमण से सुरक्षा का पुख्ता इंतजाम है। यह उस बात का परिचायक है कि यहाँ अति विशिष्ट व्यक्तियों या सम्राटों का आवागमन था और उन्हें सुरक्षा की आवश्यकता थी। ध्यातव्य है कि यहाँ निकट में मरकस का भी ठहराव था।

यह मस्जिद 20 मी0 चौड़ा एवं 11.65 मी0 ऊँचा है। इसके सामने का सहन 20 मी0 x 6 मी0 50 से0मी0 चौड़ा है। इसके तीन गुम्बद हैं। इसका मुख्य गुम्बद 18.58 मी0 एवं बगल वाले दोनों गुम्बद 17.50 की परिधि में है।

सराय नूरनगर का मस्जिद (मंसूरचक)

बेगूसराय जिला मुख्यालय से सरायनूरनगर लगभग 40 कि0मी0 की दूरी पर मंसूरचक प्रखंड में समसाघाट के निकट अवस्थित है। यहाँ बलान नदी के किनारे एक भव्य ऐतिहासिक सराय नूरनगर का शाही मस्जिद और ईदगाह निर्मित है। कहा जाता है कि नूरजहां ने इस भव्य मस्जिद का निर्माण करवाया। कहा जाता है कि नूरजहाँ ने बलान नदी में नौका बिहार भी किया था।

सरायनूर मस्जिद 40 मी0 लम्बा एवं 20 मी0 चौड़े चहारदीवारी में स्थित है। चहारदीवारी के चारो कोने पर अष्टपहल मीनार बने हुए हैं जिसकी परिधि 6.60 मी0 है। पूरब से सहन सहित मस्जिद लगभग 14 मी0 तथा उसके पीछे (पश्चिम में) अवस्थित ईदगाह 26 मी0 लम्बा है। सहन में प्रवेश के लिए 1.15 मी0 चौड़ा मुख्य द्वार है। चहारदीवारी से जुड़े आयताकार घेरे द्वारा मुख्यद्वार को अलग किया गया है जिसकी चौड़ाई 5.30 मीटर है।

मस्जिद में गलियारा या बरामदा निर्मित नहीं है। मस्जिद का निर्माण 2.20 मी0 ऊँचे आधारतल (प्लेटफार्म) पर किया गया है। मस्जिद के नीचे भूमितल में ठहरने के लिए उत्तरी दिशा में (नदी की ओर) कमरे बने हैं जिसका दरबाजा वर्तमान में बंद कर दिया गया है।

मुख्य मस्जिद 15.65 मी0 X 7.50 मी0 के आकार में निर्मित है। इसमें तीन प्रवेशद्वार हैं। मुख्य द्वार 1.85 मी0 ऊँचा एवं 1 मी0 चौड़ा है जबकि शेष दो द्वार 1.80 मी0 ऊँचा एवं 90 से0मी0 चौड़ा है। मस्जिद की दीवार 1.15 मी0 है। बीच के चार मीनार कम घेरे के हैं, जबकि शेष अष्ठपहल एवं नक्काशी युक्त है। मस्जिद में तीन गुम्बद एवं 8 मीनारें हैं। इसका गुम्बद 5.3 मी0 की परिधि में बना है। संपूर्ण मस्जिद की ऊँचाई लगभग 25 मी0 है। मस्जिद के ऊपर जाने के लिए दोनों ओर से सीढ़ियाँ बनाई गई हैं।

स्थानीय लोगों से प्राप्त जानकारी के अनुसार इस मस्जिद से संबंधित दस्तावेज मद्रास म्यूजियम में रखी हुई है।

(इस मस्जिद से संबंधित जानकारी के लिए हम स्थानीय लोगों के शुक्रगुजार है।)

* विभागाध्यक्ष,
स्नातकोत्तर प्रा. भा. इतिहास संस्कृति एवं पुरातत्व
जी.डी. कॉलेज, बेगूसराय

सौजन्य :
धरोहर
(संस्कृति एवं पुरातत्व को समर्पित शोध पत्रिका)
द्वितीय अंक – 2010, बेगूसराय

●●●

पुरातात्त्विक दृष्टि से बेगूसराय का महत्व

राधास्वामी*

क्षेत्र में अनेक स्थान पुरातात्विक महत्व के हैं। नौलागढ़ तथा जयमंगलागढ जैसे स्थानों से प्राप्त सामग्रियों के आधार पर बेगूसराय का इतिहास प्राचीन काल से लेकर आधुनिक काल तक अखंडित है। गंगा नदी के उत्तर में रहने के कारण बौद्ध साहित्य में इस क्षेत्र को 'अंगुत्तराप'[1] कहा जाता था। उत्तरी मुंगेर और उत्तरी भागलपुर का क्षेत्र अंगुत्तराप में सम्मिलित था। अंग की उत्तरी सीमा कौशिकी थी और पश्चिम में यह जनपद बेगूसराय में गंडक नदी तक फैला हुआ था। कमला और कोशी नदी के बीच का भाग अंगुत्तराप के नाम से अभिहित था। ''आपण'' इस जनपद का एक महत्वपूर्ण गांव था, जहां भगवान बुद्ध ने लगभग ने लगभग एक मास तक निवास किया था।

प्रो. राधाकृष्ण चौधरी[2] की यह धारणा है कि बेगूसराय का समस्त क्षेत्र मिथिला राज्य का एक भाग था। कमला नदी के बाद मिथिला राज्य की सीमा प्रारंभ हो जाती थी। कमला नदी के बाद के क्षेत्र में अंगुत्तराप और पुण्ड्वर्द्धन भुक्ति का क्षेत्र सम्मिलित था। अंगुत्तराप एक जनपद था। इस क्षेत्र में अनार्य संस्कृति की प्रधानता थी। अनार्यों को धर-जाति के राजपूतों ने अपदस्थ किया था। बेगूसराय के उत्तर-पूर्वी सीमा पर तथा सरौंजा और सहरसा जिले के सिंघेश्वर स्थान के निकट भर-शासन के अवशेष प्राप्त हुए हैं।

भर-राजपूत उत्तर प्रदेश और बिहार में पाये जाते हैं। भर द्रविड़ थे अथवा हिन्दू, यह प्रश्न विवादास्पद है। भर-जाति के संबंध में मेगास्थनीज के यात्रा विवरण में उन्हें उवरा के रूप में उल्लेखित किया गया। स्वर्गीय काशी प्रसाद जायसवाल के अनुसार भर राजपूत शिव के उपासक थे। शिव अनार्यों के भी देवता थे। अत: आर्यों के आगमन के पूर्व बिहार के प्रभुत्व से इंकार नहीं किया जा सकता है। भर-जाति के दुर्ग बेगूसराय में भी पाये गये हैं।

ई0 पू0 छठी शताब्दी मे बौद्ध धर्म का उत्थान हुआ और अंगुत्तराप बौद्ध धर्म का एक सबल केन्द्र बन गया। बेगूसराय जिले के जयमंगलागढ़ एवं नौलागढ़ से प्राप्त पुरातात्विक अवशेषों से यह स्पष्ट हो जाता है कि बेगूसराय का इतिहास बौद्ध काल से पीछे तक जाता है। जयमंगलागढ़ में कुछ

ढ़ले हुए ताम्बे के सिक्के मिले हैं जिससे यह स्पष्ट हो जाता है कि इस क्षेत्र का संबंध राज्य सत्ता के साथ था। मौर्यकाल में बेगूसराय मगध साम्राज्य का अंग बन गया तथा शुंगों के राजस्व काल तक यह स्थिति बनी रही।

नौलागढ़ एवं जयमंगलागढ़ का वर्तमान ध्वस्त गढ़ मौर्यकालीन दुर्ग पद्धति का सुन्दर प्रमाण उपस्थित करता है। नौलागढ़ बैंती नदी के किनारे अवस्थित है। यह तीन तरफ कृत्रिम जलकुल्या से घिरा हुआ था। कौटिल्य के अर्थशास्त्र में दुर्ग निर्माण की जो पद्धति दर्शायी गयी है, उसका स्पष्ट चित्र नौलागढ़ और जयमंगला में देखा जा सकता है। कृषि कार्य के सिलसिले में उत्खनन से प्राप्त चमकदार भाण्ड–खण्ड, भूरे भाण्ड, मनके और मृण मूर्तियां प्राप्त हुई है जो शुंगकालीन कला का उत्तम उदाहरण माना जाता है। गुप्तकाल के सिक्के और मृण–मूर्तियां भी नौलागढ़ और जयमंगलागढ़ से प्राप्त हुए हैं। एक मिट्टी की मुहर प्राप्त हुई है जिसके मुख भाग में एक त्रिशूल और पृष्ठ भाग में ''श्री समुद्र'' अंकित है।[3] श्री समुद्र ब्राह्मी लिपि में अंकित है। एक अन्य गुप्तकालीन मुद्र बेगूसराय के तेघड़ा क्षेत्र से प्राप्त हुआ, जिससे यह सिद्ध होता है कि गुप्त शासकों का एक क्षेत्र पर प्रभाव था। पालकालीन शासन के अन्तर्गत नौलागढ़ प्रशासनिक इकाई था। इसकी पुष्टि नौलागढ़ से प्राप्त अभिलेख संख्या 1 और 2 से भी होती है।[4] नौलागढ़ प्रशासन के अतिरिक्त एक महत्वपूर्ण सांस्कृतिक केन्द्र भी था। नौलागढ़ से प्राप्त ऐतिहासिक सामग्रियों से इस बात की जानकारी मिलती है कि ''इस क्षेत्र मे अनेक बौद्ध विहार थे। इन बौद्ध विहारों से चीनी यात्रियों का आवागमन होता रहता था। पाल शासक शिक्षा और संस्कृति के संरक्षक थे। उनके द्वारा अनेक मठों की स्थापना की गई थी। गंगा नदी के उत्तरी तट पर पुष्पहार या फुलहार नामक बौद्ध विहार का उल्लेख मिला है।

कला की दृष्टि से नौलागढ़ और जयमंगलागढ़ बहुत प्रसिद्ध माने गये हैं। बीहट, रजौड़ा, बरौनी, सिंघौल आदि स्थानों से कई महत्वपूर्ण मूर्तियां मिली है, जो स्थापत्य काल की दृष्टि से अद्वितीय मानी जाती है। उदाहरण के लिए बरौनी से प्राप्त सूर्य मूर्ति स्थापत्य काल की एक अन्यतम कृति है। मूर्ति में ईरानी और भारतीय विचारों का सम्मिश्रण दिखाई पड़ती है। मूर्ति का काल ईसा के छठी या आठवीं शताब्दी के बीच का रखा जा सकता है। नौलागढ़ से प्राप्त एक भग्न–मूर्ति पालकालीन कला का श्रेष्ठता का उदाहरण प्रस्तुत करती है। नौलागढ़ के पास बरैपुरा में सूर्य की एक मूर्ति है जो पालकालीन कला का एक नमूना पेश करती है। इस मूर्ति का उल्लेख मुंगेर के जिलाधीश जाँनस्टन (Johnston) ने की थी।[5] बेगूसराय में बौद्ध धर्म के साथ–साथ हिन्दु धर्म की भी प्रधानता रही थी। लेकिन विभिन्न सम्प्रदायों के बीच धार्मिक द्वेष नहीं थे। अधिकांश पाल शासक बौद्ध धर्माबलम्बी थे। जयमंगलागढ़ पहले एक महत्वपूर्ण बौद्ध स्थल था जो आगे चलकर मध्यकाल में तांत्रिक केन्द्र का रूप धारण कर लिया। नौलागढ़ और जयमंगला शक्ति साधना के भी केन्द्र थे। वराह, सूर्य, गंगा, शिवपार्वती आदि मूर्तियों से इस बात की पुष्टि होती है। पालकालीन मूतियां अधिक संख्या में बेगूसराय में उपलब्ध है।

अन्त में मैं यह प्रमाणित करना चाहता हूँ कि जयमंगलागढ़ सम्पूर्ण संसार का शिक्षा का केन्द्र था। आज भी आपके सामने यह कावर झील प्रमाणित करता है कि यहाँ संसार भर से पक्षियों का भीड़ होता है और मिलन स्थल है। प्रकृति ने हमें पक्षियों के माध्यम से यह प्रमाणित किया है कि जयमंगलागढ़ सचमुच में संसार का एक शक्ति साधना का केन्द्र था।

संदर्भ सूची:

1. बुद्धचर्या, सांकृत्यायन, राहुल पृ. 86
2. हिस्ट्री ऑफ बिहार, चौधरी; आर. के. पृ. 89
3. जी. डी. कॉलेज म्यूजियम, बेगूसराय
4. नौलागढ़ इन्सक्रिप्सन्स, चौधरी, आर. के.
5. डिस्ट्रक्ट गजेटियर, मुंगेर; राय चौधरी, पृ. 87

*स्टेशन रोड,
बेगूसराय

सौजन्य :
Jaimangalgadh
Journal of Historical Studies Vol- I, 2010
Begusarai

गोपाल मंदिर

अनिल कुमार*

उलाव बिहार राज्य के बेगूसराय जिलान्तर्गत एक प्रसिद्ध गाँव है। यह जिला मुख्यालय से लगभग 3 कि0 मी0 पश्चिम में बरौनी रिफाईनरी टाउनशीप के बगल में अवस्थित है। इसके उत्तर से राष्ट्रीय उच्च मार्ग–31 से गुजरती है एवं दक्षिण में गुप्ता–लखमिनियाँ बांध है। इसके पश्चिम में बरौनी रिफाईनरी स्थापित है। पूर्व में गंगा नदी इसके बगल से बहती थी।

उलाव स्टेट के कारण प्रसिद्ध यह गाँव आज राधेश्याम मंदिर, पंच मंदिर, गोपाल मंदिर, एस0 ओ0 एस0 एवं हवाई अड्डा आदि के कारण महत्वपूर्ण है। अतः ऐतिहासिक एवं सांस्कृतिक रूप से सम्पन्न होने के कारण यहाँ पर्यटन के विकास की भरपूर संभावनाएँ मौजूद हैं।

गोपाल मंदिर एस० ओ० एस० एवं एन०एच० 31 के उत्तर तथा सिंघौल पोखर के पूरब में स्थित है। इसके बाह्य खण्डहर दूर से ही आकर्षित करते हैं। यह उलाव के महत्वपूर्ण मंदिरों में से एक है। श्रीमति जयन्ती कुमरी ,पति श्री बनारसी प्रसाद ने अत्यन्त उत्साह के साथ सवा लाख रूपये की लागत से इस सुन्दर मंदिर का निर्माण करवाया। जिसमें सन् 1311 फसली में राधा कृष्ण की विधिवत् प्रतिष्ठा हुई। इस अवसर पर अस्सी हजार रूपये खर्च हुए।

इसका पूजन बल्लभ सम्प्रदाय की रीति से होता है। वर्त्तमान में यह बल्लभ सम्प्रदाय की पुष्टिमार्ग शाखा से जुड़ा हुआ है। पुष्टि ईश्वर की कृपा या अनुग्रह को कहते हैं जिसके द्वारा मनुष्य ईश्वर या मोक्ष की प्राप्ति कर सकता है।

मंदिर का नाम श्री ठाकुर गोपाल लाल जी महाराज के नाम पर रखा गया है और इसी नाम से यहाँ का प्रबन्धन भी होता है। मंदिर ईंटों से बना हुआ है एवं उसमें सुर्खी चूने का उपयोग किया गया है। मंदिर की सुन्दरता बढ़ाने के लिए पत्थर, लकड़ी एवं लोहे का उपयोग किया गया है। उसमें चुनार के लाल पत्थर का प्रयोग हुआ है।

मंदिर के निर्माण में महत्वपूर्ण भूमिका निभाने वालों में श्री ब्रह्मदेव प्रसाद, राय बहादुर राम सुमरन प्रसाद, गजाधर नारायण प्रसाद, पंडित श्री शिवकरण उपाध्याय, सर्वश्री शीतल प्रसाद,

मैनेजर केदार नाथ भट्ट, राम किशुन झा, मुंशी बजरंगी सहाय आदि का नाम उल्लेखनीय है।

इस मंदिर की वास्तु शैली अद्भुत है। स्थानीय लोग इसे 52 कोठरी 53 द्वार के नाम से पुकारते हैं। इसमे 52 कोठरिया एवं 53 बरामदे हैं। यहीं उलाव स्टेट का नौबतखाना था। यह मंदिर तीन मंजिला है।

मंदिर का मुख्य प्रवेश द्वार पूरब दिशा की ओर है। यह प्रवेश द्वार दो मंजिला है। स्थापत्य की दृष्टि से यह अत्यन्त आकर्षक है। इसमें लकड़ी एवं पत्थर का उपयोग हुआ है। प्रवेश द्वार की छत से कार्निस निकला हुआ है। छत के छज्जे के कार्निस के मध्य में लटकती हुई परियों की आकृतियाँ बनी हुई हैं। मुख्य द्वार में लकड़ी के मजबूत किवाड़ लगा हुआ है। इसके उपर स्तम्भों पर आधारित छत था। अब सिर्फ स्तम्भ ही शेष रह गये हैं। यह राजस्थानी शैली से प्रभावित प्रतीत होता है। इसमें चुनार के लाल पत्थर का उपयोग हुआ है। पत्थर को काट कर उस पर खूबसूरत नक्कासी की गई है।

मुख्य द्वार से अन्दर प्रवेश करते ही आयताकार खुला आंगन मिलता है। सामने गर्भ गृह पर चढ़ने के लिए सीढ़ियाँ बनी हुई है। सीढ़ी के दोनो तरफ शेर की आकृति है। ललाट बिम्ब पर गणेश उत्त्कीर्ण हैं। आंगन में अन्दर से चारो ओर छोटे–छोटे कमरे एवं बरामदे बने हुए है। दूसरी मंजिल पर चढ़ने के लिए अन्य सीढ़ियाँ मुख्य द्वार के बगल वाले कमरे से होकर जाती है।

मुख्य द्वार के सामने वाली सीढ़ी से गर्भ गृह की तरफ उपर चढ़ने के बाद दरवाजे में प्रवेश करते ही एक छोटा सा आँगन है। गर्भ गृह में राधाकृष्ण की मूर्तियाँ स्थापित है। यहाँ भी आंगन के चारो ओर कमरे एवं बरामदे की योजना है।

गर्भगृह के बरामदें पर दरवाजे के ऊपर एवं अगल–बगल दीवार के तीन तरफ खुबसूरत चित्रकारी की गई है। इसमें दशावतार के अतिरिक्त राधाकृष्ण, कृष्ण गोपियाँ, जगन्नाथ, बलभद्र एवं सुभद्रा के चित्र हैं।

मंदिर में कई कमरे की योजना है – जिनमें छप्पन भोग बनाने, गीत संगीत, प्रबंधन आदि कार्य संपादित किये जाते रहे हैं। पुजारियों के निवास के लिए मंदिर से संलग्न अलग कमरा है तथा एक संस्कृत पाठशाला के लिए अलग से प्रांगण में कमरे बने हुए हैं।

मंदिर का छत एवं बाहर की दीवारें क्षरित हो रही हैं उसे तत्काल सुरक्षित करने की आवश्यकता है। मंदिर के वर्तमान पुजारी श्री राम कुमार शुक्ल मंदिर के क्षरण से दुखी हैं एवं उद्धारक की बाट जोह रहे हैं। पुरी के जगन्नाथ मंदिर एवं अन्य जगहों की तरह वहाँ प्रतिवर्ष रथ यात्रा का आयोजन किया जाता है ।

गोपाल मंदिर के सामने एक दुर्लभ प्रजाति का वृक्ष है। 'मैंगोएस्टा' नामक यह फलदार वृक्ष भूमध्यसागरीय प्रजाति का बताया जाता है। इस वृक्ष के भी संरक्षण की आवश्यकता है। यह क्षेत्र अनेक मंदिर समूहों का प्रतिनिधित्व करता है। अतएव पर्यटन स्थल के रूप में इसके विकास की अपार संभावनाएँ हैं। संरक्षण के साथ ही प्रचार किसी भी स्थल को पर्यटन स्थल के रूप में विकसित करने के लिए आवश्यक है। इसके लिए विभिन्न तरह के समारोहों का आयोजन किया जाना चाहिए। पर्यटकों को आकर्षित करने के लिए महोत्सव भी आयोजित किये जा सकते हैं। जिससे मूर्त एवं अमूर्त संस्कृति का प्रदर्शन किया जा सकता है। उलाव में इस तरह के महोत्सव आयोजित करने की पर्याप्त संभावनायें मौजूद हैं। यहाँ पूर्व में जो भी समारोह किये जाते थे उसे फिर से प्रारम्भ करने का भी प्रयास होना चाहिए ।

शोधार्थी,
(ल० ना० मि० वि०, दरभंगा)
ग्राम–भगवानपुर
पोस्ट–धबौली, बेगूसराय

सौजन्य :
धरोहर (द्वितीय अंक)
2010

●●●

उलाव की हरिहर प्रतिमा : एक सांस्कृतिक अध्ययन

शैलैश कुमार सिन्हा*
अमिय कृष्ण

हिन्दू धर्म के देवताओं में हरिहर का एक विशिष्ट स्थान है। हिन्दू धर्म की व्यापक परिकल्पना में विष्णु यदि जगत के पालनकर्ता के रूप में स्वीकृत हैं तो शिव संहारक के रूप में। बहुपक्षीय व्यक्तित्व के स्वामी शिव को शैव धर्मावलम्वी सृष्टिकर्ता भी मानतें हैं तथा सृष्टि का संहारकर्ता भी। हरिहर शिव एवं विष्णु के संयुक्त रूप की परिकल्पना को साकार करने वाले देव हैं। इनकी एक खण्डित किन्तु आकर्षक प्रतिमा जी0 डी0 कॉलेज, बेगूसराय के प्राचीन भारतीय इतिहास, संस्कृति एवं पुरातत्व विभाग के संग्रहालय में संरक्षित है, यह जिला मुख्यालय से पाँच कि0मी0 पश्चिम स्थित उलाव ढ़ाला के निकट एक पीपल के पेड़ के नीचे असुरक्षित रखी हुई थी।

हरिहर प्रतिमा का निर्माण गुप्त काल की घटना मानी जाती है।[1] वैसे, जितेन्द्र नाथ बनर्जी हुविष्क के एक सिक्के पर बनी एक देवाकृति की पहचान हरिहर के रूप में करते हैं[2] जिससे इस देवता की प्रतिमांकन परम्परा ई0 सम्वत् के आरम्भ के आसपास ठहरती है।

ऐसा प्रतीत होता है कि शैव एवं वैष्णव सम्प्रदाय के अनुयायियों के धार्मिक मतभेदों का पटाक्षेप आदि देवों के समन्वयकारी पूजन परम्परा के कारण ही संभव हो सका है।[3] हरिहर इस समन्वयकारी परम्परा के प्रतिनिधि देव माने जा सकते हैं।[4] प्रतिमा निर्माण संबंधी शास्त्रीय विधान के अनुसार इस प्रतिमा का बायाँ भाग विष्णु का एवं दाहिना शिव का प्रदर्शित होना चाहिए। विष्णु भाग में किरीट सहित विष्णु आयुघ तथा शिव भाग में जटाभार एवं अन्य संबंधित प्रतीकों का प्रदर्शन होना चाहिए। विष्णु धर्मोत्तर पुराण के अनुसार हरिहर प्रतिमा का दक्षिणार्द्ध भाग सदाशिव का एवं वाम –अर्द्ध भाग ऋषिकेश का होना चाहिए। शिव भाग के हाथ में त्रिशूल एवं डमरू तथा ऋषिकेश भाग के हाथ में चक्र एवं कमल स्थित होना चाहिए। इसी प्रकार दाएँ भाग में वृषभ एवं

बाएँ भाग में गरूड़ प्रदर्शित किया जाना चाहिए–[5]

कार्येहरिहरस्यापि दक्षिणार्ध सदाशिवः।
वाम्मर्धे ऋषिकेषश्वेत नीलाकृतिः क्रमात।।
....
वरत्रिशूलचक्राब्ज धारिणो बाहव : क्रमात।
दक्षिणे वृषभः पार्ष्वे वामभागे विहंगराट् ।।

शिल्परत्न[6] के अनुसार–
देवं हरिहरं वक्ष्ये सर्वपातकनाशनम्।
दक्षिणे शंकरस्यार्धमर्ध विष्णोश्च वामतः।।
बालेन्दु भूषितः कार्यो जटाभारस्तु दक्षिणे।
नानारत्नमयं द्रव्यं किरीटं वाम भागतः।।
दक्षिणं सर्वराजेन भूषितं कर्णमालिखेत।
मकराकारकं दिव्यं कुण्डलंन वामकर्णतः।।

आलोच्य प्रतिमा का कटि से नीचे का सम्पूर्ण भाग, दोनो भुजाएँ एवं पार्श्व का स्टेला पूरी तरह खंडित हैं। बाई भुजा का केहुनी से ऊपर का भाग आंशिक रूप से सुरक्षित है जिससे इस प्रतिमा के द्विभुजी होने की संपुष्टि होती है। कटि के लोच एवं शरीर की आनुपातिक गति से आभास होता है कि प्रतिमा समभंग मुद्रा में रही होगी। काले बैसाल्ट प्रस्तर निर्मित 11वीं0–12वीं0 सदी की इस प्रतिमा में बाईं ओर स्वाभाविक रूप से विष्णु का अंकन किया गया है। सिर पर मुकुट का अर्द्धभाग किरीट रूप में प्रदर्शित है जिसके नीचे विन्यस्त केश राशि की बाह्य रेखा स्पष्ट रूप से देखी जा सकती है। इस भाग का कर्ण अलंकृत रत्नकुण्डल (मकरकुण्डल) से सुसज्जित है। दाहिनी ओर शिव भाग में जटाभार का अंकन है। इस भाग का कर्ण एक बड़े किन्तु अपेक्षाकृत कम अलंकारपूर्ण कुण्डल, जो सर्पकुण्डल सदृश्य है, से शोभायमान है। जटाभार के पार्श्व में फनयुक्त सर्प के मुख का अंकन किया गया है। प्रतिमा के गले में एक अलंकृत हार प्रदर्शित किया गया है जो वक्षस्थल के मध्य तक पहुँच रहा है। बाई भुजा पर भुजबन्ध का अंकन है जबकि स्कंध से होकर यज्ञोपवीत का स्पष्ट प्रदर्शन है। मुखमंडल में नासिकाग्र एवं ओठ

खंडित है जबकि चक्षु अर्द्धनिमीलित प्रतीत होते हैं।

हरिहर के रूप में शिव एवं विष्णु के संयुक्त प्रतिमा की कल्पना एक ओर यदि शैव एवं वैष्णव धर्मावलम्वियों की आपसी कटुता को दूर करने का प्रयास माना जा सकता है तो दूसरी ओर सृष्टि के उत्पादन संबंधी प्रचलित धार्मिक मान्यता। यदि हम अर्द्धनारीश्वर की प्रतिमा से हरिहर की तुलना करें तो पाते हैं कि विष्णु उमा का स्थान ग्रहण कर शिव के वामांग में स्थित हो जाते हैं।[7] कूर्मपुराण में विष्णु द्वारा स्त्री रूपधारण करने एवं शिव के साथ रमण करने का उल्लेख है[8]। 'भागवतपुराण' के एक आख्यान के अनुसार भी शिव का मोहिणी रूप धारी विष्णु के रूप पर आसक्त होकर प्रमुषितेन्द्रिय अवस्था में उनके पीछे दौड़ना इस संबंध में स्मरण किया जा सकता है।[9] विष्णुपुराण में शिव स्वयं को हरि का अर्द्धभाग बताते हैं।[10] 'पद्मपुराण' में एक स्थल पर शिव के लिंग को ब्रह्मा तथा भग को जनार्दन कहा गया है[11]। ''वायुपुराण'' में शिव के वामांग में विष्णु की स्थिति की व्याख्या करते हुए शिव को 'पुरुष' एवं विष्णु को 'प्रकृति' कहा गया है[12]।

शिव एवं विष्णु के संयोग से देव की उत्पत्ति संबंधी कल्पना का मूर्त रूपांकण भारतीय संस्कृति का अभिन्न अंग रहा है। गोपीनाथ राव के अनुसार दक्षिण भारतीय परम्परा में शिव एवं मोहिनी के संयोग से हरिहरपुत्र की उत्पत्ति संबंधी धारणा लोकप्रिय है एवं मलयालम भूभाग के संरक्षक के रूप में स्थापित इस देवता को आर्य, अय्यनार या अययानरप्पन एवं शास्ता के नाम से भी जाना जाता है।[13] श्री राव का विचार है कि हरि के मोहिनी रूप एवं हर (शव) के संयोग से उत्पन्न हरिहर (अय्यनार शास्ता) पूरी तरह द्रविड़ देवता हैं एवं आर्य परम्परा में इसका समावेश कालक्रम के अनुरूप हुआ।[14]

वर्तमान में द्रविड़ परम्परा हरिहर को ग्राम देवता के रूप में स्वीकार करती है एवं सामाजिक संस्तरण में अपेक्षाकृत निचले पायदान पर खड़ी जातियों में इनकी पूजा विशेष तौर पर की जाती है।[15] 'पद्मसंहिता' में उल्लेख मिलता है कि आर्य के मंदिर का पुजारी 'पार्श्व' (ब्राह्मण पिता एवं शूद्र माता से उत्पन्न) होना चाहिए।[16] शिव एवं विष्णु के संयोग की बात गुप्तकाल तक उत्तर भारत में भी किसी रूप में ज्ञात रही होगी। विदिशा से प्राप्त चौथी शताब्दी की हरिहर की विशाल प्रतिमा इसका प्रमाण है।[17]

बेगूसराय के उलाव क्षेत्र से प्राप्त हरिहर की यह प्रतिमा कई दृष्टियों से महत्वपूर्ण है। प्रथम तो यह कि यह इस क्षेत्र में हरिहर की एकमात्र ज्ञात प्रतिमा है। हरिहर की बहुत अधिक प्रतिमाएँ नहीं मिलती हैं। पटना संग्रहायलय में मुंडेष्वरी, कैमूर से प्राप्त बलुआ पत्थर की सप्तम् शताब्दी की एक हरिहर प्रतिमा अवश्य है किन्तु वह कलात्मक दृष्टि से आलोच्य प्रतिमा के समकक्ष प्रतीत नहीं होती। दूसरा, जिस क्षेत्र से यह प्रतिमा प्राप्त हुई है, वह अंकुरीनाथ सिमरिया महादेव के मंदिर के लिए प्रसिद्ध रहा है एवं उत्तर राजपूतकालीन अंकुरीनाथ मंदिर[18] के रूप में एक

परिवर्द्धित मंदिर आज भी स्थानीय जनों की आस्था का केन्द्र है। बेगूसराय के समीपवर्ती विभिन्न स्थलों पर सशक्त शैव–परम्परा को दर्शानेवाली पालकालीन एवं उत्तर पालकालीन काले प्रस्तर की प्रतिमाएँ उपलब्ध हैं। सामान्य शिवलिंग से लेकर चतुर्मुखी शिव लिंग तक, उमा माहेश्वर बसहा, भैरव आदि सभी प्रतिमाऐं इस ओर इशारा करती है कि पाल एवं राजपूत काल में शैव सम्प्रदाय की जड़ें इस क्षेत्र में काफी गहरीं थी। ध्यान देने योग्य है कि यह लगभग वही समय था जब संबंधित क्षेत्र में ब्रांह्मण आबादी का प्रव्रजन दो तरफ से हो रहा था– एक गंगा के दक्षिण से दूसरा मिथिला के हृदय स्थल मधुबनी से। एक तरह से बेगूसराय इस काल में शैव एवं वैष्णव मतावलंबियों की संगमस्थली बन रहा था। पश्चिम की ओर से, दक्कन एवं पश्चिम भारतीय राजपूतों का राजनीतिक दबाव भी इस क्षेत्र पर स्पष्ट रूप से था।[19] इस परिस्थितियों में 'हरिहर' के रूप में एक समन्वयकारी देवता की इस क्षेत्र में सामाजिक स्वीकृति, तत्कालीन समाज में एक स्वाभाविक परिणति हो सकती है। ध्यातव्य है कि ऐसे प्रयासों की अनुगूँज को ध्वनित करनेवाला यह एकमात्र उदाहरण नहीं। बेगूसराय जिले की दक्षिणी सीमा पर स्थित एक शिवलिंग, जिसपर विष्णु का स्पष्ट अंकन है, ऐसे प्रयासों का एक अन्य सशक्त उदाहरण है। इस सम्भावना से इन्कार नहीं किया जा सकता कि ऐसे अन्य उदाहरण अभी सामने नहीं आ पाए हो। हरिहर की यह प्रतिमा तत्कालीन समाज में व्याप्त दो सम्प्रदायों की निराधार धार्मिक कटुता से उबरने के क्रान्तिकारी प्रयासों का साक्षी बेगूसराय की धरती को अवश्य बनाती है।

संदर्भ सूची :

1. प्रा0 भा0 प्रतिमा विज्ञान एवं मूर्तिकला – बृज भूषण श्रीवास्तव, पृ0 69
2. The Development of Hindu Iconography-J.N.Benarjee, Page 544
3. श्रीवास्तव, वही
4- Elements of Hindu Iconography, Vol2, Part II, Gopinath Rao, Page 333
5. विष्णुधर्मोत्तर, 108, 35–38
6. Quoted E.H.I Page 170 प्रतिमालक्षणानि . Vol 2, Part II
7. प्राचीन भारतीय मूर्तिविज्ञान – नीलकंठ पुरुषोत्तम जोशी, पृ0 43
8. कूर्मपुराण उत्तर 38.9, 12, 27
9. भागवत 8, 13. 14–37
10. विष्णु पुराण 5,6,11–13
11. पद्दम पुराण सृष्टि 17, 63
12. वायु पुराण 2.25, 21–24
13. E. H. I Vol 2,Part II - Gopinath Rao, 485 - 7

14. वही
15. वही पृ0 487
16. वही
17. प्रा0 भारतीय मूर्ति विज्ञान, जोशी, पृ0 43
18. धरोहर, प्रथम अंक (सं. प्रो0 शैलेश कुमार सिन्हा पृ0 14)
19. द चंदेलाज इन बिहार – आर0 के0 दीक्षित, आन बिहार – बुलेटिन –(जी0 डी0 कॉलेज, बेगूसराय से प्रकाशित शोध आलेख) पृ0 3 एवं 4

*विभागाध्यक्ष,
प्रा0 भा0 इतिहास एवं पुरातत्व विभाग
जी0 डी0 कॉलेज बेगूसराय

सौजन्य :
बिहार इतिहास परिषद कार्यविवरणिका
सप्तम अधिवेशन, मुजफ्फरपुर 2011

●●●

बेगूसराय : इतिहास के आईने में

शैलेश कुमार सिन्हा*

बेगूसराय की धरती एक सुदीर्घ इतिहास को अपने अंकों में समेट एक मौनद्रष्टा की तरह ऐतिहासिक घटनाओं की साक्षी रही है। सम्पूर्ण जिले में फैले शताधिक टीले इसकी ऐतिहासिक एवं सांस्कृतिक सम्पन्नता के प्रतीक हैं। इन टीलों में बेगूसराय के अतीत की गाथा छुपी है। इन पुरास्थलों के साथ–साथ जिला भर में ऐसे बहुमूल्य पुरावशेष बिखरे पड़े हैं, जो अतीत की कालबद्धता की दृष्टि से अत्यंत उपयोगी हैं। भूगोल इतिहास की आधारशिला तैयार करता है। प्रकृति ने बेगूसराय को सात नदियों से पोषित वह विस्तृत भू–भाग प्रदान किया है, जिसपर इतिहास ने अठखेलियाँ कीं।

बेगूसराय जिला के अन्तर्गत आनेवाले कई पुरास्थल आज से दो हजार वर्ष से भी पूर्व की कहानी कहते हैं। मसूरिया डीह पर सहज प्राप्य घास–भूसे युक्त मोटे मृदभाण्ड एवं कृष्णलोहित मृदभाण्ड के ठीकरे इस क्षेत्र के इतिहास को नवपाषाण काल तक ले जाने में सक्षम है। इस पुरास्थल के उत्खनन से बेगूसराय जिला के इतिहास में नया आयाम जुड़ सकता है।

बेगूसराय जिला प्राचीन अंग जनपद (भागलपुर, मुंगेर एवं लखीसराय) से उत्तर स्थित है। बौद्ध साहित्यों में अंग से उत्तर जल से घिरे प्रदेश को '**अंगुत्तराप**' नाम से विहित किया गया है। '**महावग्ग**' एवं '**सुत्तनिपात अट्टकथा**' में महात्मा बुद्ध के अंगुत्तराप स्थित '**आपण निगम**' भ्रमण की चर्चा है। अंगुत्तराप एक विस्तृत प्रदेश था जो पूर्व में पूर्णियाँ–कटिहार से लेकर पश्चिम में बेगूसराय जिला तक गंगा के उत्तर में अवस्थित माना जा सकता था। आपण निगम को लेकर विद्वानों में मतभेद अवश्य हैं किन्तु इसकी पहचान को स्थापित करने के क्रम में तत्कालीन समाज में प्रचलित उत्तरी कृष्णमार्जित मृदभांड के ठीकरों से युक्त आवासीय गुच्छों की उपस्थिति एक प्रमुख कारक है। साथ ही उक्त आवासीय गुच्छों में एक का विस्तार इतना अवश्य होना चाहिए कि आपण निगम जैसे व्यापक एवं विस्तृत बाजार की अवधारणा साकार हो सके। उतना ही नहीं मिथिला के साथ उक्त स्थल सुगम मार्ग से जुड़ सकता है इसका ध्यान रखना

भी अपरिहार्य है। सम्पूर्ण शर्त्तों पर विचार करने के उपरांत अपने दर्जन भर कृष्णमार्जित मृद्भांड के ठीकरों युक्त टीलों के साथ बेगूसराय जिला 'आपण निगम' के रूप में चिन्हित होने के लिए अपनी सशक्त दावेदारी प्रस्तुत करता है। 'आपण–निगम उपस्थापना के बौद्धिक बहसों का निष्कर्ष जो भी हो इतना तो अवश्य है कि बेगूसराय की धरती मौर्य काल से बौद्ध काल के मध्य भी गुलजार थी। अथौराडीह, जोगिया डीह, मसूरिया डीह, रोशनाहा डीह, चाननडीह, औरे डीह, सावतडीह, नौलागढ़, जयमंगलागढ़, गढ़खौली आदि इसके सशक्त प्रमाण हैं। बेगूसराय जिला के विभिन्न क्षेत्रों से आहत सिक्कों की भी प्रचुर मात्रा में प्राप्ति हुई है जो स्थानीय संग्रहालय में संरक्षित हैं। इस क्षेत्र पर बौद्ध धर्म के प्रबल प्रभाव के भी कई प्रमाण हैं, यथा–हरसाई स्तूप श्रृंखला, मंझौल का धुंभ, गढ़पुरा के निकट स्थित स्तूप श्रृंखला, संघौल से बड़ी संख्या में बौद्ध मूर्तियाँ व प्रतीकों का प्राप्त होना, जिला भर में बौद्ध देवी–देवताओं की मूर्तियों का बिखरा होना आदि। ये प्रमाण भले ही बाद के कालों का प्रतिनिधित्व करते हों, किन्तु इतना तो अवश्य है कि ये पूर्व से चली आ रही परम्परा का ही प्रतिफलन थे। उसी परम्परा का – जो इस धरती पर बुद्ध के चरण पड़ने का संकेत करती है।

इस बात की प्रबल संभावना है कि मौर्य शासक बिम्बिसार के अंग विजय के उपरांत यह क्षेत्र मौर्य सत्ता के अधीन आ गया हो। 1957–58 ई0 में प्रो0 राधाकृष्ण चौधरी एवं प्रो0 रामशरण शर्मा की अगुवाई में इतिहासकारों के एक दल ने जयमंगलागढ़ में एक सुनियोजित काष्ठ पुल की सुडौल संरचना खोज निकाली थी। इसके आधार पर इस क्षेत्र को मौर्य स्थल के रूप में स्थापित बताया गया।

क्षेत्र के इतिहास का क्रम इसके उपरांत भी भंग नहीं हुआ। जयमंगलागढ़ से ही प्रो0 चौधरी को शुंगकालीन मृण्मूर्ति एवं अन्य छिट–पुट पुरावशेषों की प्राप्ति हुई। जी0डी0 कॉलेज, बेगूसराय के प्राचीन भारतीय इतिहास एवं पुरातत्व विभाग द्वारा, भारतीय पुरातत्व सर्वेक्षण की अनुमति से कराये गए वीरपुर–उत्खनन में उक्त स्थल के कुषाण काल में पूर्णतः स्थापित होने के संकेत मिले हैं। इतना ही नहीं, इस बात के भी संकेत मिलते हैं कि वीरपुर इस समय तक औषधि निर्माण के क्षेत्र में अपनी पहचान स्थापित कर चुका था। कुषाणकाल तक जिले में अस्तित्व में आ चुके पुरास्थलों में पूर्व में उल्लिखित नामों के अतिरिक्त अरवाडीह, चामर डीह, नटियाही डीह, छिलवा डीह, काँटी डीह, डुमरिया बाद, मनिअप्पा, बड़ी बलिया, सकरबासा डीह आदि अनेक नाम जुड़ चुके थे।

बेगूसराय जिले का इतिहास गुप्त युग में भी अनवरत जारी रहा। पुरास्थल – सर्वेक्षण के क्रम में प्रो0 राधाकृष्ण चौधरी को जयमंगलागढ़ से एक गुप्तकालीन मृण्मूर्ति के साथ उसी काल के कुछ सिक्कों के साँचे मिले थे। एक मृण्मुहर भी प्राप्त हुआ, जिस पर गुप्त ब्राह्मी में लेख अंकित है। यह क्षेत्र में गुप्त संस्कृति की उपस्थिति का द्योतक है ।

बेगूसराय जिला पाल–साम्राज्य का एक अंग था। देवपाल के मुंगेर ताम्र फलक लेख में उल्लेख मिलता है कि उसका साम्राज्य उत्तर में हिमालय तक फैला था। नारायण पाल के भागलपुर ताम्र फलक लेख में तीरभुक्ति को भी पाल साम्राज्य में बताया गया है। अतः ऐसी स्थिति में बेगूसराय जिला निस्संदेह पाल साम्राज्य का अंग था। इतना ही नहीं बलगुदर अभिलेख में धर्मपाल के शासनकाल में क्रिमिला विषय के अस्तित्व का उल्लेख है। यहाँ यह उल्लेख महत्वपूर्ण होगा कि प्रो0 राधाकृष्ण चौधरी द्वारा नौलागढ़ से अन्विष्ट एक लेख में 'क्रिमिला विषय के निवासी दाता द्वारा प्रदत्त' दान का उल्लेख है। अतः बेगूसराय जिला किसी न किसी रूप में 'क्रिमिला' विषय से संबंधित था। यहाँ तक कि हम नौलागढ़ के 'क्रिमिला विषय' का प्रशासनिक केन्द्र होने की संभावना का भी निषेध नहीं कर सकते। प्रो0 चौधरी द्वारा अन्विष्ट एवं सम्पादित लेख में 'श्री विग्रहपाल देव के राज्यारोहण के 24वें वर्ष' का उल्लेख किया गया है। प्रो0 चौधरी इसे विग्रहपाल तृतीय बताते हैं।

बेगूसराय जिला में पालवंशीय शासकों की सशक्त उपस्थिति इस क्षेत्र में पाल कला शैली में निर्मित काले बैसाल्ट प्रस्तर की प्रतिमाओं की बहुतायत में प्राप्ति से भी मुखरित होती है। वीरपुर–बरैपुरा इस सांस्कृतिक लहर का केन्द्र प्रतीत होता है। पालशासक कालान्तर में राजनैतिक परिदृश्य से भले ही ओझल हो गये हों, सांस्कृतिक पटल पर उनकी उपस्थिति उनके इस क्षेत्र में राजनैतिक अवसान के उपरांत भी बनी रही।

ऐसा प्रतीत होता है कि पालवंश के सुनहरे दिनों से लेकर सिमरॉंवगढ़ से कर्णाट शासकों के विस्तार के मध्य यह क्षेत्र राजपूत सरदारों के विशेष प्रभाव में रहा। यहाँ तक कि इस क्षेत्र पर कर्णाट शासकों के आधिपत्य के उपरांत भी राजपूत सरदारों का उल्लेखनीय प्रभाव बना रहा। इस क्षेत्र में भार, चन्देल, परमार, सोलंकी आदि राजपूत कुलों की उपस्थिति एवं चामुण्डा, रैवन्त, भैरव आदि की प्रतिमाओं की प्राप्ति से इस तथ्य को बल मिलता है। मिथिला में 1097 ई0 में कर्णाटों के उदय के उपरांत यह क्षेत्र स्वाभाविक रूप से उनके अधीन आ गया।

बेगूसराय जिला एवं पालवंशीय शासकों के आधिपत्य के सन्दर्भ में यह उल्लेख सर्वथा प्रासंगिक होगा कि जहाँ नारायणपाल के शासनकाल (854 ई0–908 ई0) के 17वें वर्ष वहीं इस कालखंड के उपरांत किसी समय मिहिरभोज के नेतृत्व में हुए गुर्जर–प्रतिहार अभियान के कारण उसे गंगा के उत्तर का अधिकांश साम्राज्य गँवाना पड़ा। गोरखपुर जिले से प्राप्त एक अभिलेख से ज्ञात होता है कि मिहिर भोज के एक कलचुरी सामंत ने पाल नरेश (गौड़ाधिपति) की प्रभुसत्ता का दलन करने में उसकी मदद की थी। 881 – 82 ई0 के आसपास सम्पन्न मिहिरभोज के 'वृहद बंग विजय' ने पाल साम्राज्य को विघटित किया होगा। इस बात के सक्षम अभिलेखीय प्रमाण हैं कि मिहिर भोज एवं उसके पुत्र महेन्द्रपाल का नियंत्रण उत्तर में पंजाब से दक्षिण में

काठियाबाड़ तथा पूर्व में पाल साम्राज्य की सीमा तक था। अपने शासनकाल के 13वें वर्ष तक महेन्द्रपाल ने गंगा के उत्तरी तट पर पूर्व की ओर बढ़ते हुए सम्पूर्ण तीरभुक्ति एवं उत्तरी बंगाल पर आधिपत्य जमा लिया। स्वाभाविक है कि ऐसी स्थिति में बेगूसराय जिला के भू–भाग गुर्जर प्रतिहारों के अधीन आ गये हों।

गुर्जर प्रतिहार शक्ति के समान ही जेजाकभुक्ति से उभरनेवाले चंदेल, पाल साम्राज्य के सम्मुख बड़ी चुनौती थे। 953–54 ई0 के खजुराहो लेख से ज्ञात होता है कि चंदेल नरेश यशोवर्मन ने गौड़ पर आसान विजय हासिल की थी। उपेन्द्र ठाकुर इस लेख में विजित क्षेत्र में मिथिला का अलग से उल्लेख किये जाने की ओर ध्यान दिलाते हुए इस तथ्य की ओर इशारा करते हैं मिथिला इस कालखंड में पाल–साम्राज्य से बाहर हो चुकी थी। इसके पूर्व के प्रतिहार अभिलेख तीरमुक्ति एवं वारेन्द्री को रौदें जाने का उल्लेख करते हैं। इस आधर पर यह निष्कर्ष निकाला जा सकता है बेगूसराय जिला के भू–भाग इस अवधि में चन्देलों एवं प्रतिहारों के संघर्ष के साक्षी बने।

पालवंश की क्षीण शक्ति महीपाल (975 ई0 से 1026 ई0) के शासन काल में पुनर्जीवित हुई किन्तु राजेन्द्र चोल के 'उत्तर भारतीय अभियान ने उसे स्थापित होने का अवसर नहीं दिया। नौलागढ़ से प्रो0 राधाकृष्ण चौधरी द्वारा अन्विष्ट दो अभिलेख इस क्षेत्र पर विग्रहपाल तृतीय (1041 ई0 – 1054 ई0) के शासन की पृष्टि करते हैं जो महीपाल के पुत्र नयपाल का उत्तराधिकारी था। यहाँ से प्राप्त एक रजत मुद्रा को भी अल्तेकर महोदय ने विग्रहपाल तृतीय का बताया है। अभिलेखीय सूत्रों से यह भी ज्ञात होता है कि कल्याणी के चालुक्यवंशी सोमेश्वर प्रथम के शासनकाल (1044 ई0 से 1068 ई0) में ही उसके पुत्र विक्रमादित्य ने महाकौशल के रास्ते कामरूप एवं गौड़ तक विजय अभियान कर विग्रहपाल तृतीय को परास्त किया एवं नेपाल की सीमा तक के प्रदश चालुक्य नरेश के अधिकार में आ गये। किन्तु उनके वापस लौटते ही पालशक्ति ने वहाँ स्वयं को स्थापित कर लिया। चालुक्यों के अभियान का एक राजनैतिक प्रतिफल यह हुआ कि उनकी सेना में शामिल बहुत से दक्षिणी एवं कर्णाटकी सरदार अपने सैनिकों एवं अनुयायियों के साथ विजित क्षेत्रों में बस गये। प्रारंभ में सामंतों की हैसियत रखनेवाले ये सरदार अपनी स्वतंत्र सत्ता के लिए सचेष्ट रहे एवं पालशक्ति के ह्रास का लाभ उठाकर कर्णाट एवं सेन शक्ति के रूप में गंगोत्तर बिहार एवं संलग्न पूर्वी क्षेत्रों में छा गये। इस प्रकार यह स्पष्ट है कि बेगूसराय की धरती गुप्तों के उपरांत निरंतर राजनैतिक संघर्ष एवं सत्ता के उथल–पुथल की साक्षी रही। मुंगेर जिला 1157–58 ई0 तक पालों के अधीन बना रहा पर बेगूसराय जिला के भू–भाग अब तक कर्णाट शक्ति के अधीन आ गये।

मिथिला पर कर्णाट–वंशीय शासकों का आधिपत्य 1324 ई0 तक बना रहा, किन्तु बेगूसराय

के भूभाग 1324 ई0 तक कर्णाट शासन के अधीन नहीं थे। दिल्ली के सुल्तान इल्तुतमिश (1211–1236 ई0) का तिरहुत क्षेत्र पर व्यापक प्रभाव था। बछवाड़ा के समीप ब्रह्मपुरा गाँव स्थित मस्जिद को इल्तुतमिश के समय दान प्राप्त होने का उल्लेख मिलता है। फिरोज एतीगिन (1291–92) के महेशवाड़ा अभिलेख से सहज अनुमान लगाया जा सकता है, बंगाल के बलबनवंशीय रूकनुद्दीन कैकस (1291–1302) के प्रभाव पूर्व की ओर बढ़कर बूढ़ी गंडक नदी के किनारे पहुँच गया था एवं तत्कालीन कर्णाट नरेश शक्तिसिंह देव को अपने पाँव उत्तर की ओर खींचने पड़े थे। प्रो0 चौधरी द्वारा 1956 में सम्पादित इस अभिलेख में वर्णित फिरोज एतीगिन का उल्लेख 'द्वितीय सिकन्दर' तथा पूर्व एवं चीन में 'खानों के खान' के रूप में किया गया है। एतीगिन रूकनुद्दीन कैकस द्वारा नियुक्त प्रशासक था। स्पष्टतः बेगूसराय बंगाल के प्रांतीय मुस्लिम शासन के अधीन आ चुका था। स्थानीय परम्परा के अनुसार अलाउद्दीन खिलजी के लखनौती अभियान के समय उसकी सेना का पड़ाव बड़ी बलिया के निकट स्थित 'छौनी' (छावनी) में हुआ था। इस क्षेत्र में स्थित एक विशाल कुँआ आज भी 'अलाउद्दीन' के साथ जोड़कर देखा जाता है जिसकी संरचना उक्त काल की साक्षी है। सूफी संत शाह अलाउद्दीन बुखारी (900 हिजरी) के काल में बड़ी बलिया प्रतिष्ठित हो चुका था। बड़ी बलिया दरगाह स्थित एक मस्जिद के ध्वंशावशेष इस स्थल की कीर्ति का सबल प्रमाण है। अलाउद्दीन के उपरांत बेगूसराय के भू–भाग 'गयासुद्दीन तुगलक' की बंगाल–अभियान से वापसी के गवाह बने। 1324 ई0 में सम्पन्न इस अभियान ने इस क्षेत्र के राजनैतिक भाग्य की दिशा निर्धारित कर दी। मुल्ला तकिया के विवरण के अनुसार तुगलक सत्ता की कमजोरी का लाभ बंगाल के हाजी इलियास ने उठाया एवं तिरहुत पर विजय प्राप्त कर इसे ओइनवार वंश के शासकों के साथ बाँट लिया। इस बँटवारे के अनुसार बेगूसराय के भू–भाग हाजी इलियास के अधीन रहा। यह प्रबंधन अल्पजीवी साबित हुआ क्योंकि फीरोज तुगलक ने इलियास साहियों को तिरहुत से खदेड़ दिया। क्षेत्र में अन्तर्कलह इतना फैल गया कि फीरोज तुगलक को सिकन्दर शाह से सन्धि करनी पड़ी। सिकन्दर शाह के पक्ष में हुई इस सन्धि के उपरांत बेगूसराय के भू–भाग रूकनुद्दीन बारबक शाह के अधीन आ गए। इस शासक के सिक्के तिरहुत के विभिन्न क्षेत्रों से प्राप्त हुए हैं। इस काल तक बेगूसराय उत्तर बिहार के अन्य क्षेत्रों की भाँति मुस्लिम शक्तियों के शक्ति–परीक्षण का केन्द्र बना रहा। 1489 ई0 के बाद सिकन्दर लोदी की सेना ने इस क्षेत्र को बंगाल की सीमा तक हस्तगत कर लिया । प्रान्तीय मुस्लिम शक्ति के रूप में अलाउद्दीन हुसैन शाह के पुत्र एवं उत्तराधिकारी नसीब खाँ नसिरूद्दीन नसरतशाह के उत्कर्ष का प्रभाव बेगूसराय जिले पर भी पड़ा। इस शासक ने गंगा पारकर बेगूसराय के भू–भाग पर अधिकार कर लिया। इस शासक का एक अभिलेख मटिहानी से प्राप्त हुआ है। नसरतशाह 1519 ई0 में गद्दी पर बैठा था एवं उसने अपने दामाद मखदम आलम को हाजीपुर का गवर्नर नियुक्त किया था। मखदम आलम ने शेरशाह के साथ मिलकर बंगाल

के सुल्तान के विरूद्ध अभियान चलाया जो बंगाल की प्रान्तीय सत्ता के लिए घातक सिद्ध हुआ। बेगूसराय अब शेरशाह के प्रभाव में था। 'बेगूसराय' नाम भी शेरशाह की प्रशासनिक व्यवस्था की दास्तान कहता है। बेगूसराय जिले का 'लोदी डीह' एवं संघौल से प्राप्त 'सुल्तान इब्राहीम शाह' अंकित ताम्र सिक्का यहाँ पर लोदी–प्रभाव की पुष्टि करते हैं। तेघड़ा , बछवाड़ा, मनसूरचक आदि क्षेत्रों के पुरास्थल इस प्रभाव को व्यक्त करते हैं। लखमिनियाँ स्थित 'मस्जिदे सुल्तानिया' के मीनार भी प्रांतीय मुस्लिम वास्तु के प्रभाव को परिलक्षित करते हैं। कालांतर में 1574 ई0 में अकबर के काल में तिरहुत मुगल साम्राज्य का अभिन्न अंग बन गया एवं इसके साथ ही बेगूसराय मुगलसत्ता के अधीन आ गया। मुगलिया सत्ता में तेघड़ा एक महाल के रूप में प्रतिष्ठित हो गया। बलिया को परगना का दर्जा मिला एवं इसके प्रशासन का दायित्व चाँद एवं अलाउद्दीन को सौंप दिया गया। इस क्षेत्र में कई न्यायिक केन्द्रों की भी स्थापना हुई जिसमें काजी रसूलपुर, रशीदपुर, रानीगोधना, बेगमसराय, बेरहामपुर आदि प्रमुख थे ।

औरंगजेब की मृत्यु के साथ ही मुगल सत्ता कमजोर पड़ने लगी जिसका लाभ उठाकर कई प्रान्तीय शासक सिर उठाने लगे। बेगूसराय इसका अपवाद नहीं था। शाम्हो के चकवार राजा बख्तावर सिंह ने मुगल सत्ता को लगान देने से इंकार कर दिया एवं 'देव–देवानाम' की उपाधि धारण कर अपनी स्वतंत्र सत्ता का शंखनाद कर दिया। एक भूमिदान पत्र से ज्ञात होता है कि उसने दलसिंहसराय तक अपना क्षेत्र विस्तार कर लिया था। ईस्ट इंडिया कम्पनी के संलेख बख्तावर सिंह को एक राजा के रूप में चिन्हित करते हैं। ये अभिलेख इस बात के प्रमाण हैं कि 1719 ई0 तक आते–आते बेगूसराय के चकवार शक्तिशाली हो गये थे एवं उन्होंने सरकार को लगान देना बन्द कर दिया था। राजा बख्तावर सिंह की मृत्यु 1730 ई0 में हो गई। तदुपरांत बहादुर सिंह ने उसका उत्तराधिकार प्राप्त किया। 1734 ई0 में अलीवर्दी खाँ बिहार का गवर्नर नियुक्त हुआ। उसने राजा बहादुर सिंह को परास्त कर लगान देने पर विवश कर दिया। इसके साथ ही चकवार – शक्ति का पतन हो गया।

बंगाल के नवाब सिराज–उद्–दौला की पराजय ने बिहार की सत्ता के द्वार ईस्ट इंडिया कंपनी के लिए खोल दिये। बेगूसराय भी कंपनी के अधीन आ गया। बेगूसराय, दौलतपुर, मंझौल, भगवानपुर आदि नील उत्पादन के केन्द्र बन गए। 1812 ई0 में मुंगेर एक पृथक् जिला के रूप में अस्तित्व में आया एवं 1832ई0 में बलिया एक परगना के रूप में उसके साथ सम्बद्ध हो गया। 1870 ई0 में बेगूसराय को एक अनुमंडल के रूप में पहचान मिली ।

बेगूसराय जिला स्वतंत्रता संग्राम के लिए भी 'उर्वर' साबित हुआ। बाबू श्रीकृष्ण सिंह ने गढ़पुरा में अपना प्रसिद्ध नमक सत्याग्रह सम्पन्न किया। 1942 ई0 के भारत छोड़ो आन्दोलन में भी बेगूसराय ने बढ़चढ कर हिस्सा लिया एवं स्थानीय शहीदों की अमरगाथा ने बेगूसराय का

मस्तक गर्व से ऊँचा रखा। बीहट बेगूसराय के वारदोली के रूप में चर्चित हो गया ।

जब भारत को 1947 ई0 में स्वतंत्रता मिली, तो बेगूसराय ने अपनी यात्रा एक अनुमंडल मुख्यालय के रूप में शुरू की। 1972 ई0 में इसे 'जिला' का दर्जा मिला एवं तदुपरांत यह अहर्निश विकास पथ पर अग्रसर है।

*विभागाध्यक्ष,
प्रा0 भा0 इति0 एवं पुरातत्व विभाग
जी0 डी0 कॉलेज बेगूसराय

सौजन्य :
मैं बेगूसराय हूँ
जिला स्थापना 2011

●●●

बेगूसराय का पुरातात्विक अन्वेषण : इतिहास के आइने में

अमिय कृष्ण*

प्राचीन भारतीय इतिहास संस्कृति एवं पुरातत्व के क्षेत्रीय हस्ताक्षर विद्वान इतिहासकारों की सेवाओं की दृष्टि से बेगूसराय सौभाग्यशाली रहा है। 1950 के दशक में ही क्षेत्रीय इतिहास के शिखर पुरुष प्रो0 राधाकृष्ण चौधरी के नेतृत्व में अन्वेषणकर्त्ताओं की एक टीम ने बेगूसराय के विभिन्न पुरास्थलों का अन्वेषण कार्य प्रारंभ किया। इस टीम में **डॉ0 उपेन्द्र ठाकुर**, **डॉ0 एम0 एस0 पांडेय**, **डॉ0 ए0 कुमार** एवं **डॉ0 आर0 सी0 पी0 सिंह** जैसे ओजस्वी इतिहासकारों के साथ–साथ इतिहास में गहरी रुचि रखनेवाले अन्य विद्वतजन सम्मिलित थे। जयमंगलगढ़, संघौल एवं बरौनी जैसे प्रमुख पुरास्थलों का अन्वेषण किया गया एवं इनके माध्यम से इतिहास की टूटी कड़ियों को जोड़ने का कार्य प्रारंभ हो गया। **1957–58 ई0** में एक अन्वेषण दल ने जयमंगलगढ़ में एक काष्ठपुल की संरचना खोज निकाली। यह पुरातात्विक दृष्टि से ऐसी दुर्लभ कड़ी थी जो इस क्षेत्र के इतिहास को मौर्य काल तक ले जाती है। इस अन्वेषण दल को बेगूसराय के राष्ट्रीय–अन्तर्राष्ट्रीय स्तर पर स्थापित इतिहासकार **डॉ0 रामशरण शर्मा** की सेवाएँ भी मिली थी। इस दल ने **प्रो0 राधाकृष्ण चौधरी** के नेतृत्व में पालयुगीन कई पाषाण प्रतिमाएँ जिले के अलग–अलग क्षेत्रों से हासिल की जो वर्तमानतः गणेश दत्त महाविद्यालय बेगूसराय के प्राचीन भारतीय इतिहास एवं पुरातत्व विभाग से संबद्ध काशी प्रसाद जायसवाल पुरातात्विक संग्रहालय में संरक्षित हैं। इस अन्वेषण दल को यदि जिले में पुरातात्विक अन्वेषकों की प्रथम पीढ़ी कहा जाय, तो कोई अतिशयोक्ति नहीं होगी। प्रो0 चौधरी के सफल नेतृत्व में इस अन्वेषण दल से जुड़े इतिहासकारों एवं इतिहास प्रेमियों ने इतिहास एवं पुरातात्विक अन्वेषण की जो अलख जगाई, वह वस्तुतः आज भी बेगूसराय की पहचान बनी हुई है। वास्तव में जिले की

प्रथम पीढ़ी के इन इतिहासकारों ने आनेवाली पीढ़ियों के लिए इतिहास–दर्शन एवं इतिहास मनस चिन्तन की मजबूत आधारशिला रखी जो आज हमारे लिए गौरव का विषय है। इन्हें हम जिले में पुरातात्विक अन्वेषण के पथ–प्रदर्शक कहें तो कोई अतिशयोक्ति नहीं होगी।

बेगूसराय जिला एवं संलग्न क्षेत्र में पुरातात्विक अन्वेषण का दूसरा दौर **1970** के दशक में शुरू हुआ जिसे **1999** तक विस्तारित माना जा सकता है। इस दौर में प्रमुख रूप से **डॉ0 पी0 गुप्ता** एवं **प्रो0 फुलेश्वर सिंह** ने नई उर्जा के साथ अन्वेषण कार्य की निरंतरता को जारी रखा। इतिहास के लिए अपने विशिष्ट प्रेम हेतु डॉ0 पी0 गुप्ता विशेष तौर पर स्मरणीय हैं क्योंकि उन्होनें चिकित्सा जैसे इतर एवं समयाभाव वाले क्षेत्र से सामंजस्य बनाए रखते हुए अपने इतिहास– प्रेम को सक्रियता के साथ प्रदर्शित किया। प्रो0 सिंह ने पुरातत्व की अपनी विशिष्ट दृष्टि का भरपूर उपयोग कर कई नए पुरास्थलों को प्रकाश में लाया। सिंघौल जैसे पुरास्थल पर पूर्व से जारी अन्वेषण कार्य को आगे बढ़ाने के साथ–साथ उन्होनें मसूरिया डीह जैसा एक नया पुरास्थल खोज निकाला जो बहुत संभव है, बेगूसराय के इतिहास की कड़ी को नवपाषाण काल तक विस्तारित कर दे। इस दौर में गणेश दत्त महाविद्यालय, बेगूसराय के प्राचीन इतिहास एवं पुरातत्व विभाग के अध्यक्ष **डॉ0 ठाकुर हरेन्द्र दयाल** ने भी व्यक्तिगत रुचि लेकर पुरावशेषों का संग्रह किया जो पूर्वोक्त संग्रहालय में संरक्षित हैं।

पुरातात्विक अन्वेषण के क्षेत्र में जिले की अन्वेषण गतिविधियों में **1999–2003 ई0** के दौरान एक नई उर्जा का समावेश हुआ जब **डॉ0 शैलेश कुमार सिन्हा** (वर्तमान विभागाध्यक्ष) ने गणेश दत्त महाविद्यालय के प्राचीन भारतीय इतिहास एवं पुरातत्व विभाग में अपना योगदान किया। विभागाध्यक्ष प्रो0 फुलेश्वर सिंह एवं डॉ0 शैलेश कुमार सिन्हा के समेकित प्रयास से स्नातकोत्तर छात्रों को इस कार्यक्रम में सक्रिय किया गया। राज्य के कई महत्वपूर्ण इतिहासकारों एवं पुरातत्ववेत्ताओं यथा – **डॉ0 मुहम्मद के0 के0 एवं डॉ0 डी0 पी0 सिंह (भारतीय पुरातत्व सर्वेक्षण, पटना), डॉ0 विजय चौधरी एवं डॉ0 जगदीश्वर पांडेय (काशी प्रसाद जायसवाल शोध संस्थान, पटना), डॉ0 ओ0 पी0 जायसवाल एवं ए0 के0 सिंह (प्रा0 भा0 इतिहास एवं पुरातत्व विभाग पटना वि0वि0) डॉ0 रामशेखर सिंह, श्री आर0 एस0 सिंह एवं श्री एस0 झा (पुरातत्व निदेशालय बिहार सरकार)** आदि ने स्थानीय सर्वेक्षण दल के साथ जिले के विभिन्न क्षेत्रों में सर्वेक्षण किया। इस क्रम में बेगूसराय जिला के लगभग तीन दर्जन पुरास्थलों को चिह्नित किया गया। इस दल ने समस्तीपुर एवं खगड़िया जिला के पुरास्थलों का सर्वेक्षण किया। वर्ष **2003** के उपरांत भी डॉ0 सिन्हा का सर्वेक्षण कार्य जारी

रहा एवं वे छात्रों के सहयोग से पुरातात्विक अन्वेषण का कार्य करते रहे। मार्च **2004** में क्षेत्रीय पुरातत्व पर गणेशदत्त महाविद्यालय में सम्पन्न राष्ट्रीय सेमीनार में वर्त्तमान **महानिदेशक पुरातत्व, भारतीय पुरातत्व सर्वेक्षण, डॉ0 गौतमसेन गुप्ता** सहित अन्य विद्वानों की सहभागिता ने जिले में पुरातात्विक अन्वेषण कार्य को गति प्रदान किया। इस दौरान विभागाध्यक्ष के रूप में डॉ0 सिन्हा कि जीवट अन्वेषण क्षमता एवं प्राचीन भारतीय इतिहास एवं पुरातत्व विभाग, गणेश दत्त महाविद्यालय के स्नातकोत्तर छात्रों की सक्रिय भागीदारी से पुरास्थल अन्वेषण संबंधित गतिविधियाँ बनी रही। डॉ0 सिन्हा ने औरेडीह एवं रोशनाहाडीह जैसे पुरास्थलों को प्रकाशित किया ।

बेगूसराय जिला के पुरातात्विक अन्वेषण के क्षेत्र में वर्ष **2007–2010** मील का पत्थर साबित हुआ जब **डॉ0 शैलेश कुमार सिन्हा** को काशी प्रसाद जायसवाल शोध संस्थान पटना द्वारा आहूत बिहार के प्रमुख पुरास्थलों के सूचीकरण कार्य में बेगूसराय एवं खगड़िया जिलों के समन्वयक का दायित्व निभाने का सुअवसर मिला। इस दौरान डा0 सिन्हा के निर्देशन में बेगूसराय जिला के शोध अन्वेषक इन पंक्तियों के लेखक एवं शंकर सुमन ने बेगूसराय के विभिन्न गाँवों एवं टीलों का गहन सर्वेक्षण किया। इस गहन सर्वेक्षण में जिला भर से लगभग 150 पुरास्थलों को चिह्नित कर सूचीकृत किया गया। इनमें गणेश दत्त महाविद्यालय के प्राचीन भारतीय इतिहास एवं पुरातत्व विभाग द्वारा पूर्व से चिह्नित किये गये पुरास्थल भी शामिल थे। इन पुरास्थलों में हिन्दू धर्म के साथ–साथ इस्लाम एवं बौद्ध धर्म से संबंधित कतिपय पुरास्थल भी थे। वर्ष **2003 से 2008** के बीच देश एवं राज्य स्तर पर इतिहासज्ञों एवं इतिहास प्रेमियों का ध्यान आकृष्ट करनेवाले कुछ प्रमुख पुरास्थल बेहतर तरीके से सामने आए। इनमें अंकुरीनाथ मंदिर एवं राधेश्याम मंदिर उलाव, हरसाईं स्तूप–समूह, गढपुरा के निकट स्थित स्तूप–समूह, बड़ी बलिया स्थित प्राचीन मस्जिद के ध्वंसावशेष आदि प्रमुख रहे। डॉ0 सिन्हा की अध्यक्षता में गठित पुरातात्विक एवं सांस्कृतिक धरोहर संरक्षण परिषद की अध्यक्ष–नीत टीम के बारंबार प्रयास के उपरांत वर्ष 2008 में भारतीय पुरातत्व सर्वेक्षण की पटना इकाई ने हरसाईं को वज्रयान से संबंधित महत्वपूर्ण स्थल के रूप में चिह्नित किया। तत्कालीन **अधीक्षण, पुरातत्व, भारतीय पुरातत्व सर्वेक्षण, पटना डॉ0 पी0 के0 मिश्र** के अतिरिक्त तत्कालीन जिलाधिकारी, बेगूसराय श्री संजीव हंस के नेतृत्व में जिला प्रशासन की इसमें महत्वपूर्ण भूमिका रही। डॉ0 सिन्हा के साथ–साथ जिला प्रशासन के सक्रिय सहयोग से हरसाई स्तूप के संरक्षण हेतु राज्य सरकार तत्पर हुई। पुरास्थलों के प्रति अपने विशेष प्रेम एवं सक्रियता के लिए वर्त्तमान जिलाधिकारी श्री जितेन्द्र श्रीवास्तव भी

इतिहास प्रेमी जिला वासियों के विशेष धन्यवाद के पात्र हैं। सम्प्रति बेगूसराय जिला के महत्वपूर्ण पुरास्थलों को **www.begusaraiheritage.com** वेबसाइट पर देखा जा सकता है जो डॉ शैलेश कुमार सिन्हा द्वारा इतिहासप्रेमियों को समर्पित एवं बेगूसराय की पहचान को स्थापित करने के लिए कटिबद्ध है। इस वेबसाइट का उद्‌घाटन जनवरी 2009 में विप्लवी पुस्तकालय, गोदरगामा स्थित सभागार में स्व0 राधाकृष्ण चौधरी की धर्मपत्नी **श्रीमति शांति देवी** द्वारा ऑन लाईन किया गया था। डॉ0 सिन्हा के सम्पादकत्व में प्रकाशित **''धरोहर''** नामक शोध पत्रिका के माध्यम से भी बेगूसराय के पुरास्थलों को समय–समय पर सामने लाया जाता रहा हैं।

शोध अन्वेषक,
काशी प्रसाद जायसवाल
शोध संस्थान, पटना

सौजन्य :
मैं बेगूसराय हूँ
जिला स्थापना, 2011

●●●

के0 पी0 जायसवाल पुरातात्विक संग्रहालय की मधुपात्रधारिणी प्रतिमा

कुमारी रंजना*

सभ्यता के उदय से ही मातृशक्ति की अराधना किसी न किसी रूप में प्रचलित रही है।[1] देवी पूजन की परम्परा मुख्यतः दो रूपों में मिलती है : (1) मातृदेवी के रूप में (2) शक्ति के रूप में। प्रारंभ में देवी की उपासना माता के रूप में अधिक लोकप्रिय थी। पुराणों की दुर्गा–स्तुति में जगन्नाथमाता या जगदम्बा स्वरूप की अवधारणा में देवी के माता स्वरूप का स्पष्ट संकेत देखा जा सकता है। विश्व की विभिन्न प्राचीन सभ्यताओं में धर्म की अवधारणा के साथ ही मातृपूजन की परम्परा भी आरंभ हुई। देवी पूजन का दूसरा रूप शक्ति पूजन के रूप में प्रकट हुआ। शक्ति पूजन के अन्तर्गत विभिन्न देवताओं की क्रियाशीलता उनकी शक्तियों में निहित मानी गयी।[2]

गुप्तकाल तक शक्ति पूजा के क्रमिक विकास के फलस्वरूप शक्ति के उपासको का एक स्वतंत्र शाक्य सम्प्रदाय बना। यद्यपि पुरातात्विक एवं पुरालेखीय प्रमाणों के आधार पर शक्ति पूजा की परम्परा का स्पष्ट निर्धारण कठिन है। किन्तु भारतीय शिल्प में लगभग सातवीं सदी ई0 के उपरांत शक्ति के विविध रूपों का शिल्पांकन प्रारंभ हुआ। विष्णुधर्मोत्तर पुराण, अपराजितपृच्छा रूपमंडन, शिल्परत्न, आदि कई ग्रंथों में शक्ति के विविध रूपों का विस्तृत विवरण मिलता है।[3]

लगभग छठी से दसवीं सदी ई0 के मध्य का काल भारत के तीनों प्रमुख धर्मो (ब्राह्मण, बौद्ध एवं जैन) के लिए संक्रमण काल रहा है। इस अवधि में तांत्रिक कार्य के परिणामस्वरूप तीनों ही धर्मो में अनेक नूतन देवी–देवताओं की कल्पना की गयी और उनके पहचानिक लक्षण नियत किये गए। तीनों धर्मो में देव–देवी लक्षणों का पारस्परिक आदान–प्रदान भी हुआ।

बौद्ध देवकुल में स्वतंत्र देवों की कल्पना के साथ ही ब्राह्मण देवकुल के अनेक देवी–देवताओं को सम्मिलित किया गया है।[4] वज्रयान मत में विभिन्न ध्यानी बुद्धों से संबंधित देवियों की कल्पना

की गयी, जिन्हें तारा कहा गया। ध्यानी बुद्ध अमिताभ के देव परिवार में देवियों की संख्या तीन बतायी गयी है। ध्यानी बुद्ध अक्षोभ्य से उत्पन्न देवियों में एकजटा (वज्रयान की अत्यंत शक्तिशाली) सभी बाधाओं से मुक्त कर सौभाग्य देने वाली, भयंकर दर्शना, प्रत्यालिढ़ मुद्रावाली देवी मानी गयी है।[5] एकजटा का वर्ण नीला तथा तीन आँखें होती है। इसे द्विभुजी, चर्तुभुजी और अष्टभुजी रूपों में दिखाया जाता है। इस देवी का शरीर नाटे कद का, उदर बड़ा और आगे की ओर निकला होता है। गले में नरमुण्डों की माला धारण किये, शव पर आरूढ़, प्रत्यालिढ़ आसन में इसे दर्शाया गया है। जबकि इससे साम्य रखती संयुक्त रूप से उत्पन्न पंच ध्यानी बुद्धों में से कुरूकुल्ला भी उल्लेखनीय है।[6] इनके कई रूप मिलते हैं। इनमें शुक्ल कुरूकुल्ला द्विभुजी, त्रिनेत्री, पशुवाहन, वज्रप्रयंक, अक्षमाला एवं पद्मपात्र (अमृत से भरा) से युक्त होती है।[7]

के0पी0 जायसवाल पूरातात्विक संग्रहालय जी0 डी0 कॉलेज, बेगूसराय में स्थापित मधुपात्र–धारिणी प्रतिमा उपर्युक्त वर्णित देवियों से अत्याधिक साम्य रखता है। यह एक नारी (मधुपात्र–धारी) प्रतिमा है जो काले पत्थर से निर्मित है। प्रो0 राधाकृष्ण चौधरी ने इसे अप्सरा की प्रतिमा माना है तथा इसकी तुलना खजुराहो एवं भुवनेश्वर की मूर्तिशिल्प से की है।[8] यह प्रतिमा नवमी से दसवी सदी ई0 के मध्य की प्रतीत होती है। इस प्रतिमा की प्राप्ति स्थली सिंघौल है जो बेगूसराय जिला मुख्यालय से लगभग 3 कि0मी0 की दूरी पर अवस्थित है। इस प्रतिमा की ऊँचाई 31 cm तथा चौड़ाई 20 cm है।

इस मधुपात्रधारिणी प्रतिमा का केवल केन्द्रीय भाग सुरक्षित है। मुख्य प्रतिमा के घुटने से नीचे तथा इसके चारो ओर का स्टेला भी खण्डित है। प्रतिमा का दाहिना हाथ केहुनी के नीचे खण्डित है। इसके बाँए हाथ में मधुपात्र प्रदर्शित किया गया है। दाहिने हाथ की गति से मधुपात्र की दिशा में मुड़े होने का संकेत मिलता है। प्रतिमा के कटि से ऊपर का भाग एक विशिष्ट लोच के साथ प्रदर्शित है। इसका देहियष्टि मांसल है। प्रतिमा के गले में हार, बांयी भुजा में भुजबंध एवं कंगन, कानों में कुण्डल, केश राशि विन्यस्त है। मुख्य आकृति की दाहिने ओर पार्श्व में दाहिने छोड़ पर गतिमान अश्व प्रदर्शित किया गया है। मुख्य आकृति के बांयी ओर के हाथ के नीचे पेड़ की शाखा से लिपटे पुरुष आकृति याचक मुद्रा में प्रदर्शित किया गया है।[9]

यद्यपि देवी प्रतिमा खण्डित एवं अपूर्ण अवस्था में प्राप्त हुई है। अतः इनकी पहचान पूर्णरूपेण करना संभव प्रतीत नहीं होता। इतना स्पष्ट है कि तंत्रयान से संबद्ध यह प्रतिमा बौद्ध धर्म से सम्बद्ध है।

संदर्भ सूची :–

1. निलिमा वशिष्ठ ; राजस्थान की मूर्तिकला परंपरा, पृ0 100
2. तिवारी एवं गिरि ; मध्यकालीन भारतीय प्रतिमा लक्षण
3. टी0ए0 गोपीनाथ राव ; पूर्व निर्दिष्ट खण्ड 'ए' भाग–2 पृ0 327–400
4. डा0 मारुतिनंदन तिवारी, डा0 कमल गिरि ; भारतीय प्रतिमा लक्षण, पृ0 242
5. तिवारी एवं गिरि ; मध्यकालीन भारतीय प्रतिमा लक्षण
6. डा0 वृजभूषण श्रीवास्तव ; प्राचीन भारतीय प्रतिमा विज्ञान एवं मूर्तिकला
7. तिवारी एवं गिरि ; मध्यकालीन भारतीय प्रतिमा लक्षण
8. ऑन बिहार, एपेन्डिक्स –III, पृ0–1 (जी0 डी0 कॉलेज बुलेटिन 4)
9. डा0 शैलेश कुमार सिन्हा ; काशी प्रसाद जायसवाल पुरातात्विक संग्रहालय–एक परिचय

शोधार्थी,
ल0न0मि0वि0, दरभंगा

सौजन्य :
धरोहर
(संस्कृति एवं पुरातात्विक शोध को समर्पित पत्रिका)
अंक – III, 2013

●●●

बेगूसराय जिला में चंदेल राजपूत

यशवीर कुमार सिंह*

आज के बदलते परिवेश में बेगूसराय के क्षत्रिय इतिहास एवं पूरा सम्पदा को बिहार राज्य एवं देश के मानचित्र पर स्थापित करने के लिए इसके समृद्ध विरासत के संरक्षित एवं उद्घाटित करने की आवश्यकता है। बेगूसराय वर्तमान मिथिला का एक प्राचीन, ऐतिहासिक एवं पुरातात्विक स्थल है। वैज्ञानिक ढ़ंग से बेगूसराय के ऐतिहासिक महत्व के स्थानों का सर्वेक्षण अभी तक बार–बार के सीमित प्रयास के बावजूद संभव नहीं हो सका है। यत्र–तत्र बिखरे हुए सामग्रियों, स्थानीय अभिलेखों एवं किंवदन्तियों के आधार पर इस क्षेत्रीय इतिहास की कड़ियों को जोड़ने का प्रयास किया गया है।

नदियों की घटती–बढ़ती धारा के अनुसार, बेगूसराय की सीमा समय–समय पर बदलती रही है। नौलागढ़, जयमंगलागढ़, वीरपुर, सिंघौल और पानापुर से पर्याप्त मात्रा में सिक्के, प्रस्तर, मूर्तियाँ, खिलौना आदि प्राप्त हुए हैं। कुछ अभिलेखों के आधार पर इस क्षेत्र का ऐतिहासिक संबंध प्राचीन काल से सम्बद्ध है। डा. ए. एस. अल्तेकर ने इस क्षेत्र में बसने वाली प्राचीन जाति को भारशिव की संज्ञा दी है जो कि यह एक राजपूत राजवंश है।[1] इसके साथ ही यहाँ पर चंदेल, परमार, सुलकी एवं चौहान राजपूत के वंशजों ने अपना शासन स्थापित किया था। नौलागढ़, जयमंगलागढ़, वीरपुर एवं पानापुर में चंदेल राजपूत के वंशज क्रमशः नवल सिंह, जयमंगल सिंह, वीर सिंह एवं पनक सिंह ने शासन किया था। इन स्थानों का यह नामकरण उसी समय से प्रचलित है।

चंदेल शासक विष्णु और शिव का उपासक हुआ करते थे। काले पत्थर के विभिन्न मूर्तियों से यह स्वतः प्रमाणित हो जाता है कि वैष्णव शैव एवं शाक्त मत का यहाँ पर प्रचार–प्रसार हुआ था। वीरपुर, वरैयपुरा में चामुण्डा की काले पत्थर की एक प्रतिमा है। यह प्रतिमा मंदिर में स्थापित है। जो राजपूत शैली में बना है। चामुण्डा की प्रतिमा एवं उसके मंदिर की शैली इस क्षेत्र में चंदेल राजपूत के शासन का एक प्रमाण है। बेगूसराय जिला मुख्यालय से वीरपुर की दूरी 14 कि0मी0, वीरपुर से नौलागढ़ की दूरी लगभग 5 कि0मी0, नौलागढ़ से पानापुर की दूरी लगभग 5 कि0मी0

एवं बेगूसराय से जयमंगलागढ़ की दूरी लगभग 18 कि0मी0 है।

हर्षवर्द्धन के मरणोपरान्त उत्तर भारत में राजनीतिक विकेन्द्रीकरण की प्रवृत्ति प्रबल हो गई। लगभग 125 वर्षों तक उत्तर भारत में अराजकता छायी रही। इसी बीच उत्तर–पश्चिम और मध्य भारत में नये–नये राजवंशों का उदय प्रारंभ हुआ। जो अपने को पुराने क्षत्रिय वंश से संबंधित होने का दावा पेश करते हुए राजपूत के नाम से विख्यात हुए। यद्यपि ये वंश प्रादेशिक सत्ता की स्थापना तक ही सीमित रहे, किन्तु इन राजवंशों ने लम्बे समय तक भारतीय राजनीति को प्रभावित कर हिन्दू संस्कृति में यथेष्ट योगदान किया।

राजपूतों की उत्पत्ति के संबंध में अनेक मतों का प्रतिपादन कया गया है। चन्दवरदायी के पृथ्वीराज रासो के विवरण में 36 प्रकार के राजपूत कुलों के उदभव का विवरण मिलता है।[2] इनके कथा के अनुसार परशुराम ने क्षत्रियों पर क्रुद्ध होकर उनका 21 बार विनाश किया था। चारों ओर धरती क्षत्रिय विहीन हो गयी। फलतः अराजकता छा गयी और लोग धर्म से विमुख हो पाप कर्म में संलग्न हो गये। अतः ऋषियों ने आवू पर्वत पर 40 दिनों तक यज्ञ किया। यज्ञ के अग्निकुंड से 36 प्रकार के राजपूत उत्पन्न हुए। कर्नल टॉड महोदय ने एनांल्स एण्ड एन्टिकयूटी ऑफ राजस्थान नामक पुस्तक में लिखा है कि राजपूत पुराने योद्धा जाति के वंशज थे।[3] कर्नल टॉड के मत का समर्थन भी0 ए0 स्मीथ ने भी अपनी पुस्तक अर्ली हिस्ट्री ऑफ इंडिया में किया है।[4]

8वीं से 10वीं शताब्दी के बीच उत्तर, पश्चिम और मध्य भारत में राजपूतों ने क्षेत्रिय और राष्ट्रीय धारा को प्रभावित कर इतिहास में महत्वपूर्ण योगदान दिया।

चंदेल राजवंश प्रारंभिक मध्यकालीन राजपूत राजवंशों में एक महत्वपूर्ण राजवंश था। 1202 ई0 में कालिंजर और गढ़महोवा पर कुतुबुद्दीन ऐबक का अधिकार हो गया। इस वंश के वीरवर्मन और भोजवर्मन 13वीं सदी के अंत तक चंदैलों की सत्ता प्राप्ति हेतु असफल संघर्ष करते रहे। मिश्रा के पुस्तक चंदेला और उनका राजत्वकाल में भी चंदेल शासकों के बिहार आगमन और उनके निवास स्थल पर प्रकाश डाला गया है।[5] उनके शासनकाल में वैष्णव, शैव, बौद्ध और जैन की वृद्धि हुई। चंदैल राजा विष्णु और शिव के उपासक हुआ करते थे। त्रिशूल शिव की उपासना का प्रतीक था। इस क्षेत्र में आज भी सबसे अधिक शिवालयों की संख्या देखी जा सकती है।

मुस्लिम आक्रमणकारियों से मात खाने के बाद चंदेल शासक अपने लिए नये आश्रय की खोज में पूरब की ओर अपने बचे–खुचे सेना को लेकर चले थे। इसका विवरण चंदेल वंश के नौलागढ़ एवं पानापुर के निवासियों के पास आज भी रिकॉर्ड के रूप में मौजूद है। वहाँ के निवासियों का यह कहना है कि गढ़महोवा (मध्यप्रदेश) से उनके वंशज जो कि चार भाई थे अपने पूरे काफिले के साथ बढ़ते हुए गंगा पार बेगूसराय के उत्तर में चार जगह पर अपना पड़ाव डाला था। यहाँ की भूमि अति उर्वर एवं संस्कारी प्रतीत होने के कारण वे यहीं पर अपना निवास स्थल

बनाने का फैसला किया। इन्हीं चारों भाई के नाम पर जो जहाँ बसे उस जगह का नाम पड़ गया।

नवल सिंह (नौलागढ़ पर शासन किये)

वीर सिंह (वीरपुर में शासन किये)

जयमंगल सिंह (जयमंगलगढ़ पर शासन किये)

पनक सिंह (पानापुर में शासन किये)

स्थानीय अभिलेख के आधार पर वीर सिंह के बारे में कहा जाता है कि उनके बगल में सरौंजा नामक एक बस्ती था जहाँ का जमींदार पासवान परिवार से संबंधित था। वीर सिंह को एक खुबसूरत लड़की थी। जिससे वैवाहिक संबंध स्थापित करके पासवान अपनी सामरिक स्थिति को और मजबूत बनाने के प्रयत्न में था। वीर सिंह के पास जब शादी का प्रस्ताव लेकर सरौंजा का दूत पहुँचा तो, उसके साहस को देखकर के वीर सिंह सिंह ने कूटनीति का सहारा लेने का निश्चय किया। उन्होंने अपनी सामरिक स्थिति को कमजोर पाकर इस प्रस्ताव को स्वीकार कर लिया और सरौंजा के जमींदार के पूरे बस्ती के साथ बारात में शामिल होने का निमंत्रण दे दिया। पासवान का पूरा गाँव इस बारात में सम्मिलत हुआ। इधर वीर सिंह जहर मिला हुआ भोजन खिलाकर पूरे बारातको मौंत की नींद सुला दिया। इस बात की पुष्टि इस बात से भी होती है कि वीरपुर के पश्चिम बलान नदी के किनारे बाँध में मिट्टी देते समय सैकड़ों नरकंकाल मिले थे।[6] इससे इस बात को और बल मिला है। वहाँ के निवासियों में यह किंवदन्ति है कि उस पासवान परिवार में मात्र एक औरत बची जो उस समय गर्भवती होने के कारण अपने नैहर चली गई थी। उस औरत के एक लड़का हुआ जिसका पालन–पोषण अपने ननिहाल में किया गया था। उस लड़का के बहुत दिनों बाद घटना की जानकारी मिली। कहा जाता है कि वह वीर सिंह से बदला लेने की कसम खाकर दिल्ली चला गया और वहाँ लम्बे अवधि तक सेवा करने के बाद उसने मुगल शासक को वीर सिंह के ऊपर हमला करने के लिए राजी कर लिया। मुगल शासक लम्बे समय से इस क्षेत्र पर अपनी निगाहें जमाये हुए था। इस अवसर के हाथ से जाने देना वह नहीं चाहता था। उचित अवसर देखकर मुगल की सेना दिल्ली से कूच करते हुए गंगा के दक्षिणी किनारे पर अपना डेरा डाल दिया।

इधर वीर सिंह का राजपुरोहित जो उस समय सिमरिया में गंगा स्नान करने के लिए गया था, उसने अपना दूत भेजकर पता लगाया कि डेरा डालने वाली सेना कहाँ की है और कहाँ प्रस्थान करने वाली है। कहते हैं कि यह दिल्ली की शाही सेना है और गंगा पार करके वीर सिंह के साम्राज्य पर आक्रमण की तैयारी में है। वीर सिंह के इस बात की सूचना उनके राजपुरोहित ने आकर दिया। वीर सिंह भी आनन–फानन में अपने सेना को तैयार कर मोर्चा संभाल लिया। लेकिन शाही सेना के सामने वीर सिंह की स्थिति को कमजोर पाकर उनके सेनापतियों ने राजा को किला छोड़ने का सलाह दिया। किला छोड़ते ही सैनिकों में भगदड़ मच गया। मामूली संघर्ष

के बाद वीरपुर के किला पर शाही सेना का अधिकार हो गया। राजा का खजाना भी शाही सेना के हाथ आ गया था। इधर वीरपुर से पलायन के बाद राजा सपरिवार धरहरा मोहनपुर (लखीसराय) में बस गये। उनका वंशज वर्त्तमान में भी वहाँ मौजूद है। इस बात की पुष्टि के लिए स्थानीय अभिलेख एवं हस्तलिखित वंशावली का सहारा लिया गया है।

कहा जाता है कि वीरपुर के किला पर अपना आधिपत्य स्थापित होने से उत्साहित होकर शाही सेना नवल सिंह के ऊपर आक्रमण कर दिया। नौलागढ़ के चारों ओर किला का निर्माण किया गया था। जो बहुत ही मजबूत था। किला में प्रवेश करने के लिए दुश्मन की सेना को कठिन संघर्ष करना पड़ा था। किले की दीवार को तोड़ने के लिए तोप का प्रयोग करना पड़ा था। जिसकी पुष्टि गढ़ के अंदर बने कुएँ के भीतर से प्राप्त तोप के गोला से भी होता है। दो दिनों क भयंकर युद्ध के बाद स्थिति में बदलाव नहीं होते देख सेना ने तोप का इस्तेमाल कर दीवार को ध्वस्त करके किला के अंदर प्रवेश कर गई।

राजा के विश्वासपात्र मंत्रियों और सेनानायकों ने दुश्मन को प्रबल पाकर राजा को गुप्त ढ़ंग से बने हुए सुरंग के माध्यम से किला छोड़ने की सलाह दी। राजा किला के अंदर बने सुरंग में प्रवेश कर गये। कहा जाता है कि नवल सिंह को दो पत्नियाँ थी। एक ने यह सारा भेद आक्रमणकारी को बता दिया।[7] इसके बाद राजा को सुरंग में ही घेरकर मार दिया गया। इस युद्ध में पूरे राज परिवार को मौत की नींद सुला दिया गया। फलस्वरूप नौलागढ़ पर भी आक्रमणकारी का शासन स्थापित हो गया।

यहाँ पर अपनी विजय पताका लहराने के बाद आक्रमणकारी जयमंगलागढ़ (जयमंगलगढ़) के ऊपर हमला कर दिया। पूरे किले को घेर लिया गया। भयंकर संघर्ष के उपरान्त यहाँ पर भी आक्रमणकारी की ही जीत हुई। जयमंगल सिंह निःसंतान ही मारे गए, फलस्वरूप जयमंगलागढ़ से भी चंदैल शासन का अंत हो गया। इसके बाद आक्रमणकारी पन्नक सिंह के ऊपर आक्रमण कर दिया जो पानापुर में स्वतंत्र रूप से रह रहे थे। पन्नक सिंह को यह पता चल गया था कि डटकर मोर्चा लेने पर हार निश्चित है, इसलिए ये अपने सैनिकों के साथ छापामार युद्ध का सहारा लिया। पानापुर के पूरब और उत्तर में घनघोर जंगल था। ये उसी जंगल में प्रवेश कर गए। आक्रमणकारियों को इस क्षेत्र के भौगोलिक स्थिति की जानकारी नहीं थी। इसलिए यहाँ पर रहने के बाद भी पनक सिंह का दमन नहीं कर सके। समय बीतने के साथ ही पन्नक सिंह के पुत्र धिरजु सिंह ने अपने पैत्रिक भूमि को हस्तगत कर लिया। वर्तमान समय में पानापुर में इन्हीं पन्नक सिंह के वंशजों का निवास है। इस बात की पुष्टि हेतु पानापुर निवासी शिवजी सिंह के पास उपलब्ध स्थानीय अभिलेख एवं हस्तलिखित वंशावली का सहारा लिया गया है।

वर्तमान समय में संघौल के उत्तर पचम्बा, वरैपुरा और जयमंगलागढ़ से शिवलिंग और उमा महादेव के अतिरिक्त काले पत्थर की मूर्तियों के अतिरिक्त चामुण्डा की मूर्ति मिली है। चामुण्डा

चंदेल राजपूत की कुल देवी माना गयी है।[8] वीरपुर (बरौनी प्रखंड) के पास वरैपुरा के वसहा स्थान के पास पोखर से 1957 ई0 में राजपूत कालीन काले पत्थर की पूर्ण और भग्न मूर्तियों का विशाल भंडार मिला था। इनमें सबसे बड़ी संख्या शैव्य मूर्तियों की थी। उसमें मात्र एक शिवलिंग और बसहा की मूर्ति बची हुई है। भयंकर युद्ध के बाद स्थिति में बदलाव नहीं होते देख सेना ने तोप का इस्तेमाल कर दीवार को ध्वस्त करके किला के अंदर प्रवेश कर गई।

इस काल में बेगूसराय में वैष्णवों और सूर्य उपासना में भी समान रूप से विकास देखा जाता है। इससे बेगूसराय में हिन्दूओं के प्रायः हर धर्म के देवी–देवताओं की मूर्ति मिलने से यह प्रमाणित होता है कि यह इलाका राजनीतिक तौर पर ही महत्वपूर्ण नहीं था, वरन आर्थिक तौर पर सम्पन्न होने के कारण तत्कालीन सांस्कृतिक चेतनाओं से भी सम्पन्न था।

उपर्युक्त विश्लेषण से यह ज्ञात होता है कि वीरपुर में चामुण्डा प्रतिमा की उपस्थिति चामुण्डा मंदिर का राजपूत शैली में निर्मित होना इस क्षेत्र में राजपूत शासन का प्रमाण है। चंदेल राजपूत परिवार के पास उपलब्ध हस्तलिखित वंशावली, स्थानीय अभिलेख, भूमि विवाद संबंधी दस्तावेज आदि भी इस क्षेत्र में राजपूत की उपस्थिति का प्रमाण है। इनके वंशज के हजारों परिवार अभी इस क्षेत्र में वर्तमान है।

सदर्भ–सूची :

1. डा. ए. एस. अल्तेकर, प्राचीन भारत का इतिहास, पृ0 330
2. डॉ. ठाकुर हरेन्द्र दयाल सिन्हा, वीरपुर की पाषाण प्रतिमाएँ
3. चन्दवरदायी – पृथ्वीराज रासो, पृ0 27
4. कर्नल टॉड – एनांल्स एण्ड एन्टिकयूटी ऑफ राजस्थान
5. भी. ए. स्मीथ – अर्ली हिस्ट्री ऑफ इंडिया
6. मिश्रा जी. पी. चंदेला और उनका राजत्व काल, पृ0 279
7. प्रो. फुलेश्वर सिंह, बेगूसराय का इतिहास, स्वर्णभूमि, जी. डी. कॉलेज, बेगूसराय,
8. हवलदार त्रिपाठी सहृदय बिहार की नदियाँ, पृ0 249
9. क्षत्रियवंशावली – ठाकुर उदय नारायण सिंह, पृ0 32

* शोधार्थी
ल. ना. मि. विश्वविद्यालय,
दरभंगा

सौजन्य :
धरोहर
(संस्कृति एवं पुरातत्त्व को समर्पित शोध पत्रिका)
अंक – IV-V - 2006

●●●

बेगूसराय जिले की प्रारंभिक मध्यकालीन मूर्तिकला का अध्ययन आवश्यक

सुशान्त कुमार*

अरबों के आक्रमण के बाद आठवीं एवं नवीं शताब्दी के तत्कालीन तीन प्रमुख शक्तियों (पाल, प्रतिहार और राष्ट्रकूट) के बीच साम्राज्य विस्तार करने के लिए कई चरणों में लगभग दो शताब्दी तक त्रिपक्षीय संघर्ष हुआ। बिहार बंगाल के क्षेत्र में पालों की शक्ति बहुत मजबूत थीं। इस काल तक प्रशासनिक इकाई भुक्ति में विभाजित रही। तत्कालीन बिहार – बंगाल का सम्पूर्ण इलाका छः भुक्ति में विभाजित था, जिसमें एक ओर आधुनिक सोनभद्र–मिर्जापुर का इलाका था तो दूसरी ओर आधुनिक बंगलादेश स्थित राजशाही का इलाका। ये भुक्तियां थीं, यथा – तीर भुक्ति, नगर भुक्ति, पुण्ड्रवर्धन भुक्ति, वर्धमान भुक्ति, दंड भुक्ति और पराग–ज्योतिष भुक्ति। इन भुक्तियों में से तीर भुक्ति का सम्पूर्ण इलाका और पुण्ड्र वर्धन भुक्ति का पश्चिमी इलाका कमोबेश आज गंगा का सम्पूर्ण उत्तरी भाग है, जिसमें चम्पारण से पूर्णिया तक का सारा क्षेत्र आ जाता है। भुक्तियों के इस प्रशासनिक एवं भौगोलिक विभाजन में वर्तमान बेगूसराय जिला का सम्पूर्ण इलाका तीर भुक्ति के अधीन था।

पालों का प्रसार क्षेत्र मुख्य रूप से गंगा के दक्षिणी हिस्से में अधिक रहा है और गंगा के उत्तरी हिस्से में सीमान्त इलाकों यथा नोलागढ़ (बेगूसराय), इमादपुर (वैशाली), बनगांव (सहरसा) के क्षेत्र से मिलता है। प्रारंभिक मध्यकाल में तीर भुक्ति क्षेत्र से इसके अतिरिक्त पाल शासन के कोई अन्य पुरातात्विक प्रमाण नहीं हैं। ऐसी स्थिति में जब बेगूसराय जिला से संबंधित प्रारम्भिक मध्यकालीन प्रतिमाओं का अध्ययन करते हैं तो कतिपय प्रश्न उभर कर आता है। बेगूसराय जैसे छोटे से क्षेत्र में छोटे बड़े कमोबेश सत्तर पाषाण प्रतिमाओं के ज्ञात होने की जानकारी है। ये प्रतिमाएं काशी प्रसाद जायसवाल पुरातात्विक संग्रहालय, जी. डी. कॉलेज बेगूसराय, बेगूसराय संग्रहालय, बेगूसराय के अतिरिक्त मन्दिरों एवं खेतों में रखे हुए हैं। बीरपुर–बरैपुरा, जयमंगलागढ़, बरौनी, बीहट, पचम्बा, बलिया, रजौरा, कंकौल आदि जगहों से प्रतिमाएं मिली हैं। उपलब्ध

प्रतिमाओं में अधिकांशतः खंडित प्रतिमा हैं। कुछ प्रतिमाएं ही पूर्ण रूप से बिना किसी टूटन के दिखाई देती है। एक अनुमान के मुताबिक जिले के आठ दस प्रतिमाओं की चोरी भी हो चुकी है, जिसमें विष्णु, नृवराह, नरसिंह, चामुण्डा, अवलोकितेश्वर जैसे देवी देवता हैं। सर्वाधिक चोरी वीरपुर जैसे क्षेत्र से हुई है। बेगूसराय जिला में वीरपुर मूर्ति निर्माण परम्परा का एक महत्वपूर्ण केन्द्र के रूप में विख्यात रहा होगा क्योंकि आज भी एक दर्जन से अधिक की संख्या में प्रारंभिक मध्यकालीन पाषाण प्रतिमाओं के उपलब्ध होने की जानकारी वीरपुर–बरैपुरा से मिलती है।

तीर भुक्ति के क्षेत्र में पाषाण प्रतिमाओं का विकास गुप्त शासकों के अधीन प्रारंभ हो चुका था। पाल शासकों के बारे में यह जानकारी मिलती है कि इन्होंने मूर्ति कला के क्षेत्र में महत्वपूर्ण योगदान दिया, फलतः मूर्ति कला के क्षेत्र में एक विशिष्ट कला शैली का जन्म एवं विकास पाल काल में हुआ। इस कला के महत्वपूर्ण केन्द्रों में नालन्दा, कुर्कीहार, अन्तिचक आदि था, जहाँ मूर्तियों का निर्माण जाता था। पाल काल में अधिकांशतः बौद्ध प्रतिमाओं का निर्माण हुआ जिसमें बोधिसत्व, अवलोकितेश्वर, मंजुश्री, तारा प्रमुख रूप से हैं। ब्राह्मण प्रतिमाओं का निर्माण अपेक्षाकृत कम हुआ जिनमें, विष्णु, सूर्य, उमा–महेश्वर मुख्य हैं। ये प्रतिमाएं एकाश्म काले बेसाल्ट पत्थर में शारीरिक सौष्ठव और शालीनता के साथ बनी हुई दिखाई देती है। भारतीय कला के विकास में पाल कला का महत्वपूर्ण स्थान रहा है लेकिन बिहार और बंगाल के क्षेत्रीय कला के रूप में इसकी ख्याति बन कर रह गयी है।

गंगा एक महत्वपूर्ण नदी है जो सालों भर अत्यधिक जल के साथ आच्छादित रहती है। गंगा के दक्षिणी भाग में पालों का साम्राज्य लम्बे काल खंड तक स्थापित रहा है। बेगूसराय की प्रतिमाओं में पाल कालीन प्रतिमाओं की विशेषताओं से अलग दिखने वाली प्रतिमाएं आसानी से दिखाई देती है, जिसके संबंध में अभी तक किसी कला विशेषज्ञ या इतिहासकार ने कभी कोई सवाल खड़ा नहीं किया है। तीर भुक्ति से संबंधित पाषाण प्रतिमाओं के अवलोकन से स्थानीय स्तर पर शैलीगत एवं कालगत अन्तर आसानी से दिखाई देता है। पालकालीन प्रतिमाओं का स्टेला गोलाकार होता है किन्तु यहाँ की अधिकांश प्रतिमाओं का स्टेला त्रिकोणात्मक प्रतीत होता है। पालकालीन स्टेला के ऊपरी हिस्से में किसी तरह का कोई अलंकरण दिखाई नहीं देता है जबकि बेगूसराय के जयमंगलागढ़ से प्राप्त और मोहनपुर में स्थापित विष्णु, कंकौल से प्राप्त विष्णु, बरौनी, हरिहरपुर (वीरपुर), बरैपुरा आदि जगह से प्राप्त सूर्य की प्रतिमाओं में कीर्तिमुख बना हुआ दिखाई देता है।

अधिकांशतः पालकालीन प्रतिमाएं द्वि आयामी बनी हुई है जबकि यहाँ की प्रतिमाओं में कटाव के कारण त्रि आयामी दृश्य उभर कर आता है। यह कटाव द्विदलीय कमल से कमर तक के हिस्से में आसानी से देखा जा सकता है। गंगा के दक्षिणी भाग में इस तरह के कटाव वाली प्रतिमाओं को पाल सेन कला के नाम से जाना जाता है या फिर इन प्रतिमाओं को ग्यारहवीं

बारहवीं शताब्दी की प्रतिमा मानी जाती है। पालों की प्रतिमाओं में बौद्ध धर्म का ज्यादा प्रभाव है जबकि बेगूसराय से प्राप्त प्रतिमाओं में विष्णु के अवतारवाद नृवराह, नरसिंह, चामुंडा, गणेश, नवदुर्गा आदि वैष्णव एवं शैव प्रतिमाएं प्राप्त होती है। पालकालीन प्रतिमाओं के स्टेला के दाहिने एवं बाएं हिस्से में अंकित ग़ज़ वयाल का अंकन और बेगूसराय जिले में अवस्थित प्रतिमाओं के ग़ज़ वयाल का अंकन दूसरे रूप में होता है। इस तरह के कई उदाहरण हैं जो बेगूसराय एवं बेगूसराय से उत्तर तीर भुक्ति के इलाके में पाल प्रतिमा एवं पाल प्रतिमा से अलग होने की जानकारी देते हैं।

कला में इस तरह के अन्तर को समझने के लिए तीर भुक्ति के भूगोल और राजनीतिक नेतृत्व को भी देखने की आवश्यकता है क्योंकि जब पाल शासक बौद्ध मत को प्रश्रय दे रहे थे तो इस क्षेत्र में वैष्णव एवं ब्राह्मण धर्म से संबंधित प्रतिमाओं की अधिकता क्यों और कैसे हो गयी। जब पालों की प्रतिमाओं के स्टेला में कोई अन्तर नहीं दिखाई देता है तो इस क्षेत्र के स्टेला में अन्तर कैसे हो गया है। इस तरह के कारण की तलाश आवश्यक है, पालों के पास बड़ी नों सेना के होने की जानकारी नहीं मिलती है। बेगूसराय जिला गंगा जैसी बड़ी नदी का उत्तर स्थित तटीय क्षेत्र है और पालों के पास इस तरह आने का कोई महत्वपूर्ण कारण नहीं था क्योंकि यह क्षेत्र कन्नौज के रास्ते पर नहीं था। तीर भुक्ति के उत्तरी एवं मध्य क्षेत्र से पाल शासकों से अगल अन्य शासकों के अभिलेख मिलते हैं लेकिन बेगूसराय में ऐसे किसी अन्य अभिलेख की जानकारी उपलब्ध नहीं है। बेगूसराय से उपलब्ध चामुंडा की प्रतिमाएं और पूर्वमध्यकालीन सिक्के किसी अन्य शासन की ओर आंशिक इशारा करती है क्योंकि चामुंडा राजपूतों की देवी है और यहाँ से प्राप्त चाँदी के सिक्के वज़न में चार ग्रेन से कम के हैं जो गुर्जर प्रतिहार शासकों के द्वारा जारी किये गए थे।

बेगूसराय जिला तीर भुक्ति के दक्षिणी हिस्से में एक ऐसे छोटे क्षेत्र का प्रतिनिधित्व करता है जो गंगा, बुढ़ी गंडक, बागमती, बैंती, बाया आदि छोटी–बड़ी नदियों से घिरा हुआ है। बुढ़ी गंडक नदी के समीपवर्ती क्षेत्रों से पूर्वमध्यकालीन सिक्कों की प्राप्ति बेगूसराय के आर्थिक सम्पन्नता की ओर इशारा करता है, फलतः साम्राज्यवाद के विस्तार हेतु राजनीतिक नेतृत्व का प्रयास भी बार–बार होता रहा। इस तरह की तमाम परिस्थितियों के बीच प्रारंभिक मध्यकालीन बेगूसराय जिला से संबंधित पाषाण प्रतिमाओं का मूल्यांकन अभी तक नहीं हुआ है और इस विषय पर गंभीरता से कार्य करने की आवश्यकता बनी हुई है।

भास्कर भवन, शिवपुरी,
बेगूसराय (बिहार)

सौजन्य :
लोकतंत्र की बुनियाद
(राष्ट्रीय मासिक पत्रिका)
अगस्त, 2019

●●●

अंगुत्तराप का क्षेत्रीय पुरातत्त्व एवं इतिहास
विषयक
राष्ट्रीय सेमिनार

सार–संक्षेप

2–3 मार्च, 2004

स्वर्ण जयंती
प्राचीन भारतीय इतिहास एवं पुरातत्त्व विभाग
सह
के. पी. जायसवाल पुरातात्त्विक संग्रहालय
जी. डी. कॉलेज, बेगूसराय

उद्घाटन सत्र

प्राचीन इतिहास एवं पुरातत्त्व हमारी गौरवशाली संस्कृति का अमूल्य धरोहर है जिसको बचाए रखने की जिम्मेवारी हम सबों की है। पुराने अवशेषों की नए सिरे से खोज करना निहायत जरूरी है। जो कार्य पूर्व के विद्वान इतिहासकार अधूरा छोड़ गए, उसे पूरा करना भी हम सबों का दायित्व है।

आज इस बात की आवश्यकता है कि युवा इतिहासकार मेहनत कर प्राचीनकाल के इतिहास को उजागर करें ताकि आनेवाले समय में वे समाज के लिए उपयोगी हो सकें।

डॉ० गौतम सेन गुप्ताए, निदेशक
पुरातत्त्व निदेशालय, पश्चिम बंगाल

तर्कपूर्ण एवं निष्पक्ष इतिहास की स्थापना के लिए क्षेत्रीय पुरातत्त्व एवं इतिहास का गहन अनुसंधान समय की माँग है। अंगुत्तराप जैसे महत्वपूर्ण महत्वपूर्ण अध्याय पर इस सेमीनार से महत्वपूर्ण प्रकाश पड़ेगा, ऐसी प्रत्याशा है। इतिहास एवं पुरातत्त्व की दृष्टि से समृद्ध बेगूसराय में ऐसे कार्यक्रम का आयोजन सराहनीय है।

डॉ० सीताराम राय, पूर्व निदेशक
पुरातत्त्व निदेशालय (बिहार)

बेगूसराय की पहचान इतिहास के क्षेत्र में पहले भी थी और आज भी है। यहाँ का वीरपुर गाँव ऐतिहासिक है। गुप्तकालीन सिक्के नौलागढ़ से प्राप्त हुए हैं। अंगुत्तराप की सही व्याख्या हो जाए तो पुरातत्त्व की दृष्टि से एक महत्वपूर्ण कार्य सम्पन्न होगा। पुरातात्त्विक अन्वेषण की दृष्टि से जी.डी. कॉलेज, बेगूसराय के प्रोफेसर इतिहासकार राधाकृष्ण चौधरी जी के योगदान को भुलाया नहीं जा सकता है।

डॉ. अखिलेश्वर कुमार
पूर्व प्राचार्य, जी.डी. कॉलेज, बेगूसराय

●●●

विषय प्रवर्तन

प्रो0 फुलेश्वर सिंह

प्राचीन पाली बौद्ध साहित्य के कुछ विवरणों से ज्ञात होता है कि गौतम बुद्ध के समय गंगोत्तर बिहार को 'अंगुत्तराप' के नाम से पुकारा जाता था। गंगोत्तर बिहार का कौन सा भाग 'अंगुत्तराप' कहलाता था, यह स्वयं शब्द के संधि–विच्छेद (अंग+उत्तर+आप) से स्पष्ट है। अतः मेरी मान्यता है कि अंग जनपद के उत्तर में गंगा पार क्षेत्र को 'अंगुत्तराप' कहा जाता था। इसका प्रसार वर्तमान के बेगूसराय, खगड़िया, उत्तरी भागलपुर और सहरसा से लेकर पूर्णियाँ तक रहा होगा।

अस्तु! अंगुत्तराप की स्थापना एक ऐसा महत्वपूर्ण विषय है जिसके लिए क्षेत्रीय इतिहास एवं पुरातत्त्व का गहन अन्वेषण आवश्यक है। पुरातात्त्विक उपादानों एवं साहित्यक साक्ष्यों के अनुसंधानात्मक विश्लेषण तथा विषय के मर्मज्ञों की बौद्धिक परिचर्चा के बल पर हम क्षेत्रीय इतिहास के इस महत्वपूर्ण किन्तु पृष्ठभूमि में पड़े विषय को उद्घाटित कर सकते हैं। इस दृष्टि से यह आयोजन मील का पत्थर साबित होगा, ऐसी आशा करता हूँ।

विभागाध्यक्ष,
प्रा0भा0 इतिहास एवं पुरातत्व विभाग,
जी.डी. कॉलेज, बेगूसराय।

●●●

पालिबौद्ध साहित्य में अंगुत्तराप

जगदीश्वर पाण्डेय

पाली बौद्ध–साहित्य में अंगुत्तराप को विशिष्ट स्थान प्राप्त है। भगवान बुद्ध का यह प्रिय चारिका–स्थल रहा है। 'मज्झिम निकाय' की 'अट्ठकथा' में इसे अंग जनपद (पुराना मुंगेर एवं भागलपुर जिला) के उत्तर में माना गया है। अंग के सटे गंगा नदी के उत्तर में जो 'आप' अर्थात पानी है उसे अंगुत्तराप कहते हैं। 'महाभारत' में इसे 'जलोद्भव' देश कहा गया है जिसकी स्वतंत्र सत्ता थी। 'ललितविस्तर' में इस प्रदेश को पूर्व विदेह कहा गया है जिसकी अपनी स्वतंत्र पूर्व–विदेह लिपि भी थी।

बुद्ध बेरंजा में अपना 12वाँ वर्षावास बिताकर अपने जीवन के 48 वें वर्ष में अपने भिक्षुसंघ के साथ भद्दिया पधारे थे जिसकी पुरातत्विक साक्ष्यों पर आधारित खोज आवश्यक है। पुनः वे जनशून्य स्थल से गुजरते हुए अंगुत्तराप के आपण निगम पहुँचे जो बहुत बड़ा व्यापारिक केन्द्र था। यहाँ पोतलिय नामक गृहपति के बुद्ध से भेंट करने की कथानक 'पोत्तलिय–सुत्त' में वर्णित है। यहाँ के वेणिय एवं सेल नामक ब्राह्मणों का भी बुद्ध से साक्षात्कार हुआ।

बेगूसराय जिला स्थित संघौल संभवतः सेल के संघ का मुख्य केन्द्र रहा हो क्योंकि यह क्षेत्र तत्कालीन अंगुत्तराप के अन्तर्गत आता है।

●●●

अंगुत्तराप : पाल कला का पारगमन केन्द्र

सुरेन्द्र कुमार

पूर्व मध्यकाल में नेपाल में पाल कला शैली का बड़े पैमाने पर प्रसार हुआ। यह प्रसार नालंदा, विक्रमशिला एवं बंगाल–बिहार के अन्य क्षेत्रों से हुआ। ऐसा लगता है कि पाल कला के नेपाल में प्रसार का पारगमन केन्द्र अंगुत्तराप था।

अंगुत्तराप क्षेत्र (पू0 समस्तीपुर, सम्पूर्ण बेगूसराय, खगड़िया, उत्तरी भागलपुर और सम्पूर्ण कोसी अंचल) से पालयुगीन कलाकृतियाँ बड़ी संख्या में मिली हैं। अंगुत्तराप में मिली मूर्तियों एवं नेपाल में मिली मूर्तियों के बीच भी अदभुत समानता है। पूर्व मध्यकाल में नेपाल का मतलब सिर्फ काठमांडू घाटी था जिसमें कान्तिपुर, भक्तपुर एवं ललितपुर जैसे नगर अवस्थित थे। काठमांडू घाटी में प्राप्त सूर्य की मूर्तियों एवं बेगूसराय के बरौनी से प्राप्त सूर्य की मूर्ति में काफी एकरूपता दिखलाई पड़ती है। बेगूसराय के ही संघौल में भूमिस्पर्श मुद्रा में जो बुद्ध की मूर्ति मिली है, वैसी असंख्य मूर्तियाँ काठमांडू घाटी में मिलती है।

ऐसा प्रतीत होता है कि नालन्दा, विक्रमशिला एवं बंगाल में विकसित पाल कला शैली का नेपाल की ओर प्रसार अंगुत्तराप के द्वारा हुआ। बेगूसराय का इलाका पाल कला का महत्वपूर्ण केन्द्र बना, और यहीं से पाल कला का प्रसार नेपाल में हुआ। नेपाल की ओर पाल कला का संक्रमण बेगूसराय के रास्ते हुआ, इसका सबसे बड़ा प्रमाण यह है कि सम्पूर्ण उत्तर बिहार में बेगूसराय क्षेत्र में एक स्थान पर जितनी पाल कलाकृतियाँ मिलती हैं, उतनी और कहीं नहीं मिलती हैं।

अंगुत्तराप क्षेत्र नदी मार्ग से सीधा नेपाल से जुड़ा था। 11 वीं सदी में अतिश दीपंकर ने विक्रमशिला से नेपाल की यात्रा सिमरनगढ़ से होकर की थी। यह यात्रा निश्चित रूप से अंगुत्तराप के रास्ते ही हुई होगी।

अंगुत्तराप की मिली–जुली संस्कृति से इस प्रसार को संरक्षण एवं बढ़ावा मिला।

रीडर, इतिहास विभाग,
पटना कॉलेज, पटना।

●●●

अंगुत्तराप का पुरातात्त्विक एवं ऐतिहासिक अध्ययन

रामचन्द्र पासवान
डी.सी.एल.आर. खगड़िया

बौद्ध साहित्य में वर्णित 'अंगुत्तराप' अब ऐतिहासिक पहेली नहीं रह गई है। पुराविद् एवं इतिहासकार यह मान चुके हैं कि यह एक क्षेत्र विशेष का भौगोलिक नाम है जिसकी सीमा क्षेत्र के अन्तर्गत सदियों से मानव सभ्यता का विभिन्न रूप में प्रादुर्भाव हुआ और संस्कृति ने अठखेलियाँ की।

भगवान बुद्ध के 45 वर्षों के यात्रा–प्रवास में भद्दीया, आपण और अंगुत्तराप की चर्चा कई बार आई है। विनय पिटक में उल्लेख है कि भगवान एक बार वाराणसी से भद्दीया गए थे और इसके समीप जातीय वन में ठहरे थे। पुनः, भद्दीया में इच्छानुसार विहार कर मेंडक गृहपति से बिना पूछे ही साढ़े बारह सौ महान भिक्षु संघ के साथ भगवान जहाँ अंगुत्तराप था, वहाँ चारिका के लिए चल दिए। भद्दीया एवं आपण की सही पहचान से 'अंगुत्तराप' जनपद की ऐतिहासिक पूर्णता सम्पन्न हो सकेगी। जैन साहित्य में भी एक बार भगवान महावीर के यात्रा प्रसंग में भद्दीय ग्राम की चर्चा आई है। जिस सहज ढ़ंग से भद्दीय से वैशाली और फिर भद्दीय से अंगुत्तराप एवं आपण निगम में भ्रमण की कथा आई है, उससे यह सहज ही कहा जा सकता है कि भद्दीय और आपण निगम सहज रूप से सड़क मार्ग से जुड़े थे, नदी पार करने की चर्चा नहीं है।

अंगुत्तराप सामान्य रूप से तीन शब्दों के मेल से बना है – अंग + उत्तर + आप। सामान्य अर्थ में हम कह सकते हैं – अंग के उत्तर का पानीवाला भाग। यह सर्वमान्य है कि अंग प्रदेश

में मोटे तौर पर आज का भागलपुर, मुंगेर, जमुई, लखीसराय, शेखपुरा, बेगूसराय, खगड़िया, मधेपुरा, सहरसा का दक्षिणी भाग और समस्तीपुर जिला के पूर्वी भाग को सम्मिलित माना जा सकता है जिसके उत्तरी भाग बेगूसराय, खगड़िया, सहरसा, मधेपुरा, उत्तरी भागलपुर, समस्तीपुर जिला के पूर्वी भाग अर्थात् दलसिंहसराय और विद्यापति नगर प्रखंड के भू–भाग को मिलाकर 'अंगुत्तराप' कहा जाता था।

अब तक के अध्ययन के आधार पर यह भी कहा जा रहा है कि सहरसा, मधेपुरा के दक्षिण और मध्य खगड़िया (अलौली प्रखंड के पश्चिम और मध्य भाग को छोड़कर) जिला की मिट्टी का निर्माण पाँचवी सदी के बाद हुआ है। इस तरह अलौली के बाद ही अर्थात् बेगूसराय क्षेत्र में ही आपण निगम की खोज करनी होगी।

मेरा मत है कि बौद्धकालीन अंगुत्तराप का आपणनिगम, बेगूसराय जिला का बखरी बाजार है जो आज अनुमंडल कार्यालय का मुख्यालय है। बखरी के चारों तरफ के गाँव ऐतिहासिक एवं पुरातात्त्विक साक्ष्यों को समेटे हुए हैं। नौलागढ़ एवं जयमंगलागढ़ की प्राचीनता किसी से छिपी हुई नहीं है। बागमती की एक धारा बखरी भउहरसिंह गाँव को छूती हुई प्रवेश करती है। निकटवर्ती गढ़पुरा से बौद्ध स्तूप मूर्ति मिले हैं। सुत्तनिपात के 'सैल सुत्त' में उल्लिखित सैल ब्राह्मण बखरी के ही थे। बखरी की सहचरी सलौना मेरी समझ से शैल बभना (शैल ब्राह्मण) का संक्षिप्त एवं अपभ्रंश रूप है। फिर, अंगुत्तराप की जलीय स्थिति के मद्देनजर भी बखरी का आपण निगम होना उपयुक्त लगता है। जलमार्ग से इसका सहज सम्पर्क दूर–दूर के प्रदेशों से था।

अतः साहित्यिक वर्णन, भौगोलिक स्थिति, व्यापारिक दृष्टिकोण, पुरातात्त्विक उपलब्धता, नामकरण का औचित्य तथा आज तक व्यापारिक महत्ता – सभी आधार पर हम विश्वासपूर्वक कहने में सक्षम हैं कि बौद्धकालीन अंगुत्तराप का आपणनिगम और कोई नहीं, बेगूसराय का बखरी है।

अंगुत्तराप का प्राचीन भूगोल

प्रो0 फुलेश्वर सिंह

प्राचीन बौद्ध पाली साहित्यों में गंगोत्तर पूर्वी बिहार को 'अंगुत्तराप' के नाम से पुकारा गया है। 'अंगुत्तराप' शब्द के संधि विच्छेद से 'अंग जनपद के उत्तर में जलप्लावित क्षेत्र' का बोध होता है। बौद्ध साहित्य से स्पष्ट होता है कि गौतम बुद्ध 48 वर्ष की उम्र में राजगृह में 12 वाँ पावस आवास व्यतीत करने के बाद चारिका (धर्म प्रचार) के लिए निकले। राजगृह से भद्दीयग्राम होते हुए घने जंगल को पारकर ग्रीष्म ऋतु में उन्होंने अंगुत्तराप में प्रवेश किया था। अंगुत्तराप के 'आपण निगम' में गौतम बुद्ध 1250 भिक्षुओं के साथ एक सप्ताह से भी अधिक समय तक ठहरे थे।

प्रश्न उठता है कि गौतम बुद्ध के समय में गंगोत्तर पूर्वी बिहार की भौगोलिक स्थिति क्या थी ? मानव आवास योग्य कौन–कौन से स्थल थे ? इसके आधार पर बुद्धकाल से लेकर उत्तरोत्तर ऐतिहासिक काल तक इस क्षेत्र की सभ्यता एवं संस्कृति को आँका और परखा जा सकता है। कुछ विद्वान गंगोत्तर पूर्वी बिहार को अंग जनपद से जोड़कर देखने का प्रयास करते रहे हैं जो एक ऐतिहासिक भूल है। पालि बौद्ध साहित्य इसे 'अंगुत्तराप' के नाम से तो ब्राह्मण साहित्य 'जलोद्भव प्रदेश' तथा 'पूर्व विदेह' के नाम से पुकारता है। रामायण में तो इसकी अपनी एक अलग लिपि और भाषा की चर्चा आयी है।

अंग महाजनपद की सीमा के आधार पर अंगुत्तराप की सीमा का निर्धारण किया जा सकता है। पश्चिम में हाथीदह नदी एवं पूर्व में राजमहल की पहाड़ी अंग जनपद की सीमा थी। इसी के उत्तर गंगा पार की भूमि को पालि साहित्य में अंगुत्तराप के नाम से पुकारा गया है। वर्तमान में गंगोत्तर बिहार के उस क्षेत्र को अंगुत्तराप की सीमा रखा जा सकता है, जिसका विस्तार पश्चिम में समस्तीपुर के बरैला चौड़ एवं सिंघिया चौड़ तथा उत्तर में बागमती, करेह, बलान, तिलयुगा और कोसी के संगम द्वारा विभाजित भूमि से लेकर पूर्व में महानन्दा तक के क्षेत्र में था।

अंगुत्तराप का पूरा क्षेत्र नदियों, उसके छारन, झील और ताल–तलैया से भरा हुआ है। इसके चलते यह कई उपखण्डों में बँटा हुआ नजर आता है। इसके चलते यह कई उपखण्डों में बँटा हुआ नजर आता है। अध्ययन की सुविधा के लिए इन्हें आठ उपखण्डों में बाँटते हैं :–

1. समस्तीपुर जिला का विशाल बरैला चौड़।
2. गंगा और बूढ़ी गंडक के बीच का भू–खण्ड।
3. बूढ़ी गंडक और बागमती, करेह, कोसी के संगम का छारन द्वारा विभाजित भूखण्ड।
4. बूढ़ी गंडक–गंगा और बागमती का मानसी–महेशखूँट के बीच गंगा का छारन।
5. गंगा और बागमती तथा कोसी के बीच का भूखण्ड।
6. बागमती और कोसी के बीच का भूखण्ड।
7. कोसी का पश्चिमी अंचल।
8. कोसी का पूर्वी अंचल।

बरैला चौड़ का सबसे प्राचीन भाग पूर्वी भिंड है। परन्तु मध्य बरैला चौड़ और उत्तरी बरैला चौड़ के समस्तीपुर मुख्यालय तक के क्षेत्र की धरती मध्यकाल में आवासित प्रतीत होती है।

गंगा और बूढ़ी गंडक के बीच के भूखण्ड में भी कई उपधाराएँ हैं। गंगा की देवकी नाम की उपधारा के दोनों किनारे पर बेगूसराय जिले में मानव आवास के सबसे पुराने टीले के अवशेष बछवाड़ा से कोला चौड़ तक विद्यमान हैं। इसी क्षेत्र में वीरपुर से भीठ पुल तक बलान निर्मित नाला है। अनुमान लगाया जा सकता है कि प्राचीन काल में बैंती और बलान नदी के द्वारा नौलागढ़ के विशाल आवास को बूढ़ी गंडक और गंगा के जलमार्ग से जोड़ा गया था।

बूढ़ी गंडक और बागमती के बीच के भूखण्ड में भी कई छारन हैं। बेगूसराय जिला में बूढ़ी गंडक द्वारा विभाजित उत्तरी भाग में विशाल कावर झील फैला है जो एक 'गोखुर झील' है। इस झील के चार उपखण्ड हैं जिनके भींड पर प्राचीन बस्तियों के आवास के टीले पाये जाते हैं।

बूढ़ी गंडक और गंगा तथा बागमती के बीच के भूखण्ड पर भी कई छारनों को सक्रिय देखा जा सकता है। खगड़िया के पश्चिम और बखरी–अलौली के पूर्व में बागमती तथा करेह की संयुक्त धारा और कहीं–कहीं अलग धारा के छारन विद्यमान हैं जिसका जल निकास इमली स्टेशन के पास से बागमती की मुख्य धारा में है। यहाँ मानव आवास के कई प्राचीन टीले हैं।

कोसी क्षेत्र की पश्चिमी धारा में भूतही बलान, तिलयुगा और कमला नदी के संगम ने द्रोणी का निर्माण किया। कोसी अंचल के पश्चिमी भाग में कन्दाहा, घोड़ाडीहा, वनगाँव–महेशी से लेकर सुपौल जिला में गढ़बरूआरी, कपिलेश्वर स्थान, समदाहा गढ़ आदि से मानव आवास के

सबसे पुराने प्रमाण मिलते हैं। कोसी की प्राचीन पूर्वी और मध्य धारा से अररिया, पूर्णियाँ और कटिहार के पश्चिमी भाग की द्रोणियों का निर्माण ढ़ाई–तीन सौ वर्ष पहले हुआ था। वनमनखी के सिकलीगढ़ से ही हमें इस क्षेत्र में प्राचीन आवास के प्रमाण मिलते हैं। शेष भाग अररिया, किशनगंज, पूर्णियाँ और कटिहार में मध्यकाल के उत्तर भाग यानि 16 वीं सदी से बंगाल की मुगलिया सत्ता के प्रसार से मानव प्रसार के साथ राजसत्ता की स्थापना शुरू होती है।

निष्कर्षतः कहा जा सकता है कि गंगा और उसमें दक्षिण बिहार से आनेवाली नदियों के जलौढ़ से गंगा, बूढ़ी गंडक और बागमती द्वारा विभाजित द्रोणियाँ पटकर मानव आवास योग्य पहले बना। यह भाग समस्तीपुर के दलसिंगसराय, सम्पूर्ण बेगूसराय, रोसड़ा और खगड़िया जिला का अलौली तथा सहरसा का भू–भाग है। इसलिए इस बड़े भूखण्ड में नवपाषाणिक कृषकों की कई बस्तियों से इसका इतिहास शुरू होता है और ताम्रपाषाणिक तथा उत्तर वैदिक काल के आते–आते एक दर्जन बस्तियाँ अस्तित्व में आ जाती हैं। गौतम बुद्ध के समय में इस भूखण्ड में ढ़ाई से तीन दर्जन बड़ी–बड़ी बस्तियाँ और छोटे–बड़े पाँच व्यापारिक नगरों की स्थापना से हो जाती है। इसलिए बुद्ध अपने धर्म के प्रचारार्थ इस क्षेत्र में आए थे। पालि बौद्ध साहित्य इसे 'अंगुत्तराप' तथा इसके प्रमुख नगर को 'आपण–निगम' कहता है।

A glimpse into the sculpture of Anguttarapa Janapada Area

Dr. P.Gupta
Dr. Prabal gupta

In our preliminary exploration of Saharsa, Khagaria, Begusarai and Samastipur to find out the identity of Anguttarupa, a Janapada referred to the Buddisht Literature, we came across with a plethora of lithic sculpture belonging to early medieval period - largely contemporaneous with the Pala Dynasty and in some cases associated with the post-pala chronology.

Tabulation of Specimen :

1. Saharsa District

a) Surya image and Door frame of Kandaha.

b) Shivalingas, Nandis, Crocodile - shaped water spout, broken Vishnu images, door jambs with several motifs and many broken pieces at Deona dih (Kabra Block).

c) Tara and Parinirvana - Buddha of Mahisi.

d) Broken figure of Vishnu at Okahi village.

e) Varaha with Prithvi, Surya images, damaged icon of Kubera at Kapileshwar sthan of Baruari on

Khardaha River.

2. Khagaria District

Sadyojata of Alaoligarh

3. Samastipur District

Ganesh, Chamunda, Mahisa Mardini, Vishnu and Shivlinga at Keos.

4. Begusarai District

a) Buddhist Pantheon

Buddha in Bhumisparsa and Padmasana mudra from Balia, Bhumisparsa and Sthanaka Buddha from Sanghaul, Marichi at Rajwara near Barauni, Avalokiteshwara at Birpur - Barepura, a small male specimen bearing in legend 'Birupa' at Sanghaul.

b) Brahmanical Pantheon

Varaha (inscribed) at Rajaura ; Syncrestic Varaha and Sivalinga at Itwa ; Nr. Simha at Birpur Barepura (stolen) ; Sivalinga at Birpur Barepura and Ulao ; Uma Mahesvara at Birpur ; Bull at Birpur - Barepuri, Genesa at Sanghaul ; Dancing Ganesa at Birpur (stolen) ; Surya at Birpur Barepura,

Kaith, Barauni ; Revanta at Barepura ; Navagraha at Barepura, Jaimangalgarh (stolen); Camunda at Barepura, Pachambha, Birpur ; Mahish Mardini at Barepura.

Iconographic and stylistic Narration of Icons.

It is a historical puzzle that the Brahmanical icons numerically overwhelm the Buddhist Pantheon in our region. So far, we have not noticed a singal Jaina image. The problem can possibly be soved if a thorough archaeogical investigation are carried out of major archaeological mounds like mangalgarh (Samastipur), Naulagarh (Begusarai), Jaimangalgarh (Begusarai), Alaoligarh (Khagaria) etc.

Being on the northern side of Anga, we may find seminal linkage with plastic art of Anga. The Pala Sculpture of our area has not been studied as yet in its evolutionary lineage as per the allied parameters such as time, space, iconography and aesthetics which includes the styles. The corelation of the local styles associated with smaller centres of polity lika Alaoligarh, Jaimangala garh, Naolagarh, Mangalgarh etc. With the main genre of the Pala art can be properly comprehended when proper archaeological exploration of these mounds will be undertaken.

In Certain places of our areas say Birpur, We come across an unfinished sculpture. So apart from the art of diaspora, there is corresponding evidence of fashioning icons by the itenarenat sculptors in the spot. Uptil now no major workshop catering the entire area has been found out. Most likely icons were imported from the different ataliers functioning outside our area possibly Anga.

Anguttarapa and Apan-Nigam: a truth of History

Umesh Kumar Singh
DIG of Police, Kosi Range

Anguttarapa and Aapan-Nigam like many other issues are still warranting due care and attention of historians, regarding fixation of their exact location, physical identification and evidence-based exploarative opinion. In different periods, opinions have been differently formend and some scholars accepted "Aapan Nagam" in Mahismati of Saharsa district whereas others took it to Naulagarh and Jaimanglagarh in Begusarai district.

In the sikth centiurey B.C, out of sixteen Janpadas, Anga was one of the strorgest Janpadas with its capital at Champa Nagar (modern Bhagalpur). Anguttarapa was the name of territory, falling north of the river of Anga janapada, i.e. river Ganga. Lord Buddha visited Anguttarapa twice and stayed with township namely Aapan - Nigam, which was at that time, having two ot twenty thousand shops. It is also described that Lord Buddha crossed the river Ganges, near the village 'Bhaddiya'; situated on the southern bank of the river. He trevelled through a thick forest to reach 'Aapan-Nigam', where keniya, the shresthi of the Nigam warmly greeted and welcomed him. Here, Buddha's transcendental personality overshadowed the Brahmin teacher-shail and he alongwith his disciples accepted Buddhism. Lord Buddha left Aapan Nigam for Kushinagar, the capital of the Mallas,in U.P.

To identify and locate the exact place and territory of Anguttarapa and its eloquent township-Aapan Nigam, different hypothesis and views with their separate justifications are enumerated below -

1. Pandit Rahul Sankritiyayan had indicated the identification of village 'Bhaddiya', on southem bank of the river Ganges as that of Monghyr and fixed the territory of moderm Khagariya and Begusarai districts as Anguttarapa.

2. Some of Pali scholars are of the opinion of indicating 'Bhaddiya' village with

that of a village in the vicinity of Bhagalpur and Anguttarapa, the area of Naugachiya, Birpur and Kursela (Katihar).

3. A Section of scholars speculate a village of the same name near Muhaddi Nagar (Samastipur) to be 'Bhaddiya'.

This is based on the view that Buddna had not crossed any river to reach Anguttarapa (Mahabagga).

4. Some writers, quoting Jain and Buddhist literature, say that Anguttarapa, a part of Tirbhukti was assimilated to the kingdom of Anga and the present regions of Kosi division constituted a part of the kingdom of Anga in the 6th century B.C.

Mahismati, Bangaon and Kandaha areas of saharsa district are referred in contemporary Buddhist poli literature and many historians have also endorsed the fact of Lord Buddha's visit to Saharsa in Anguttarapa. Geographically this regio in north of territory of Anga across the river Ganges, difined region of Anguttarapa of history. According to'Suttanipat' river Mahi flew in Anguttarapa and capital of Angattarapa is said to be on the north bank of river Mahi. In Buddhist literature, Mahi river in modern Kosi. River Mahi used to flow in the vicinity of the village Mahesi where Lord Buddha had stayed. There are many places even now existing, which resemble and are synonyms of Buddhist Pattern such as Buddhbare Gotra of Mahesi, Bangaon and a village named Buddhai also denote sufficient indications of Lord Buddha's visit and his extraordinary influence over the area. In Kosi rigion, there are many mounds and ancient historical sites, which need excavation and further probes. Punchmark coins have been found from the remains of a stupa at Mahesi and from Madhepura.

Anguttarapa and Aapan Nigam are to be searched in undisputed and convincing location and corroborated in contemporary Buddha Pali literature also. We must refrain from shortcut decisions and conclusions to avoid stains of partiality.

●●●

अंगुत्तराप : एक पुरातात्विक सर्वेक्षण

बेगूसराय एवं खगड़िया जिला के सन्दर्भ में

शैलेश कुमार सिन्हा

यह निर्विवाद है कि प्राचीन बौद्ध पालि साहित्य में वर्णित 'अंगुत्तराप' प्राचीन अंग की उत्तरी सीमा तय करने वाली गंगा के उत्तर का बिहार है। उत्तरी बिहार के पूर्वार्द्ध का वर्तमान कौन–कौन सा जिला अंगुत्तराप का गठन करता था, यह शोध का विषय है। अंगुत्तराप की पूर्वी, पश्चिमी एवं उत्तरी सीमा के विषय पर मत–मतान्तर संभव है किन्तु कोई भी तार्किक संरचना वर्तमान बेगूसराय एवं खगड़िया जिला को सम्मिलित किये बिना संभव नहीं है। यहाँ ध्यान रखना होगा कि 'अंगुत्तराप' एवं 'आपणनिगम' की भौगोलिक स्थापना हेतु पृथक दृष्टिकोण अपरिहार्य है। 'अंगुत्तराप' एक व्यापक अवधारणा है जबकि 'आपणनिगम' अपेक्षाकृत उसमें शामिल एक लघु इकाई। अतः 'अंगुत्तराप' की भौगोलिक स्थापना के क्रम में पुरातात्विक दृष्टि से शर्तों को पूरी करने वाले पुरास्थलों पर ही 'आपणनिगम' की खोज हेतु ध्यान केन्द्रित करना होगा। यहाँ गंगोत्तर बिहार के पुरातात्विक दृष्टि से महत्त्वपूर्ण दो जिलों–बेगूसराय एवं खगड़िया के पुरातात्विक सर्वेक्षण पर ध्यान केन्द्रित किया जा रहा है।

बेगूसराय जिला :–

1. बेगूसराय सबडिविजन के प्रमुख पुरास्थल

1. संघौल 2 उलाव 3 पचम्बा 4 लोदीडीह 5 कंकौल

6 हरदिया 7 रजौड़ा 8 साँख तरैया 9 जोगिया डीह

10 मसुरिया डीह 11 कैथ–बरैठ 12 दमदमा 13 कुशमहौत

14 मैझलापुर 15 मटिहानी 16 मनिअप्पा 17 मझनपुर

18 वीरपुर–वरैयपुरा 19 फाजिलपुर 20 चाननडीह 21 सहूरी

उपरोक्त सभी पुरास्थल उत्तरी कृष्णमार्जित मृद्‌भांड परंपरा से पालकालीन सांस्कृतिक परंपरा तक के पुरावशेषों से संपन्न हैं। पालकालीन प्रतिमाओं की दृष्टि से भी इनमें से संघौल, पचम्बा, कंकौल, हरदिया, कैथ–बरैठ, मटिहानी, वीरपुर–बरैयपुरा आदि विशेष महत्वपूर्ण हैं।

2. तेघड़ा सबडिविजन के पुरास्थल

1 बदुरवाडीह 2 नुरपूर, 3 मंसूरचक

3. बलिया सबडिविजन के पुरास्थल

1. बलिया 2. सुघरन 3. गोदी डीह 4. मरट्‌ठा डीह 5. सरैया डीह

4. मंझौल सबडिविजन के पुरास्थल

1. मंझौल 2. जयमंगलागढ़ 3. हरसाई 4. गढ़खौली डीह

5. एजनी–परोड़ा 6. नकटाही 7. सोनीडीह 8. झीकटाही 9. रोशनाहाडीह

10 औरे डीह 11. नारायण–पीपड़ 12. चिरैयाडीह

उपरोक्त स्थलों से भी मौर्यकाल से पालकाल तक के पुरावशेष मिलते हैं।

5. बखरी सबडिविजन के पुरास्थल

1. गढ़पुरा इंटर कॉलेज वाला टीला एवं गढ़पुरा टीला 2. एकम्बा 3. रामपुर 4. सोहरैया डीह 5. डीहवार

खगड़िया जिला :–

1. अलौलीगढ़ 2. मुरलीडीह 3. संतोश डीह 4. बेला–सिमरी 5. मारर

6. झिकटाही 7. जरगामा 8. चनवा डीह 9. भेलवा डीह

उपरोक्त वर्णित पुरास्थलों में से लगभग आधा उत्तरीकृष्णमार्जित मृद्‌भांड के अवशेषों से युक्त हैं। भौगोलिक विचार एवं भू–परिदृश्य की दृष्टि से परिगणित टीलों में से कुछ – यथा नौलागढ़, जयमंगलगढ़, वीरपुर आदि ऐसे हैं जिनकी अनदेखी कर 'आपणनिगम' की खोज करना सर्वथा अतार्किक होगा। प्रथम चुनौती तो इतने विस्तृत उत्तरीकृष्णमार्जित मृद्‌भांड के अवशेषयुक्त टीलों की अन्यत्र खोज से संबंधित हैं। तदुपरान्त इतने व्यापक समकालीन मानवगुच्छ से युक्त पुरास्थलों की उपस्थिति से किसी सदृश विस्तृत पुरास्थल को संबद्ध कर ही 'आपण निगम' की खोज की जा सकती है।

Birpur Tara : An Iconographic Study

Amiya Krishna

It is unquestionable that Mahatma Buddha had visited the land of Anguttarapa and it used to be a stronghold of Buddhism. It is natural that Buddhism started flourishing in the region with Buddha visiting here and overshadowing the Brahmin Guru Shail during one of his short stay in the summer. Whatever be the centre of Aapan Nigam, it is evident that Begusarai district used to coustitute the political division of Anguttarapa. Apart from many other features of Buddhist influence, the whole area of Begusarai is litter of with many intact and broken stone sculptures. Many Buddhist icons have been placed in the garbhagriha of Hindu temples and are being worshipped as Hindu god or goddess. The concerned icon is one of them. Placed in a newly constructed temple at Birpur, almost 12 kms North to district headquarters, this Buddhist icon is a fine piece of Pala sculpture. It is being worshipped as Brahma-Baba by local Hindu devotees. The stone is black basalt. The image is intact and superb glaze can be seen on it. The deity is seated in *Lalitasana* on the double-petalled lotus. Right leg of the deity is pendent on Mahambujapitha while the left is bent to rest on the Aasana. The right palm is exposed in the *Varadmudra* while the left holding the stalk of a lotus is in the *Abhayamudra*. Keyur, greevahar, nupur, katimekhala, kundala etc. are adornment of the deity. Five Dhyani Buddha are apparent on the top of the stelae. The four associating deity in the lower part of the stelae are quite important for identification of the central deity. These can be identified as Ashokanta, Ekjata, Janguli and Mahamayuri. The Best possibility of specification advocates it being an important sculpute of **Varad Tara**.

●●●

Report on the Inscriptions Preserved in The K. P. Jayaswal Archaeological Museum Department Of Ancient Indian History, Culture and Archaeology G. D. College, Begusarai, Bihar

This report contains the text and gist of ten stone inscriptions, two terracotta sealings and three terracotta votive tablets copied from the K. P. Jayaswal Archaeological Museum, Department of Ancient Indian History, Culture and Archaeology, G. D. College, Begusarai, Bihar.

Of the ten stone inscriptions, two are written in Sanskrit language and Early Nagari characters of about 8th century A.D, three are in Sanskrit language and Nagari characters of 9th-10th century A.D, two more are in Sanskrit language and Gaudiya characters of about 10th century A.D, and three others are in Sanskrit language and Gaudiya characters of 10th-11th century A.D.

Of the two terracotta sealings, one is written in Sanskrit language and Brahmi characters of 4th century A.D, and the other is in Sanskrit language and Early Nagari characters of about 7th century A.D.

All the three terracotta votive tablets are written in Sanskrit language and Early Nagari characters of 9th century A.D.

STONE INSCRIPTIONS

Acc. No: 36, Findspot: Naulagarh, Birpur block, Begusarai district, Bihar

Text

1 . . . *hētu prabhava hētu*

2 . . . . . *gatō hyavada tē*

3 . . . . *[ni]rōdha ēvaṁ vādi*

4 . . . . *ṇaḥ* //

Fragmentary. Records the Buddhist formula. In Sanskrit language and Early Nagari characters of about 8th century A.D.

Acc. No: 29, Findspot: Naulagarh, Birpur block, Begusarai district, Bihar

Text

1 . . . . *tēsāṁ hētuṁ tathāgatō avacha*

2 . . . . . *dhō ēvaṁ vādī mahāśamaṇō* II

Fragmentary. Records the Buddhist formula. In Sanskrit language and Early Nagari characters of about 8th century A.D.

Acc. No: 30, Findspot: Not known, Birpur block, Begusarai district, Bihar

Text

Siddhaṁ Dēvadharmmōyaṁ śrī . . . . . .

The inscription is damaged, the word *siddhaṁ* is expressed in symbol. It seems to record that the image was the pious gift of some individual (name lost). In Sanskrit language and Nāgarī characters of 9th-10th century A.D.

Acc. No: 08, Findspot: Rampur, Maithani block, Begusarai district, Bihar

Text

[Dhā]sasya

Seems to record that the image was the gift of an individual named Dhāsa. In Sanskrit language and Nāgarī characters of 9th-10th century A.D.

Acc. No: 14, Findspot: Rampur, Maithani block, Begusarai district, Bihar

Text

Śrī Bhaṭabhadhrapradhā . ka .

Worn out. Seems to record that the image was made by a person named Bhaṭabhadra. In Sanskrit language and Nāgarī characters of 9th-10th century A.D.

Acc. No: 12, Findspot: Sanghaul, Begusarai tehsil and district, Bihar

Text

Dēyadharmmōyaṁ dānapa[ti] lauhākāra Rājabadhra [ka] . . .

Incomplete. Records that the image was the pious gift of a person named Rājabadhra, a blacksmith (*lauhākāra*) by profession. In Sanskrit language and Gauḍīya characters of 10th century A.D.

Acc. No: 20, Findspot: Not known, Begusarai tehsil and district, Bihar

Text

1 *[Siddhaṁ] [Dē]ya[dhā]rmmōyaṁ Bha . . . ta . . .*

Worn out and built-in. The word *siddhaṁ* is expressed in symbol. Seems to record that the image was a pious gift of some individual (name lost) . In Sanskrit language and Gauḍīya characters of about 10th century A.D.

Acc. No: 1, Findspot: Naulagarh, Birpur block, Begusarai district, Bihar

Text

1 *Siddhaṁ Śrī Vigrahapāladēvarājyasaṁvat 24 krimilīya śau-*

2 *ṇḍika Mahāmati duhitrā Dahāmmaji patnyā Āśōkayā kā[ri]tāḥ ॥*

The word *siddhaṁ* is expressed in symbol. Records that during the 24th regnal year of Śrī Vigrahapāladēva, a lady named Āśōka, daughter of Mahāmati, a *śauṇḍika* (distiller and vendor of spirituous liquors) by profession and wife of Dahāmmaji, has donated the image. In Sanskrit language and Gauḍīya characters of 10th-11th century A.D.

Acc. No: 7, Findspot: Rampur, Maithani block, Begusarai district, Bihar

Text

1 *yē dharmma hētu prabhavā hētu tēsāṁ tathāgatō hyavadat tēsāṁ ja (cha) yō [ni]rōdha ēvaṁ vādi mahā[śamaṇaḥ ॥]*

2 *pramōpāsaka*

3 *Mādgakasyaḥ* //

Lines 2 and 3 are written to the left corner of the pedestal, before line 1.

The record begins with Buddhist formula and states that the image was donated by Mādgaka, a lay disciple (*pramōpāsaka*). In Sanskrit language and Gauḍīya characters of 10th-11th century A.D.

Acc. No: 7, Findspot: Rampur, Maithani block, Begusarai district, Bihar

Text

1 . . . . . . *lāśatōja* . . . . *ścha dha* . *ma* . . . .

2 . . . . *rshadha Udrākasya* //

Seems to record that the image was donated by a person named Udraka. In Sanskrit language and Gauḍīya characters of 10th-11th century A.D.

SEALINGS

Terracotta sealing retrieved from archaeological excavation at Birpur

TEXT

Sūtrakasya

Seems to record that the seal was issued by Sūtraka. In Sanskrit language and Brāhmī characters of 4th century A.D.

Terracotta sealing retrieved from archaeological excavation at Birpur

TEXT

. . bhapa

In Sanskrit language and Early Nāgarī characters of about 7th century A.D.

VOTIVE TABLETS

Acc. No: 11, Findspot: Naulagarh, Birpur block, Begusarai district, Bihar

Text

Yē dharmma hētu prabhavā hētu tēshāṁ tathāgata [hyavadat] tēshāṁ cha yō nirōdha ēvaṁ vādī mahāśramaṇaḥ

Records Buddhist formula. In Sanskrit language and Nāgarī characters of 9th century A.D.

Acc. No: 10, Findspot: Naulagarh, Birpur block, Begusarai district, Bihar

Text

Yē dharmma hētu prabhavā hētu [tēshāṁ tathāgata hyavadat] tēshāṁ cha yō nirōdha ēvaṁ vādī mahāśramaṇaḥ

Records Buddhist formula. In Sanskrit language and Nāgarī characters of 9th century A.D.

Selected Photographs

K.P. Jaisawal Archaeological museum, G.D. College, Begusarai (Bihar)

Goddess

Surya

Buddha

Padestal of **Vishnu**

Madhupatradharini

Buddha

Harihar

Begusarai District Museum, (Bihar)

Buddha

Buddha

Buddha

Door frame

Broken piece of stela having **Dhyani Buddha**

Buddha

Vishnu

Ankurinath Mahadeva Temple, Ulao, Begusarai

A Front View of
Radhe Shyam Temple, Ulao, Begusarai

Paintings in
Radhe Shyam Temple, Ulao, Begusarai

Close View of a painting inside the Radhe Shyam Temple, **Ulao, Begusarai**

Writers with the Exploration Team of A.S.I., Patna on the top of Hersai Stupa (Above) and in the middle height (Below).

Distant and Close views of Hersai Stupa

Baraipura, Birpur, Begusarai (Bihar)

Chamunda,

Tara,

Raivanta, Vishahar Sthan

Sun, Sun Temple,

Sun , Basaha Sthan,

*Baraipura, Birpur, Begusarai (Bihar)
Sculptures at Present traceless

Narsinh ,

Vishnu

Dancing Ganesha ,

Courtesy: Bihar District Gazetteers Munger 1960 Appendix